VOID

Library of
Davidson College

Social Change in a Yemeni Highlands Town

The new *sūq* in ʿAmran

Social Change in a Yemeni Highlands Town

Thomas B. Stevenson

University of Utah Press
Salt Lake City

Copyright © 1985 University of Utah Press
All rights reserved
Printed in the United States of America

Library of Congress Cataloging in Publication Data

Stevenson, Thomas B., 1945–
   Social change in a Yemeni highlands town.
   Bibliography: p.
  Includes index.
    1. ʿAmran (Yemen)—Social conditions. I. Title.
HN664.A8S73   1985   306′.0953′32   85-5322
ISBN 0-87480-112-5

To
Susan
and
Hajj ᶜAbdalla

Contents

Preface ix
Note on Transliteration x
Introduction xi
Location and Physical Geography xii.
Religious, Cultural, and Social Divisions xiv.
Modern Yemeni History xv   The Fieldwork xvii.
Presentation of Data xxii.

PART I: ʿAMRAN PRESENT AND PAST

Chapter 1. A Day in ʿAmran 3

Chapter 2. ʿAmrani Views of the Past 39
The Origin of Social Differences 42.
ʿAmran's Jewish Population 44. The Wall 47.
ʿAmrani Relations with the Turks 50.
Life before the Revolution 52.   The Town's Expansion 55.
Conclusion 57.

PART II: AFFILIATION, OCCUPATION,
AND MARRIAGE AND KINSHIP

Chapter 3: Affiliation: Changing Bases of the Social Order 61
Who Is an ʿAmrani? 61.
The Connection between the Tribal and Nontribal Peoples 63.
The Kinship Basis of Affiliation 66.   Forms of Alliance 69.
Alliance and Tribal Organization 74.
The Tribe in the Postrevolutionary Era 81.   Conclusion 88.

Chapter 4. Occupation: Ascription and Achievement 91
Occupation and Status 91.   The Ascriptive System 93.
The Hierarchy in ʿAmran 95.   The *Sūq* and the Hierarchy 105.
Saudi Arabia, Migration, and the Decline of Agriculture 108.
Returned Migrants and New Modes of Adaptation 110.
The Nonmigrants 116.   Land and Status 118.   Conclusion 120.

*Chapter 5. Marriage: Individual Connections and
Status Assessment* 123
Relations within and between Kin Groups 123.

Marriage Patterns 127.   Patrilateral Parallel Cousin Marriage 132.
Marriages for Other Tribesmen and *Sayyid* Families 136.
Bride-Price 140. The Brother-in-Law Relationship 143.
Mobility and the Arrangement of Marriages 146.   Conclusion 149.
*Chapter 6. ʿAmrani Perceptions of Social Change:
Acceptance and Denial* 151
Flexible Bases of Status Assessment 152.
Pseudo-Kinship Relations 158.   The Cooperative Election 160.
Conclusion 168.

Notes 173
Glossary 178
References 181
Index 185

MAPS

1. Sketch map of Yemen xiii
2. Sketch map of ʿAmran 2

TABLES

1. Sample of Hierarchies Described by Scholars 94
2. Social Categories and Divisions Based on Defining Feature and Real Tasks 96
3. Distribution of Shop Use 112
4. Ownership of Freezer Units in General Merchandise Shops 114
5. Ownership of Shops 119
6. Advisory Board Election Results 162

CHARTS

1. Variable Expressions of Descent and Affiliation: The Kinship Model 68
2. The Two Bases for Alliance Membership 71
3. Patterns of Alliance Formation 74
4. The Alliance Relationships between Villages and the Town 76
5. Hypothetical Depiction of Internally Ranked Descent Groups 126
6. Marriages of the *Shaykh*'s Household 134
7. Marriages of a Medium-Level Minimal Agnatic Group 137
8. Marriages of a Low-level Minimal Agnatic Group 138
9. Multiple Exchange Marriages among Medium-Level Families 144
10. Multiple Exchange Marriages among Low-Level Families 145

Preface

This book is a study of social organization in ᶜAmran, a rapidly expanding market town in the Yemen Arab Republic. It focuses on emerging changes in the town's social structure and the townspeople's response to them. I intend to show that the rigid hierarchical model that was and is the basis of the social order represents a cultural ideal. As an increasingly rough approximation of social reality, the model has accommodated the variations that are emerging as new or modified aspects of the town's social structure while still retaining its importance in social status assessment.

Social Change in a Yemeni Highlands Town is a revision of my dissertation submitted to the Department of Anthropology at Wayne State University, published by University Microfilms under the title *Kinship, Stratification, and Mobility: Social Change in a Yemeni Highlands Town*. I am grateful to members of my doctoral committee —Drs. Barbara C. Aswad, Michael J. Bell, James B. Christensen, and Bernice A. Kaplan—for their encouragement. Dr. Aswad, my committee chair, made many suggestions and prompted new approaches, yet allowed great latitude. Dr. Jon C. Swanson offered critical insights and valuable comments on the reworking of the manuscript. Throughout all phases of this study, from its inception to its publication, my wife, Susan Dorsky, has been a continuing source of encouragement and advice.

Naturally I owe a great debt to ᶜAmranis who made this study possible. As I promised them, all names appearing in the text, with the exception of those found in written sources, are pseudonyms. I modified some details and altered some situations to protect the privacy of individuals while retaining the salient points of their case histories. It has not been possible to disguise the identities of all office holders, however. I hope ʿAmranis accept these disclosures as incumbent on men of high status and not as a violation of our agreement.

The research for this book was conducted from January 1978 to July 1979 under a grant from the Social Science Research Council and the American Council of Learned Societies. I also received support from a Wayne State University Graduate Fellowship. Some of my dissertation write-up expenses were underwritten by a separate grant from the Social Science Research Council.

NOTE ON TRANSLITERATION

The transliteration system I use in the text and the glossary follows that of *Arabian Studies* (Middle East Center, University of Cambridge). I have not transliterated place names, but have used common spellings. In accordance with Yemeni pronunciation, I have changed the letter *qaf* to *gaf*. In ʿAmran, *gīm* is pronounced *jīm*. Words beginning with an ʿ*ayn* have an "a" following the initial sound for ease of reading.

Introduction

This book is a description and analysis of social change in ʿAmran, a market town in the tribal highlands of the Yemen Arab Republic. The study focuses on emerging modifications in the town's social structure during a period of rapid economic growth and political change. The data were collected in 1978–79 as part of a doctoral research project.

I decided to investigate social change in 1977 while I was preparing to do the fieldwork. At that time the literature on Yemen, at least in Western languages, was rather scant, largely because of the difficulty foreigners had in obtaining permission to enter the country. The few available sources made it clear that until 1962, when the ruling imam or religious head of state was overthrown, Yemen was isolated from the rest of the world. Although the British had colonized Aden and the Ottomans twice had controlled sections of the country, highland Yemen had remained free of either foreign ideology or technology. Just as the world knew little of Yemen, the Yemeni knew little of the world, or, for that matter, much about their own country. In neither case was this accidental. The imams who ruled Yemen for nearly a millennium had sought actively to retain Yemeni independence and their own power by minimizing foreign contacts. Whereas a rudimentary infrastructure allowed for some central government control, it also assured that, beyond the elite, most Yemeni peasants knew of little outside their local regions. Characterizations that prior to the revolution Yemen's social and technologic complexity was equivalent to that of sixteenth-century Europe probably are overstatements, but it is clear that when the military overthrew the imam, the Yemeni were thrust abruptly into the twentieth century.

Yemen is culturally diverse, an easily missed fact since most available information dealt with the population centers in the highlands. The following sketch of Yemen's geography, social and religious divisions, and recent history is based on that information, which I used to formulate my research plan (cf. Wenner 1967; Stookey 1978; Peterson 1982).

In this survey I have not mentioned the Yemeni living on the arid coastal littoral of the Red Sea. In a broad sense they are Shafi'i Muslims, many of whom had African ancestors. Inland dwellers cultivate seasonal water courses; coastal dwellers either combine cultivation and fishing or are traders.

LOCATION AND PHYSICAL GEOGRAPHY

The Yemen Arab Republic, situated in the southwestern corner of the Arabian Peninsula, borders the states of the Kingdom of Saudi Arabia and the People's Democratic Republic of Yemen (South Yemen). (See map 1.) Yemen enjoys a temperate climate unique to its location. The high mountain range that extends longitudinally from Saudi Arabia southward through the center of Yemen before gradually decreasing in elevation in South Yemen affords much of the country with moderate weather and provides a rain shadow for the annual Indian Ocean monsoons. Although popular images of Arabia portray its people as camel nomads or coastal fishermen and traders, the area's relatively well-watered, arable plateaus have made farmers of most Yemeni.

The majority of Yemen's estimated 5.3 million inhabitants live in the central mountain range, the area referred to generally as Arabia Felix (Central Planning Office 1978: pt. 1, 73; map). Highlanders subsist on crops grown in the plateaus and valleys composing the central mountain massif. Although a single mountain chain, the massif is punctuated by many valleys and rugged peaks that have created natural boundaries separating portions of the population from regional centers and from each other. The environment as well has hindered attempts to centralize political authority.

The essentials of highland subsistence are, of course, rainfall and arable soil. Al-Attar (1964:141) estimates that only 15 percent of Yemen's land is arable. So scarce are fertile plots that villages often are perched on mountain peaks, both as a defensive measure and to

Introduction / xiii

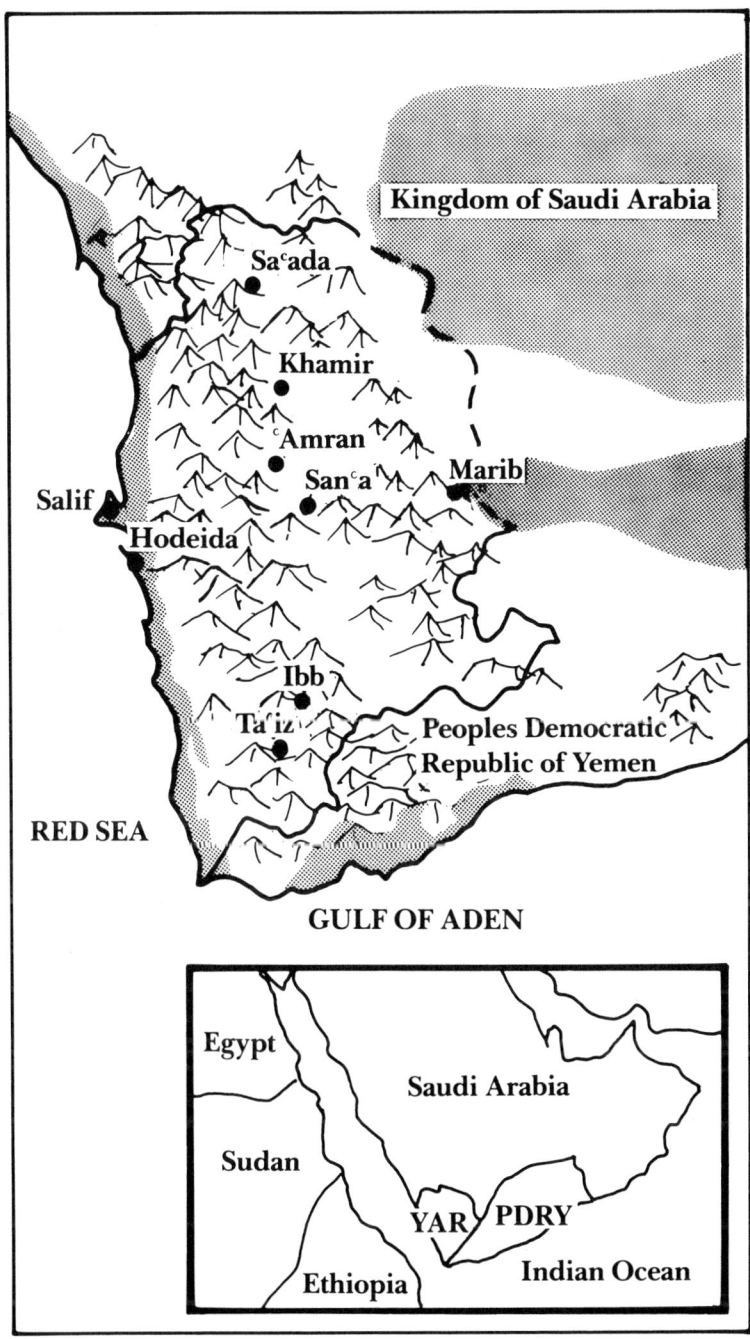

Map 1. Sketch map of Yemen

leave the valleys and hillsides free for cultivation. Even though limited in technology, Yemen has a highly developed agriculture. Throughout the highlands, particularly in the southern areas around Ibb, elaborate terraces have been built to maximize land area and retain and utilize rain runoff. Terracing is less extensive in the north where the combination of less heavy rains and plateaus has produced lower yields.

Yemen is often reputed to have been self-sufficient agriculturally. This may have been the case in the past, but since 1928 some foodstuffs have been imported (Macro 1968:113). In the beginning these may have been a supplement to local wheat, barley, maize, sorghum, and lentils. However, by the 1950s Yemen was depending increasingly on imported foodstuffs (al-Attar 1964:161–62); by 1973, 50 percent of all imports were food (Arab Report and Record 1976:19; cited in Abraham 1977:4). This trend has continued.

Cash crops are limited to coffee, cotton, *gāt* (*Catha edulis*), fodder, green vegetables, and a few fruits. Although Yemen has long been famous as the source of mocha coffee, the annual production has declined almost continuously since 1945 (Halliday 1974:88). In recent years coffee growers have turned to the more profitable cultivation of the mild narcotic, *gāt*, a shrub whose leaves are chewed. In Yemen, *gāt* is used as a local cash crop and has no direct impact on the balance of trade.

RELIGIOUS, CULTURAL, AND SOCIAL DIVISIONS

Virtually all Yemeni are Muslims. Highlanders in the area north of Ibb adhere to the Zaydi sect of Shiʿa Islam introduced to Yemen by Iraqi Zaydi under Imam Yahya ibn Hussayn in the ninth century. Zaydi influence began in the extreme north and its spread involved not only religious conversion but also acceptance of the imam's political authority. The Zaydi imams and their followers, descendents of the Prophet Muhammad's nephew ʿAli, were a small group. The Zaydi elite or *sāda* relied on the northern tribes for military support. Even as converts to Zaydism, these tribes resisted the imposition of Islamic law (Shariʿa) and other aspects of the imam's rule. Skillfully balancing opposing forces, the imams had achieved tenuous political control over most of the country by the seventeenth century. Although subject to the imam's authority, inhabitants in the southern highlands as well as the lowlands—followers of the Shafiʿi legal school of Sunni Islam—never accepted Zaydism.

Although Zaydi and Shafi'i views of Islam are quite similar, the two populations differed culturally and ecologically as well as in their relation to the imam. Both groups dealt with the imam through his representatives in local areas, members of the Zaydi elite, the *sāda*, but were treated differently.

Shafi'i in rural areas were subjected to particularly harsh taxation. Halliday (1974:87-88) implies that tax assessments in Shafi'i areas were always inequitable and the *sāda* used their political positions to amass large tracts of land. In urban areas, Shafi'i merchants were often at odds with the royal family with whom they competed for control of markets and products.

Northern tribal areas could not be governed by giving the *sāda* free rein. Although the tribes recognized the imams' spiritual and temporal power, they were quick to rebel against challenges to their local autonomy. As a result, taxation was less severe in tribal areas, but the *sāda* were still able to accumulate substantial land holdings.

Religious differences posed only one aspect of social diversity. Yemen's social structure was characterized by a rigid hierarchy. The *sāda* constituted the highest social stratum, their position deriving from both their dominance of government offices and their descent from the Prophet. The tribes clearly affected the political balance and it was the *shaykh*, as leader of an autonomous group of warriors, who was most influential. Descriptions of the social structure generally placed the *shaykh* and his followers in the intermediate stratum even though the tribesmen, whose status seemed to derive from warfare, were predominantly peasants. The lowest stratum was composed of a cadre of merchants and providers of service sometimes labelled *walad al-sūq*. Their low rank was connected to their market-based occupations, which ranged from the ordinary butcher and barber to the unusual bleeder and town crier.

MODERN YEMENI HISTORY

Yemen's recent history is divided generally into pre- and post-revolution eras. The first era, 1918 to 1962, spans the post-Ottoman period during which the imamate first consolidated authority over most of the country and then fell victim to its own excesses. The second, 1962 to the present (1978-79), covers the post-coup d'etat, republican era.

Yemen's independence from Ottoman rule was closely tied to the decline of the Ottoman Empire. To maintain order, the Turks had lavished payments on the imam who, in turn, bought the loyalty of the tribes. When the Turks withdrew, the imam could no longer afford these subsidies, and the tribes revolted. Imam Yahya, using a small force of expatriate Turks as a core, fashioned an army to subdue the rebels and drew upon tribes he conquered for additional manpower. To insure tribal loyalty he extracted oaths of allegiance, installed as tribal leaders those who agreed to support him, and took as hostages members of important tribal families. Using these tactics he was able to extend his power over most of the country and to weaken the major tribal confederations, the Hashid and the Bakil.

Although Imam Yahya, and later his son Ahmad, succeeded in establishing control over most of Yemen, their authority did not prevent opposition. Reform-minded *sāda* attempted coups d'etat in 1948 and 1955, but, lacking clear goals and broad support, they failed. In 1962 a broader coalition of merchants, military, and intellectuals successfully ousted the new imam, Ahmad's son, Muhammad al-Badr. But al-Badr escaped to rally tribal support. Openly supported by Saudi Arabia, these royalist forces battled the new republican regime for eight years before peace was restored. The republican leaders were influenced by Nasserist ideals, but the revolution's success was due to the support it received not only from Egypt but also from urban Shafiʿi merchants and the Hashid confederation of northern tribes. Neither side was able to count on permanent support and the civil war was marked by groups vacillating between republican and royalist camps, usually following, if only briefly, the highest bidder.

Before peace was restored in 1970 both sides had suffered heavy casualties. It was bargaining between imam supporters and the new government, rather than the defeat of either side that ended hostilities. The coalition government formed was a consortium of Zaydi tribal leaders and Shafiʿi intellectuals, an alliance acceptable to both Saudi Arabian and Egyptian interests.

During the postrevolution years, Yemen embarked on a plan to create a modern infrastructure. Underlying the associated projects was an equally ambitious program of political unification and economic development. Progress was not uniform, and modernization in the conservative tribal areas was slow. Nonetheless there were noticeable changes. The *sāda* no longer monopolized government offices. The development of roads made communication with the capital and regional centers easier. Private sector development was stimulated by vast sums of money repatriated by Yemeni wage laborers working in Saudi Arabia and the Gulf. Small-scale economic activity boomed.

It was with this background that I decided to study social structural change. I was impressed by the republican constitution's abolition of ascriptive occupations and statuses. I reasoned that regardless of the rigidity of the social hierarchy described in the literature, new sources of wealth and new avenues to power in the post-civil war years would make upward mobility not only possible but likely. Only after I had been in Yemen for several months did I realize that while some social restraints had eased, others had endured.

THE FIELDWORK

My wife, Susan Dorsky, an anthropologist, and I chose ʿAmran, a town of about 6,000 people, for study because it was located in a tribal area and had a reasonably high rate of male out-migration. Situated on a large plateau, the region seemed to have a strong agricultural base, with ʿAmran an active market town. This site seemed suitable for testing my hypotheses and for Susan's study of the effects of long male absence on women's lives. At the outset, however, ʿAmran appeared to lack the "charm" of other towns we had visited.

Our selection of ʿAmran was not based purely on academic concerns. During the two months we lived in the capital, Sanʿa, awaiting research clearance, we found commuting to ʿAmran an easy hour's taxi ride. This proximity allowed us to set up a household, more or less in absentia, and afforded me the opportunity to meet many ʿAmrani secondary school students living in Sanʿa.

It also gave me time to practice Arabic. I had a good background in standard Arabic and an acquaintance with southern Yemeni dialect, but it took me some time to learn the particular Arabic spoken in the ʿAmran area. Although English is taught in secondary schools, the students I met had no conversational ability. Arabic was therefore essential; all activities required Arabic. Although I learned quickly, my comprehension was always superior to my speaking ability. I was easily understood, but many ʿAmranis must have tired of my continuous errors. I preferred speed and ease of conversation to grammatical perfection.

Through our connection with ʿAmrani students, Susan and I were able to rent a house in the *guriyya*, the former Jewish quarter in ʿAmran, which became our home for the next sixteen months. Our landlord had bought the house when the Jews left, but thirty years later it still had many distinctive features. In contrast to the reconstructed houses of our neighbors, our house stood only two stories high and showed evidence of the open courtyard typical of Jewish architecture.

Today, like residential areas in the rest of ʿAmran, the *guriyya* population was a cross section of society. Our neighbors included families of all statuses and occupations, some rich, others quite poor. Our house was on a cul-de-sac, and it was here that we made our first acquaintances.

We were accepted with some difficulty. Few foreigners, certainly no non-Muslims, had lived in ʿAmran. There was suspicion, both at the outset and occasionally later, that I was a spy. Some of the initial difficulties were caused by my own and my student friends' misunderstanding of the local government structure. I had met with the government administrator (*ʿāmil*) and received his approval for conducting research. However, between the time he welcomed us to ʿAmran and our moving in, he was replaced. Later I learned that ʿAmranis know little about the administrator, who commutes from Sanʿa, or his role. My letters of introduction from Sanʿa officials did little to ease their concern over my presence. It was only after another series of documents was obtained that the objections, raised originally by two political opponents, each seeking to enhance his stature, subsided.

My explanation for being in ʿAmran, that I was an anthropologist and interested in studying their way of life, was interpreted by ʿAmranis to mean I was going to record their "customs and traditions." Word of my proposed subject soon spread and eased most fears. I rejoiced in my acceptance; but later I realized that their misconception of my purpose, which I had allowed to go unchecked, blocked some avenues of inquiry. When I deviated from the path ʿAmranis felt I should follow, new suspicions arose. Eventually, with the aid of friends, I was able to overcome some of the problem.

ʿAmran, like the rest of Yemen, is sexually segregated. Some of the fears about me may in fact have been related to concerns that I was a threat to family honor. It was fortunate that Susan was with me. Aside from moral support, the warmth she generated within the neighborhood and throughout the town made me appear less a menace. Susan maintained extensive ties with women, but I could not count any among my informants. Aside from what I learned during occasional chats with a few neighbor women, what I know of ᶜAmrani women comes from Susan. Her lively and detailed discussion of women's lives and perspectives in this period of dramatic social change provides another view of ᶜAmran society (cf. Dorsky 1981).

ᶜAmrani male and female domains rarely overlap (and then not in the presence of even intimate outsiders). Men's activities are broad and their interactions many. Women's lives, apart from daily parties, are more restricted. Female modesty is important; and women, except about their houses, are heavily veiled. My informants only occasionally mentioned their wives, usually in reference to the latter's encounters with mine. Even in houses I visited regularly, I did not know the women. In general, I was scrupulous in avoiding them, much like ᶜAmrani men. Even though the men might occasionally stop and talk to a woman they knew (identified by her gait), I almost never did.

From the moment neighborhood women and girls carefully laid out our furnishings and Susan was whisked off to a women's party, our lives were molded into ᶜAmrani patterns like those described in chapter 1. Islam exerts a profound influence on all aspects of life, linguistic as well as social. Our behavior and speech soon approximated most of these standards. I did not, however, enter the mosque. This was my own choice. I felt to do so would be intrusive since I did not intend to study this aspect of religious practice. During Ramadhan, the month of dawn-to-dusk fasting, it became clear I had made the right decision.

Although we did not fast, we did enjoy the evening feast in neighbors' homes. In addition, I attended many religious ceremonies (wedding parties, wakes, and celebrations of the Prophet's birth) not centered at the mosque. I was often present when men prayed in their homes; I listened to accounts of the Friday "sermon" and engaged frequently in religious discussion. I disappointed many who hoped for my conversion.

Apart from some religious activities, Susan and I conducted our lives much as any ᶜAmrani family. Susan spent her mornings in informants' homes, on social calls, or with neighborhood women. Frequently she was a culture broker between the expatriate medical staff and ᶜAmrani women and children she accompanied to the clinic. Her afternoon activities included making the rounds of obligatory women's parties for new mothers and at pre- and post-wedding celebrations (cf. Dorsky (1981).

In the morning, after shopping in the marketplace, I usually returned there to seek friends or other individuals from whom I hoped to get information. Being without a discernible "occupation," I was initially concerned by how and where to spend my time. Soon I realized that many men had little to do, at least on a full-time basis, and I was more or less like them in simply spending time in conversation. "Hanging out" in the market was also an easy way to observe the flow of daily life, since most activity is centered there and in nearby government offices. My contact with the government was limited. I had hopes of viewing tax records, but was never able to gain access to them. Officials could not understand my interest in taxation, but this was really their way of saying that tax records are sensitive documents and not open to most ᶜAmrani. I soon dropped my inquiry and concentrated on commerce, an area readily accessible by observation and through helping men in their shops. I often took over for a friend away from his shop on business.

I also spent time in the fields helping friends with planting, harvesting, and threshing. While my efforts, particularly in planting, were not always up to ᶜAmrani standards, the retelling of my activities did much to help my image and acceptance. Even an oft-repeated account of my sowing sorghum, in which I was usually called upon to furnish the "punch line" that only a few dozen plants sprouted, provided me an important connection with the town and eased the fact that I was never able to obtain detailed accounts of land ownership.

Indeed, my most important link to ᶜAmran came through the assistance of a once-prominent family, who, in a manner of speaking, accepted me as "attached" to their household. They taught me many basic elements of ᶜAmrani social organization. More important, they provided me a stage on which to display my ability to understand social structure. Routinely, while chewing *gāt*, they posed questions to which they knew I had the answers. Once it became clear that I understood at least the rudiments of social organization, ᶜAmranis were much more willing to converse at length with me on many topics.

Through these discussions many ᶜAmranis came to understand, although some not too clearly, that I was interested in more than a "record of their customs and traditions." At the same time, our conversations led to my being confused on several points. ᶜAmranis tended to assume I knew more than I did and often omitted the obvious, believing I already understood the basics. It was only after a long period of frustration, for example, that an informant explained that a major kinship and political term, *ḥabl*, actually had more than one meaning. Drawing on informants' statements, I had been trying to give the word one definition, a term referring to a descent line in a larger group. However, this definition did not describe most groups to whom the term was applied. It was only when I learned that the term implied a type of relationship, acting as close kinsmen, that the additional uses of the word to describe distant kinsmen and political allies became clear.

Aside from close friends, I had several primary informants. None could actually be considered a research assistant, although two students helped me with a mapping project. Occasionally I questioned them extensively; but, like almost all of the educated younger men, the "children of the revolution," they preferred to appear apart from, if not above, their social system.

My associations were with "older" men, those in their mid-twenties and above, who were active participants in ᶜAmrani society. Like ᶜAmranis, I had the least connection with recent settlers who are considered outsiders. Even though I talked to men in all social strata, this study presents the tribesman's perspective. Regardless of my informants' backgrounds, they expressed the tribal viewpoint, an indication of its importance.

I gained the greatest insights by joining men in their daily afternoon social gatherings: *gāt* chews. *Gāt* (*Catha edulis*) is an essential element in ᶜAmrani daily life. When chewed, the tender leaves of this shrub stimulate and depress, leaving one with a mild sense of euphoria. Although some men do not chew, the majority do at least several times a week. *Gāt* is a luxury, but one most men can afford. My daily expenditure, twenty-five to thirty Yemeni riyals (one YR = U.S. $.22), was probably slightly below average, and accounted for over half of our daily household expenses. Generally we attempted to keep our overall total expenditures within a budget of fifty YR a day, the daily wage for unskilled laborers at that time.

Most ᶜAmranis have fixed locations for chewing *gāt*. I was somewhat less rigid, and usually chewed in houses where I felt I learned the most. For example, while I spent a few afternoons chewing with *gāt* sellers, I became disinterested in the constant banter over sums paid and received and problems of a *gāt* surplus (a rarity!) or shortfall. Instead, I chose places where current social, economic, and political issues were discussed. I also avoided houses in which television viewing had replaced conversation. Although I tried to control where I chewed in order to maximize the information gained, many times social obligations required that I join in the greeting of visitors, welcoming of men back from Saudi Arabia, or consoling of bereaved families. Conversation at these affairs, as at weddings, was usually lighthearted and filled with jokes.

Occasionally during *gāt* chews I sought to steer the conversation to topics uppermost in my mind. Generally, however, I obtained more useful information by letting informants tell me what was important to them and pursuing these issues. These were often blind alleys, but sometimes they led to new avenues of inquiry. During a discussion of marriage, I learned about the change in status of one occupational group, my first indication that the social structure was not as rigid as informants described.

This discovery of course was part of a larger process. It was a long time before I realized that the obvious bases of social differentiation —endogamy, ancestry, and occupation—were not the only status determinants. Affiliations were also important and contributed to ranking within social strata. Wealth, alliances, prestige, and access to power also influenced the status of individuals within the same descent group, resulting in internal stratification. There were in fact a variety of standards, tangible and intangible, used in assessing social position.

These criteria also defined who was included in a particular social context. The predicament facing the newcomer is of special interest, since a person's social position is determined by what is known about him. The more detailed the information, the easier it is for ᶜAmranis to define the social context. Newcomers—about half of the town's population today—are thus excluded from virtually all local, non-commercial affairs. ᶜAmranis view new residents as different, without known histories or loyalties, and lacking the requisite cultural paraphernalia for inclusion.

PRESENTATION OF DATA

Social position is based as much on the past as on the present. Description of the present social structure is therefore possible only through reference to the social environment that existed before the 1962 revolution. I have attempted to weave informants' depictions of the past, which were often static and discreetly edited, into the present dynamics of actual, observable events. This has not been possible in every case, since my informants tended to see and describe the periods before and after the revolution as if they were not connected. For ᶜAmranis (as for most peoples whose history includes a major dramatic event) a sharp break, often appearing as a chasm, separates what is seen as the *ideal*, prerevolutionary era from the present, sometimes uncomfortably *real* situation that they see as commencing in 1962.

The revolution did, of course, create a new social climate, but the ᶜAmran of today is still closely linked to its past. Its social structure was never as absolute or straightforward as informants described or would have liked me to believe. Even before the revolution some social structural modification had taken place, and it is from this series of gradual alterations that I trace the relaxation of social constraints evident today. I emphasize ᶜAmranis' depiction of their social structure, for it is against this model that the present is compared and judged. To support my focus on social structural change, I use ethnographic data to create the local context in which, from the ᶜAmrani perspective, the social modifications have been and are occurring. Following standard anthropologic practice, I have put the descriptions and discussions in the ethnographic present. ᶜAmranis date most recent events to about ten years before my fieldwork. I have followed their chronology.

In Part I, I describe ᶜAmran's present and past. In Part II, I narrow the focus to a discussion of three central social structural elements: affiliation, occupation, and marriage and kinship. Each is presented in terms of the formal model and present-day practice. Finally, I present an interpretation of ᶜAmranis' response to the modifications of their social structure.

PART I

ᶜAmran Present and Past

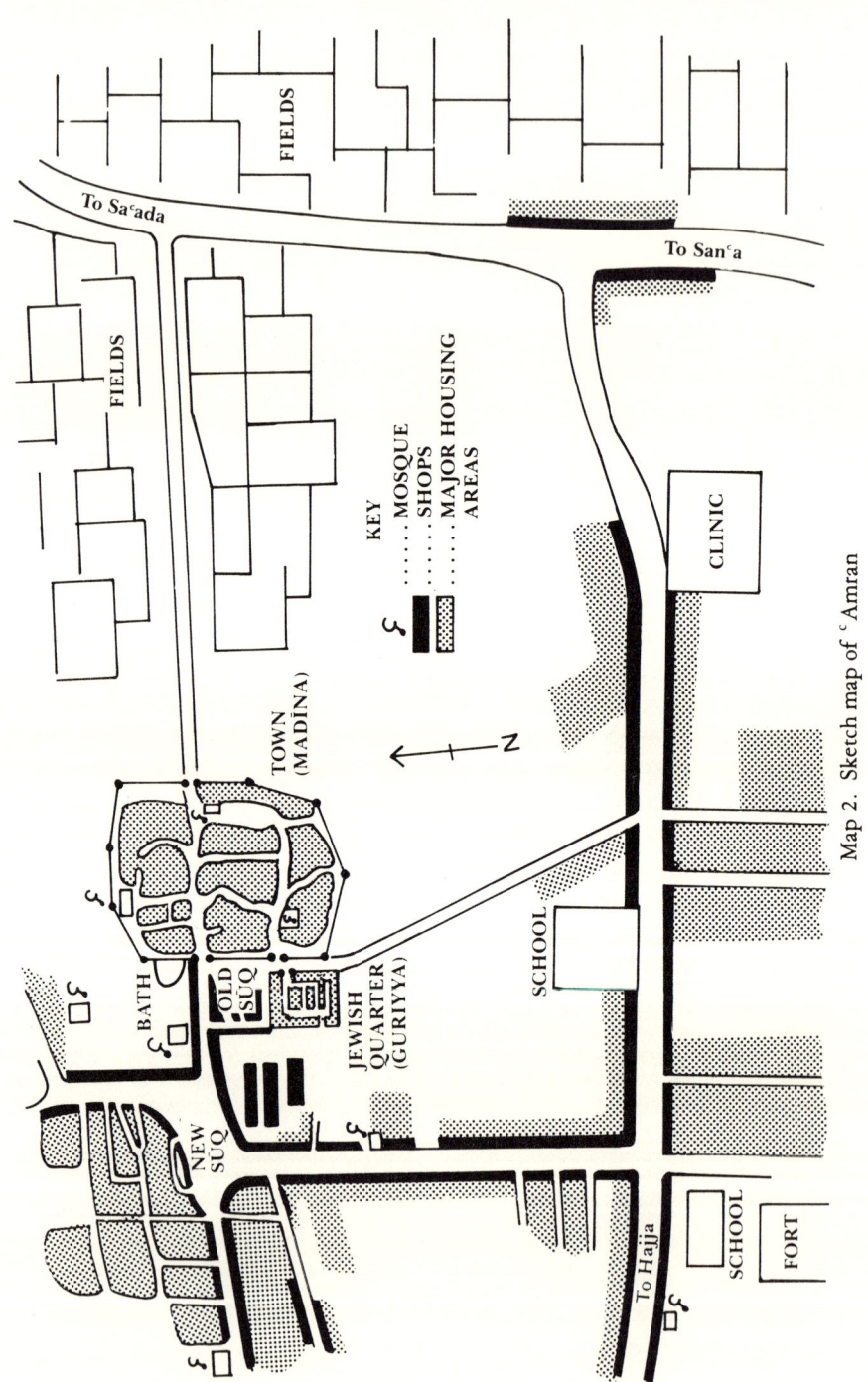

Map 2. Sketch map of ʿAmran

1

A Day in ᶜAmran

Allah al-akbār
Allah al-akbār
Ashhad an la alah ila Allah
Ashhad an la alah ila Allah
Muḥammad rasūl Allah
Ḥiya ᶜala al-ṣalah
Ḥiya ᶜala al-ṣalah

It is *fajir* (first light of the new day). Loudspeakers atop mosques proclaim the first of five appointed times of prayer. Although it is early, some men rise in response to this statement of faith and call to prayer. Many perform the ritual ablutions and prayers in their homes while others attend to these ceremonies in a nearby mosque. Prayer is a religious obligation. At the mosque it is also a social event, providing a time for men to gather and talk, to reaffirm their faith and demonstrate their connection with the community. Throughout the day, men on their way to pray encourage others to accompany them, for religious reasons and for the pleasure of sharing the experience.

It is the *mu'dhdhin*'s (announcer of the hour of prayer) call that signals the start of daily activities and the almost immediate appearance of men in the streets. Throughout the day people often ask, "Have they called prayer yet?" This is their way of keeping time and maintaining the order and tempo of daily life. Despite the proliferation of wristwatches, all important activities are defined in relation to one's religious obligations.

While men go out to pray, women, who are prohibited by custom from entering mosques, begin to bake bread and brew *gishr* (a beverage made from dried coffee bean husks) for breakfast. Yemen is famous for coffee, but the local product, like many others, is too expensive for frequent consumption. As fires are lit, smoke belches forth from small exhaust holes in the sides of houses, indicating that the open hearths are being readied for cooking.

At this early hour, with its very first hints of light, landowners and sharecroppers, who work plots in remote fields, make their way to the day's labors. Some walk beside donkeys balancing the plow, harrow, or nets to be used in the day's work. If there is no need for "heavy" equipment, the men ride their donkeys. With the decline of interest in agriculture in recent years and the concurrent growth of the mercantile sector, only a few townsmen pursue cultivation on a full-time basis. For the rest of the residents, the day begins with sunrise.

As the sun climbs and begins to burn off the haze and the chill that settle in the valley almost nightly, many fires are already going and preparations for the day are fully under way. In the narrow streets of the town, merchants remove boxes of supplies and wares from storerooms around their houses, load them in wheelbarrows, and start off for the *sūq* (market).

The slow steady flow of merchants coming to open their shops begins; and the guards leave the *sūq*, which they have protected throughout the night. The merchants are in no hurry; the market will not begin to bustle for at least an hour. A number of small temporary businesses have been set up to sell coffee, tea, and *gishr* to merchants and men returning from prayer. Fires have been laid in large empty cans and shallow bins cut from fifty-five-gallon drums; the kettles are nestled in the coals. Men gather around these vendors for a warm drink to fight the chill. Although the climate is temperate, a heavy dampness hangs in the early morning air. The men in the *sūq* huddle close about the fires or seek out a spot warmed by the first rays of the sun.

As the activity in the *sūq* increases, the coffee vendors close and leave for their full-time jobs. Customers now must wait for the permanent tea shops to open. Even as the vendors depart, their open-air locations are filled by other, more permanent sellers. Since they do not own or rent shops, these vendors pay a small fee levied by the municipality for use of public space.

Several hundred yards outside the market, in an area surrounded by new houses, sheep and cows have been slaughtered for the day's sales. The butchers' tall tripods, used to drain the animals' blood and to facilitate the gutting and skinning, stand empty. Each animal is slaughtered according to religious doctrine. The butcher faces the animal toward Mecca and just before slitting its throat, says, "In the name of Allah, the merciful, the compassionate." As the sun climbs, the butchers filter into the market carrying the meat, still steaming, in wheelbarrows. Some of the men are accompanied by their apprenticing sons, who carry cutting boards, knives, and the occasional balance scale.

In the center of the *sūq*, in the older shops, the ambitious begin to unpack items for display. All merchandise is put away at night to discourage theft. In front of the shops bins of Yemeni raisins, California almonds, American rice, *gishr*, and other foods are laid out. Intricate displays of imported ready-made clothes are set up. Individual items are placed on hangers and arrayed along the length of chains hanging from the supports of improvised sheet-metal sun and rain shields. Chinese plastic shoes, the popular tennis shoes (*būti*), and Czechoslovakian leather shoes are laid out in pairs. Stacks of plastic pails, boxes of sugar crystals, displays of razor blades, and Indian leaf tobacco all have assigned locations. Many items overflow into the narrow display area that is also the street, making room for the seller inside his shop. Later, when the crowds come, this will hamper traffic, but now it is not a problem. Wheelbarrows; all sizes of pots, pans, and kettles; chain; lanterns; nails; and assorted tools are arranged in front of "hardware" shops. The pattern for locating and displaying items is inflexible. The dried red pepper (*bisbās*) must go here; the sugar (*murāsi*) must go there.

It is still quiet. While sharecroppers and landowners set off to observe conditions in their nearby fields, day laborers gather around the many construction sites. Villagers coming to the market avoid the main road, wending their way through piles of sand, stone, dirt, and other building materials scattered about these sites, before reaching a street leading to the *sūq*. Since this is not a "market day" (one of two days in a regional market round that attracts customers from distant villages), those who come today are men who live in nearby villages in ᶜAmran district. Some bring a donkey load of alfalfa (lucerne) to be sold for cash to a broker in the market. Others come carrying bulging cloths filled with spring onions and scallions from mosque-owned and private gardens. Still others bring crates of tomatoes and sacks of onions and potatoes harvested from their fields. Some of these men will sell their produce to a greengrocer; the rest will set up shop in the area where produce is sold.

An hour after sunrise the tempo in the *sūq* nears its peak. The streets are filled with hurrying, jostling people trying to see the goods for sale. In the midst of the sounds of many conversations is heard the occasional shout or burst of laughter.

"*Sabāh al-khīr*! (Good morning!)," someone shouts to a man just entering the main market area.

"*Sabāh al-khīr wal-ᶜāfiya* (Good morning and good health)," comes the reply as the two shake hands and each makes a gesture of kissing his own hand.

They exchange a bit of news or, most often, trade formal greetings and excuse themselves, using the formalized expressions "Can I do anything for you? (*Ay khadma?*)" or "By your leave (*Khādirik*)." Then they continue on with their morning rounds.

In the residential areas, mothers send their children off to play in the streets. At 7:30 A.M. the national anthem is broadcast through loudspeakers atop the elementary and the joint middle-secondary schools. Even before the music begins, small parties of children are ambling through the old, unattended cemeteries and around construction sites, on their way to school.

The Egyptian teachers, identifiable by their larger size and Western clothing, stroll along the paved road that leads past the two schools. They offer a sharp contrast to the wiry, more graceful Yemeni striding toward the market in "traditional" dress, either long, flowing calf-length shirts or skirts and modern sport shirts, and a Western sport coat. Each man wears a large sheath (*jihāz*) fastened about his waist in which he keeps his dagger (*janbiyya*), the male symbol of adulthood. Each wears a brightly colored cloth around his head. Most also take an old or worn cloth, tossed over the shoulder or draped about the handle of the dagger for carrying items home from the *sūq*.

In the market, men have begun to shop for the day's food, purchasing only essentials this early in the day. Later there will be time to look for a good price on a 50- or 100-kilogram sack of imported flour, sugar, or rice.

"Give me a chicken for ten riyals," demands a villager and the shopkeeper's head disappears into a French-made freezer, his dagger thumping the plastic front.

"No, not this one. It still has blood on it," says the villager, pointing to a bit of rose-colored ice. He passes the chicken back and the shop owner searches for another one, taking time to fill the orders of a few customers who have clustered about the front of the shop. Finally he offers a second chicken.

"Give me another one, this is too small. Give me a bigger one," demands the customer.

"At your service," comes the reply in a most matter-of-fact tone. "Do you want one for twelve riyals?"

"I want a bigger one for ten riyals. Give me a nice one like yesterday!"

"We don't have any more. They're coming in a few hours!" yells the shopkeeper, referring to the daily carloads of frozen chickens brought from the capital.

As the shopkeeper attempts to fill the orders of other buyers, the first customer tries to complete his business.

"All right, give me the first one. How much is this rice? Is it American?"

"Six riyals a kilo. See its trademark," replies the shopkeeper as he extracts a small oval piece of paper from amid the grains identifying the rice as a product of Louisiana in both English and Arabic.

ᶜAmranis state a preference for locally grown foods, but most cannot afford their higher price and buy a variety of imported items like eggs, frozen chicken, flour, and fruits. With worldwide inflation, the influx of monies from Saudi Arabia, and labor-intensive farming practices keeping prices of local goods beyond consumers' reach, many ᶜAmranis have found it more profitable to enter the commercial sector than to continue agricultural production.

Vendor-customer squabbles are more pronounced in the vegetable and meat sections of the market. Butchers and greengrocers hold a low status within the social system and, since prices are not fixed, customers believe these vendors are more inclined to cheat them. People of all statuses frequently allege that the butchers are the least honest of all men in the *sūq* and feel they should be more strictly regulated. This attitude reflects the fact that butchers have a commodity people now consider essential, although this was not always the case.

"Give me half a kilo of calf meat," demands a customer, tossing a twenty-riyal note in the butcher's lap. "That isn't from a calf, it's from a bull," he shouts as the butcher pulls the cowhide cover back, revealing the meat.

The butcher points to the calf's head sitting on the edge of his cutting board, a sign of what he has to sell, and swears it is from the animal he slaughtered this morning.

"Trust me," replies the butcher calmly.

"That's the same head you had yesterday!" says the customer, although he lacks conviction.

"The liar is a Jew," comes the reply. "This is from today. Strike me blind if I lie," he declares as a mild affirmation of the truth and proceeds to cut bits from various sections of meat.

"Give me some more! This isn't worth twenty riyals, and take away the fat. I don't want any bones!" demands the customer as he makes a feint at grabbing back his money.

Finally satisfied, he demands a plastic bag in which to carry the meat and moves on to look for other items.

"How much is a kilo of potatoes?" he asks a greengrocer seated in the center of this older section of the *sūq*.

"Five riyals, and that's cheap. The bag cost me fifty-two," replies the vendor as he sucks on the stem of his water pipe.

"Five!" bellows the customer attempting to attract the other vendors' attention.

"Everyone is selling for five today," comes the retort with an air of certainty.

The customer glances about and, seeing no one beckoning with a lower price, squats to select his potatoes. After they are weighed and bagged, he will probably haggle a bit over the price. If the vendor wishes, he may add a few more potatoes to the purchase; if not, the customer will add a few of his own choosing in spite of the vendor's fainthearted objections.

A characteristic inquisitiveness accompanies some purchases. "Why are you getting mutton today? Is someone sick? Did your wife give birth? Do you have guests?" These are typical questions that arise over any perceived change in buying habits. Mutton or lamb is considered essential for certain occasions and proper for others if within one's means. People are quick to notice when one has changed his buying patterns. Such critical observation extends well beyond the affairs in the *sūq*.

While the haggles and squabbles are common and repeated daily at most stops, they are less frequent in the new commercial sections on the main road where prices and quantities tend to be fixed. Only a few items can be bargained for, particularly local produce and some imported goods. Others, like imported eggs, frozen chickens, and fruit, have fairly rigid prices. Each man has a somewhat fixed series of shops he tends to visit, either because he is a friend of the owner, thinks he gets better prices, or because he has an established credit relationship.

It takes only slightly more than half an hour to make most of the essential purchases. Soon men are carrying their food home in bulging scarves, meeting and exchanging pleasantries with others going to and from the market. Occasionally they enlist someone to drop purchases off at their homes. A few, particularly those with highly successful businesses or other sources of wealth, hire low-status individuals to make their daily purchases. This practice was more common in the past when men of status considered the market an area to be avoided.

ᶜAmrani men do not like to return home during the day. After purchasing items from the *sūq*, a man will stand in the street in front of his home and call the name of his eldest son—a signal for someone to come down and take the food. It is shameful (*ᶜayb*) to call an adult woman by her name in public. Addressing her by her eldest son's name in this situation is considered protective of her honor; and, as some informants suggest, it is also a way of protecting against the evil eye.

By nine o'clock the level of activity begins to slowly wind down, since most people have completed the bulk of their essential shopping. Now that the necessities are at home, it is time for most men to concentrate on the business of the day. Often they merely wander about, checking prices of bulk goods, meeting friends, or drinking tea in the *sūq*. Most men have some place to go, and it is often said that one advantage of having a shop is that it affords a place to be.

Many men have been at work since shortly after sunrise and, because of the demands of farm chores and construction work, will not find time to get to the market. If they are day laborers, their boss (the owner of the construction project) may pay for and even make the purchase of the day's meat in addition to giving them a cash wage. Men at work in the fields usually have a friend or a family member make their purchases.

Since the end of the eight-year civil war, the market has mushroomed in size. The area known as the *sūq* lies just outside the

High Gate of the *madīna*, which literally means "city," but which actually refers to the walled portion of the town. The *sūq* is a concentrated area of shops, some forty or more years old, others built within the last six to eight years. Most are small, and many are simply used as storerooms for new shops in other sections of the town. The *sūq* shops are distinct in their older style of construction: uniformly of stone, with large wooden doors and with floors raised several feet off the ground to prevent rainwater from seeping in and damaging goods, which in the past were primarily grains.

Several traditional, status-linked occupations are practiced in this older commecial section of the market. Clustered in open areas amid the shops along the narrow, primary road leading to the High Gate are the butchers, greengrocers, itinerant beggars, and the disabled men who perform religious tasks. Like vendors without shops, they take up positions in front of shops used for storage. The butchers' special section, with stalls raised high above the ground, is in poor repair and meat usually is sold in improvised locations nearby.

In this same section are the blacksmiths' shops. Although their fires are small and clean-burning, this portion of the market is often buried beneath a dense low-hanging cloud of smoke coming from the public bath (*ḥammām*). The baths are heated with fires made by burning bones from butchered animals and hard wood, a combination that produces a thick black smoke, particularly when the fires are first lighted. As the only public bath in the district, it is always busy. In line with the segregated nature of Yemeni society, specific days are assigned men and women for bathing.

Government offices, located in rooms above the High Gate, overlook the *sūq*. This gate is one of three openings in the tall, thick wall that surrounds what was, only seventeen to eighteen years ago, almost the entirety of ʿAmran. The *sūq* and the public bath lie just outside the wall. The area surrounding the High Gate is considered the center of the town and the hub of many activities, but its importance is waning as residential and commercial areas are springing up elsewhere.

The shops along the tarmac road have a character different from those in the *sūq*, and they reflect the town's strong commercial base. These newer shops are rented primarily by nonnative ʿAmranis, men who have left their villages to relocate in the town. This is where they intend to invest the earnings of years of work in Saudi Arabia. Many of their shops are distinct from the older ones. In addition to common imported goods like the Chinese air-pot thermos, or a variety of canned goods and perfumes, emigrant shopkeepers sell specialties such as clothes and shoes, building materials, or (in one case) cars and trucks. There is even a laundry. All of the shops are open and bright. The newest are larger, with goods neatly arranged on shelves and all wares kept inside.

Interspersed among these shops are hotels (often merely large rooms filled with cots), restaurants, and barbershops that meet the needs of a growing, often itinerant, population. Even for those without capital, ʿAmran has become a place to make a living. Many come to work on the numerous construction sites that dot the area, others to take up positions in restaurants and hotels acting as "servants," positions no ʿAmrani will accept. Crowds often gather in front of shops offering the latest cassette tapes from Sanʿa.

In front of the newer shops, taxis await a full load of passengers. Drivers roam about, calling "Sanʿa" or "Rayda" depending on their destination. Taxis bring villagers to ʿAmran to shop or for medical treatment in pharmacies or at the government operated clinic and also to take villagers and ʿAmranis to the capital, an hour's drive away.

Along with taxis and other vehicles busily transporting people, there is an almost daily arrival of large Mercedes trucks loaded with cement, flour, sugar, rice, salt, lumber, steel, freshly bottled Pepsi Cola, or an array of canned goods destined for wholesalers. The rumbling of these trucks attracts small bands of young men who chase after the vehicles in hopes of finding a few hours of work unloading and storing the goods.

Most activity seems concentrated in the commercial sector, but the transport and sale of goods and the provision of services are only part of the occupational structure of the economy. The demand for new houses and shops has created many jobs and encouraged specialization in carpentry and construction.

In the past, construction techniques allowed for little variation, and all houses were similar in architecture and even in interior furnishings. New building techniques are now common. Cut stone was part of traditional construction, but its use was limited to the foundation and the first floor. Now it is fashionable to use stone for as much of a house as one can afford. Today one hears the constant pinging of hammers on chisels as the skilled, highly paid stonecutters chip away at large rocks, forming smooth faces for the exteriors of homes and storefronts.

Construction areas resound with the clinking of metal on stone, and the thunderous roar of truckloads of stone and dirt being dumped. The moistened dirt is mixed with straw to bond the stones together. Cement blocks, made in "block factories" along the main roads, are used when money is scarce. Sometimes stone, cement block, and the traditional mud and straw bricks (*liban*, s. *libna*) are combined in one house.

The newest homes are single-story dwellings with perimeter walls enclosing a garden or open space and the house. The basic house design includes a central hallway with rooms on each side, virtually all of which are living areas. This architectural style reflects the fact that their owners are not engaged in agriculture and do not need rooms for storage of annual produce or agricultural implements. Even though there is an enclosed compound, most families do not keep livestock. Exceptions to this pattern occur among long-time residents who have built new houses but maintain storage areas in their old homes.

The older houses provide a striking contrast. They are tall, usually four stories high, and share walls with neighboring houses. In the *madina*, the first two floors of houses are used for storage of animals, tools, and grains. Living quarters are found only on the top one or two floors, where the bathroom and kitchen are located. Usually the upper floor room with the best view is used as the main reception room. The *madina* is then an area of row houses, with the new residential areas best described as suburbia.

Despite the modernity of the newer houses located elsewhere, some people still consider the *madina* the place to live. Many men view its narrow winding streets, where only friends and neighbors enter, as a safe place for their women. Here women can conduct their daily chores with little concern that their modesty and family honor will be compromised. Perhaps to avoid "compromising" situations is the reason men do not like to return to their homes during the day. Certainly, many, particularly older men, travel through the streets mumbling bits of the Quran, giving public notice of their presence. Yet, despite the "safety" of the *madina*, it is not uncommon to find the narrow streets blocked by cars, the occasional pickup truck disgorging a load of firewood, and the small street-corner shops run by children selling Pepsi, candy, and *shrub* (a mixture of water and juice concentrate) to equally small customers.

By midmorning, the pinging of hammers on stone is smothered by the rhythmic thumping of exhausts from diesel-engine powered generators in the carpenter shops where electricity drives imported band saws, table saws, routers, and other tools. Although the carpenter shops open late in the morning, they have a booming business in making doors and windows for the many new homes, and they stay open until nearly eleven at night. ʿAmran does not have an electric power station, so the carpenters' long hours serve a dual purpose. First, the generated electricity is available for running the power tools; and second, it can be sold to others. The principal demand period for electricity is in the evening for television sets (broadcasts begin in late afternoon) and lights, so carpenters work late to meet the demands of both their businesses. Numerous power lines, streaming from each of the many workshops, are suspended precariously from makeshift poles, and large trucks often snag these lines and pull them down. Even though viewed by most as a minor inconvenience, this is a serious problem for shopkeepers who need electricity for five or six hours daily for their feezers full of imported chickens. Generator or engine breakdowns bring a flurry of activity as shopkeepers enlist friends to help them string new lines to a working power source.

About midmorning when the carpenters begin work, men who have nothing of importance to do or who have a bit of free time go to the *sūq* for breakfast (although they could just as easily eat at home); many bring freshly baked bread with them. In the market they are assured of meeting friends. There are restaurants and tea shops as well as vendors in the market selling boiled potatoes and hard-cooked eggs and, in season, slices of watermelon. In many shops a person can buy a Yemeni-made Pepsi and munch on Yemeni-manufactured biscuits or share the shopkeeper's breakfast. Regardless of where he spends the morning, he will have some breakfast. The disabled and poor are given bread and tea as they sit in the entrances of mosques awaiting anyone wanting prayers said or part of the Quran read for the recently deceased or seriously ill. They are rarely left idle, for it is both an obligation and a blessing to help the unfortunate and also to commemorate a death with Quranic reading in the mosque or at home.

While men gather in the *sūq* to meet friends, women do the same in the relative safety of their neighborhoods. It is not uncommon to see women (who quickly veil themselves at the approach of a man) in the more secluded residential areas, gathered on stoops, chatting as they pick bits of dirt and chaff out of locally grown grains. All the while, they exchange bits of information and make plans for the afternoon's visiting. Snatches of gossip also are traded. The worlds of men and women rarely overlap, but many of the daily patterns are similar.

The rumble of motors is not limited to the town. During the day, it is heard in the countryside where water is pumped from wells and sent flowing in irrigation ditches. Not all fields are irrigated, although the town lies in a region with a good water table. The main variable is one's distance from a good water source. Some areas that could be irrigated mechanically are not because they are close to natural watercourses that fill and flow during the rainy season. Landowners and sharecroppers alike move quickly to stem the flow to one field while opening the channel to another. Prudent use of water is essential because it is expensive. The cost is based on the expenses of operating the pump, and some crops require more water than others. Even as men are adjusting the water distribution, other groups of men and women are squatting in fields cutting alfalfa, an important cash crop. As the crop matures, it is harvested to meet the demands of livestock owners in town and nearby villages. Middlemen sell most of the alfalfa in ʿAmran's *sūq*, but occasionally growers market it at other stops in the weekly market round.

In spite of, or because of, the thriving economy, leisure has become a new "occupation" for some. For men who have no particular work—the elderly, those recently returned from Saudi Arabia, fathers with sons working in Saudi Arabia, students on vacation—or who have only temporary day-to-day employment, the *sūq* has become a place to wander and hang out. Tradition-oriented ʿAmranis frown on this behavior, and men of importance pass through and rarely stop in the *sūq*, but it has become an acceptable place for many people to spend time. This new image of the *sūq* has emerged because groups of men who traditionally avoided the mercantile sector now play a major commercial role in the town. It is natural that their neighbors, friends, and acquaintances spend some time visiting during the morning while these "new" entrepreneurs tend their shops. Emigrants congregate in shops run by those from their village or natal area.

As the midday prayer call approaches, the level of activity in the *sūq* picks up. Most of the interest is centered on the *gāt sūq*. Here one always finds crowds perusing the day's supply of *gāt*, checking prices, types, freshness; but as noon approaches men are keenly aware of the need to buy their supply of leaves for the afternoon's chewing.

While interest grows in the *gāt sūq*, other sectors of the market begin to close down. Only a few butchers are left trying to sell the remains of the day's slaughter. The gold, silver, and money exchangers slowly stow their valuables. Most of their customers are villagers, who come to convert some of their Saudi riyals to Yemeni riyals; by midday they are on their way home. Gun and ammunition vendors also are closing shop, as men's interest shifts to *gāt*.

ᶜAmrani men always bargain for *gāt*. No one pays the price asked except when the supply is limited. Buyers are as suspicious of *gāt* sellers as they are of butchers, but for reasons not related to status. Sure they are being robbed, customers strive to get the best deal. A man may even show his purchases to friends announcing the cost as somewhat lower than it was.

"What have you got?" asks a man muscling through the crowd around a *gāt* seller. "Give me a look. Where is this *gāt* from?"

Picking up a wrapped bundle, a buyer carefully opens the covering to see how much *gāt* is actually under the many layers of protective, non-*gāt*, leaves. He is particularly careful to note the number of tender young leaves since these make for the best chewing.

"How much is it?" he asks.

"Forty," comes the reply.

"What's your final price?" he queries.

"Thirty-five, and I'm only making two riyals," responds the seller.

"Thirty," offers the customer, but the vendor simply takes back the *gāt*.

Later, the customer finds some other *gāt* to his liking or comes back to the first seller. If demand is heavy by then, the price may have gone up.

"Give me long branches of *gāt*," shouts a man.

"Here's some locally grown," says the vendor and hands long stalks to the customer.

"Where's it from?"

"From Dhaᶜwān."

"How much?"

"Fifty."

"Forty."

"Forty-five," says the seller. "That's my final price."

"Okay, but give me something for cigarettes."

They settle for forty-two riyals as the loudspeakers on the mosques begin to announce the noon prayer. Since there are ten mosques, the calls begin at slightly different times and the various *mu'dhdhins'* litanies blend into each other. A few men begin to close their shops for the day, but most leave them under the eye of a guard (often a younger brother, son, or other household youth) as they go off to pray and then to their homes for lunch. With the prayer call, clouds of smoke begin to rise from houses throughout the town as the women ready the fires for baking. They know their husbands and sons will linger a while in the mosque or chat with friends on the way home; the bread will be ready in time.

Lunch is not a time for relaxing. It is a necessity, and men do not linger over it. Although it is the largest meal, usually four to five courses, most men manage to eat in less than twenty minutes. In large extended households, or if guests are present, men eat separately from women and children. Once they have finished and adjourned to another room for tea, *gishr*, or perhaps a brief rest, the women begin their lunch.

Despite the separation of male and female spheres, men find time to play with their children, but prefer to do so outside, away from the house. After lunch they usually take time to chat in the street with neighbors, to joke with their children or give them money for candy.

It is only an hour and a half after the noon prayer call when men begin to trickle back into the *sūq*. In many respects, they are starting a new day. Although afternoon activities for many men are far removed from those of the morning, they begin in the marketplace. Once again it is time for tea and, though the pace is leisurely as in the morning, men harbor concerns about their final selection of a suitable place to spend the afternoon. Those who have no fixed chewing site, or are merely seeing if there are better locations, make such decisions in the tea shops. Here men gather; discuss where they are going to chew; inform their friends of any special events; inspect with a trained eye the quantity and type of *gāt* their friends have purchased; and perhaps, if the supply of *gāt* is good, buy an additional bunch. Those who were unable to get to the *gāt sūq* earlier, now crowd around the sellers in what often appears a frenzied effort to get some leaves at an affordable price.

Theoretically, men do not begin to chew until the midafternoon prayer has been called and answered. Actually, some begin almost as soon as they have finished lunch. Despite their passion for *gāt*, many men, if not all, realize that chewing is an expensive pastime and that they may spend twice as much money on *gāt* as food. Many like to cite the apparent evils of chewing, most notably its effects on sexual performance. In spite of jokes and hand signals used to demonstrate powerful erections produced by some types of *gāt*, it is well known that the limp wrist sign is a more apt indicator of the temporary impotence that accompanies heavy chewing. Still, although they complain, they chew.

Most men have a relatively fixed site for chewing. Merchants like to chew in their shops so they can conduct business even though consumer traffic is light in the afternoons. Those who do not have a business select various locations, but usually follow a pattern. Most men like to chew with the same people, at the same place, for weeks or months at a time. Only after they have become tired of the same company do they begin to look for a new place.

As in other areas of social life, there are rigidities in *gāt* chewing patterns. The degree of ritualization depends primarily on the number of people gathered and how long they have been coming to the same location. With familiarity, informality increases.

Houses in which men regularly gather are open to all, without invitation. Special announcement or invitation is required only for an event, such as a wedding or an out-of-town guest, or when a man first decides to open his house to friends. In the latter case, once the information becomes public anyone may attend. Men prefer to chew in houses with a *mafraj* (a well-appointed men's room often located on the highest floor) that affords both good company and a good view. Guests arrive about midafternoon and are extremely cautious in entering the house, since the women do not leave home for their own gatherings until after performing the afternoon prayers. A courteous visitor always calls "Allah" as he climbs the winding dark staircases to the *mafraj* to warn women that a non-family member is entering the house and to allow them time to dart for cover. (All men should give warning whenever they enter a house, whether their own or a friend's. This shows consideration not only for the women of the household but also for any others who may be visiting.)

Although women clean the *mafraj* every morning (which includes sweeping out the remains of *gāt*, stacking the thick rectangular arm cushions, setting the water pipes and hoses off to the side, and straightening the floor and back cushions lining the room), there are final preparations yet to be made. When the guests arrive they remove their shoes either in the hall outside the room or just inside the door. At large gatherings, some men carry their shoes so they will not have to search for them in the dark when they leave. As the men enter the *mafraj*, each takes an arm cushion or two and possibly a blanket, then seeks a suitable location where he arranges the cushions and blanket for maximum comfort. Early arrivers almost always arrange their own seats. Later guests may find the room has been laid out by members of the household. After settling into their spots, men usually get ready to chew. If they are regular visitors and are early, however, they may help with some of the other chores. It is common for the children or grandchildren of a house to set up and "build" the water pipe. First they prepare tobacco and then place its holder, covered with hot coals, atop the pipe's long stem. Thermoses also must be filled, ashtrays and spittoons laid out, and cushions and blankets set in place. Guests usually provide a share of the necessities. Men who smoke the water pipe bring a small contribution of tobacco or charcoal.

Once the room is ready and a few men are seated, chewing begins. By the time latecomers arrive the room is filled, each man reclining against thick back cushions with his left leg folded beneath him and his left arm resting on an arm cushion. The right leg is bent so the foot rests on the floor, to avoid insulting anyone by showing him the sole of the foot.

As each new arrival is comfortably seated, he begins to open and inspect the contents of his plastic bag. After selecting a bunch of *gāt* with a good number of nice leaves, he stows the others in the bag to preserve their freshness and begins to chew. The process is simple. He breaks the tender young shoots from the stem, places them in one side of his mouth, and chews. He swallows the juices, and the masticated leaves are pushed off to the side. As he adds new leaves, the wad in his cheek grows. He discards the stems with large rough leaves. Shortly these form a large pile in front of the chewer. Chewing produces a hearty thirst and the amount of water he consumes has an influence on the type and speed of the *gāt*'s effect.

Virtually all aspects of *gāt* activity are referred to by the word *khazin*, which literally means "to store." The process of chewing is *khazin* as is the process of buying *gāt*. Men often ask each other, "*Khazant?*" In the morning this means "Have you bought your *gāt?*" and, in the late afternoon or evening, "Did you chew today?"

Each meaning refers to the process of storing the leaves in one's cheek.

Early in the *gāt* chew, the conversation is lively, centering on bits of information about the day's activities; stories and jokes are exchanged as well. It is not uncommon for one man to become the butt of jokes for thirty minutes to an hour. By this time the chewers are beginning to feel a mild sense of euphoria. Also, the larger the wad in the chewers' cheeks the less lively the conversation, until eventually only quiet prevails, broken only by the gurgle of the water pipe. At the beginning of the afternoon, the anticipation of the *gāt*'s effects serves to direct conversation to important matters after the interlude of joking and laughing has passed. It is such talk that ultimately fades as men continue to pack ever larger numbers of leaves into their cheeks and begin to contemplate their lives in a rather dreamy way.

Discussions often center on religion, sometimes focused on the decline of Islam and morality since the revolution, more often on particular passages from the Quran. It is not uncommon for Quranic commentaries to be read aloud. At many *gāt* chews, readings are an integral part of the afternoon's activities, and often men seek out houses where religious discussions are held. This religious interest naturally reaches its zenith during the holy month of Ramadhan.

Where people elect to chew is often related to the nature of their work or other connections. *Gāt* sellers chew in one *diwān* (a large meeting room outside a house) attached to the storeroom of a major *gat* broker. The Prophet's descendents, the *sāda* (s. *sayyid*), and tribesmen who do not have shops chew in houses. Members of a status group tend to chew with others of similar rank, but there are no absolute patterns. Many *gāt* chews are quite cosmopolitan, which may be a result of the new ideas that came with the revolution.

Gāt chews also illustrate cultural expectations related to the host-guest relationship. The host should always provide services for his guests and, therefore, occupy the poorest seat, the one nearest the door so he can easily leave to get new supplies of water or to "rebuild" the water pipe. At the same time he should be sure that his guests are comfortable and that those viewed as socially important have the best seats. In reality, a household head relies on his sons to provide these services. In a formal *diwān*, such as that of a government official, these patterns are more sharply drawn and service is provided by a man hired for the task.[1]

For the few who do not chew *gāt*, the afternoon is a time for sleep, for strolls in the countryside, and perhaps to meet others in the *sūq*. The great majority of men chew, however, regardless of the situation, even if they find it necessary to undertake any sort of work in the afternoon. Taxi drivers and passengers, for example, calmly chew as they commute back and forth from the capital.

Men also chew *gāt* when making obligatory calls on sick friends, seeking resolution of disputes, or arranging the sale of property. Occasionally a worker chews in the house of his employer. Under these circumstances, as at weddings and funerals, lighthearted conversation is the rule.

Shortly after the midafternoon prayer has been announced from the mosques, most women are on their way to call on mothers who have recently had a baby, console the bereaved, or attend parties in the home of a prospective or new bride. Although they may attend one or two social gatherings in an afternoon, they are careful to return home soon after the sunset prayer call. It is considered inappropriate for women to be far from home once evening falls; the sunset prayer call tells women that they should be in their neighborhoods.

The sunset prayer call notifies men that the day's chewing is drawing to a close. They gauge their supply of *gāt* so that it will run out about a half-hour before the first evening prayer is announced. Leave-takings are marked by quiet sounds; the brushing of *gāt* leaves off clothes, the rustle of coats being pulled on, the squeak of leather as daggers are straightened, and the crunching of *gāt* branches under foot. At the door, men pause to locate and put on their shoes and, as they did upon entering the room, mumble "*Salām ʿalīkum*" (Peace upon you) and disappear down dark stairways. Although sunset usually means the end of *gāt* chews, they sometimes continue into the evening if important matters are still under discussion. The fact that most men leave at sunset may be related to the obligations of prayer and, perhaps, to the knowledge that women will be returning to their homes.

Whether they spit out their *gāt* wad in the house or chew a few more minutes outside, most men will return to the market. Some go directly to pray; others sip a glass of tea and then proceed to the mosque. The prayers for sunset and evening are usually said together. With sunset and the turning on of electricity in many shops, the incandescent light gives the *sūq* a surreal appearance. Except for the shouting and squabbles among adolescent boys, the early evening is quiet. The affairs of the day have been completed and, having chewed gāt, men have little left to say.

This time of day is like the early morning hours when men gather to be with each other but spend most of the time in quiet contemplation. Those not tied to shops in the market gather in groups of two or three to engage in private conversation or to sit in silence together. Although the sūq is clearly the public domain, in the early evening it also becomes, under darkness, the private domain. Men do not like to sit at home, and they use the night to create private space outside the home.

Evening activity in the market is slow. Men look for the occasional purchase—some fruit to eat while watching television, kerosene for a lantern—or they arrange for workers for a special project.

Even this spotty activity begins to slow down about an hour after the evening prayer call. In the old sūq, most shopkeepers begin to stow the assorted containers of goods and slowly padlock their shops. A few, mostly the newer shops, stay open late hoping to attract business simply by being open. Carpenters, getting double use out of their generators, do not notice the change and continue to make windows and door jambs for new houses.

When the last taxi leaves for Sanʿa, the driver, anxious to get a full load, drives along the paved road calling for riders. Some men have gathered in restaurants and hotels to drink tea and watch television. By nine o'clock the tea shops in the sūq are closed.

As the noises of the market subside, the muffled sounds of televisions, cassette tape players, and radios begin to fill the streets. Television is the most popular entertainer, with its serials and soap operas from Egypt and Syria offering a new form of amusement. Arabic programs are intermixed with old American shows like "Fury" and "The Fugitive." At nine o'clock the familiar strains of the national anthem are heard as ʿAmranis tune in the evening news.

Although most of the town is at home watching television and eating bits left over from the noon meal, some men continue to wander. They visit friends to watch television if they do not own one or merely roam, looking for others with whom to stroll and chat. By eleven o'clock, when television signs off, most of the town is asleep. With the end of the broadcast, the day is officially over. Generators are stopped, and, except for barking dogs, the town is quiet for the night.

This description of a typical day in ʿAmran does not reveal the multitude of events, large and small, that quickly change the tempo of daily life. Both common and varied, some of these events are scheduled, others simply happen.

On Friday and Saturday, the *sūq* is filled with many times the normal number of shoppers and a large number of itinerant traders. The latter take part in a regular, but increasingly less important, market round. Later in the week, particularly on Monday and Tuesday, many of the permanent ʿAmran vendors are off selling items in regional markets. In contrast to the bustle of ʿAmran's *sūq* days, these days are notable for their lack of action and the feeling that the real action is elsewhere. Taxis conduct a flourishing business shuttling people back and forth to the markets nearby. Many men merely travel to these markets to keep in touch with events elsewhere. Often their accounts are the central topic of discussion in the afternoon *gāt* chews.

With the end of the cold, rainy months (November to February), planting begins. This has little visible effect on most people; but when the crops have ripened, the harvest will change the daily pattern sharply. Relatively few men are required to plow and sow, but many are needed to reap the crops quickly to save them from sudden rains. In harvest season, men (often shopkeepers) may spend the whole day in the fields cutting sorghum, wheat, barley, and other crops, or in specially prepared threshing areas laboriously separating the grain from the stalks and the chaff. Women also participate in the harvesting chores, and they bring breakfast and sometimes lunch to workers in the fields.

It is natural that major religious holidays change daily patterns, and in ʿAmran these days bring sharp contrasts to regular daily routines. In Ramadhan, with its month-long fast, the activities of day and night are reversed. Many men spend hours in the mosques, praying and reading passages from the Quran. Others spend the evening and the night wandering through the *sūq*, which becomes a carnival of sorts, or playing special games. During the day, the *sūq* is closed until late afternoon; the shopkeepers are home asleep, and only those with pressing business are awake. Women's activities are altered less sharply because they must still tend the children, who do not fast.

Both the *ʿayd al-fatr* and the *ʿayd al-kabīr* or *ʿayd al-adhha*—the holidays after Ramadhan and at the time of the pilgrimage, respectively—bring the *sūq* to a standstill. There is no activity; and shops remain closed for three, four, or more days before normal operations

Although in disrepair, the wall and bastions still circle the *madīna*

The great mosque of ʿAmran

Traditional houses face a large, open area in the *madīna*

Children play in an open area in the walled town

A typical winding street in the *madīna*

The new *sūq*

A tribesman and a friend in his well-stocked shop in the old *sūq*

30 / *A Day in ʿAmran*

Men pass the afternoon chewing *gāt*, smoking the water pipe, and talking

On the wedding night, relatives and friends escort the groom (far left) from the mosque to his home

New houses clustered about the new *sūq* are reflected in pools left by heavy rains

A Day in ʿAmran / 33

Reinforced concrete pillars outline new shops on the main road

34 / A Day in ʿAmran

Grains are still threshed by driving donkeys in a circle over dried stalks

Two brothers and their mother harvest lentils in a terraced field

The main road of ʿAmran is lined with new shops

are resumed. Even then they are open only in the morning, closing in the afternoon as men gather to chew *gāt* with friends. ʿAmranis spend the days visiting friends and relatives, parading about in new holiday clothes, and leisurely strolling with companions. In the evenings, adolescents and young men play special physical and verbal games.

These are the major weekly and annual events. Even though they are remembered and awaited, they are not as interesting to many people as less formal events that punctuate the rest of the year. Part of this lack of excitement is due to the formal nature of the major holidays. Visiting patterns are known, daily activities are well defined, and everyone knows who will be found playing games until late in the evening.

Less formal and fixed events draw greater interest. Gatherings for weddings and funerals, or for returnees from the pilgrimage or work in Saudi Arabia all require attendance. These are social obligations, and friends, relatives, and invited guests must attend to avoid insulting their hosts. Reciprocity plays an important part in daily life. Wedding days give rise to questions concerning who will represent the family or, in the case of several weddings on a single day, which man will chew at the different houses. There is actually little discussion of where to chew *gāt*, but rather a common concern over the higher prices for leaves and problems of getting a sufficient supply to last through the afternoon and evening chewing. Wakes and welcoming guests also require nonkin participation. Days later people are asking for information about who attended the event, how large were the wedding gifts, who chewed in which room, who were the guests. Accounts of a returnee's days in Saudi Arabia often circulate for weeks. These events attract men both because of their obligation to attend and because of the opportunities to reminisce.

2

ᶜAmrani Views of the Past

ᶜAmran has experienced dramatic growth since the start of the revolution in 1962 and even since the civil war ended in 1970. There is a boomtown atmosphere with construction and expansion occurring so rapidly that even long-term residents have difficulty staying abreast of who is building what, where, and for how much. Many, even the postrevolution children, remember the town in a way no longer visible. People can point to a spot in what has become the "old" *sūq* and state that this is where Muhammad al-Hazb grew alfalfa in the early days of the revolution.

Yet beneath the impressive outward appearance of economic development, there are doubts about its effects. Residents openly question what has become of the town, what will be their future, and lament the loss of past virtues. The alternate forces shaping ᶜAmranis' conflicting views are characterized in the following statements. Invariably, when one opinion is expressed, someone counters with the other; and the stance a man adopts one day might be changed the next.

> Before the revolution, under the imam, we were all *masākīn* [literally humble, with overtones of humility, religiosity, and an inability to influence the events of one's life]. Everyone helped each other. We were all poor. We ate what we grew and were strong. We respected each other and everyone knew their places. Now everyone is rich and they don't care about others. They only care about themselves.

> In the past we were better [meaning more religious] and we followed the customs and traditions of our ancestors. But we didn't have money or opportunity. Now we can do as we like. We have free time to sit and talk and have fun. In the past we could only work.

Many variations of these statements are expressed in accounts of the past. Often ʿAmranis' remembrances are inaccurate, purposely exaggerated to make a point, to detail past glories, and, therefore, to call into question the modern world and the new values it has begun to inject. Although there is no written history of ʿAmran—in fact the town is rarely mentioned in historical accounts—local tales piece together a picture of how things are perceived to have been. There are inconsistencies and oversights (including, no doubt, accounts ʿAmranis did not want me to hear), but many of these appear to go unnoticed by listeners. In the reverie of *gāt* chews, for example, during which I collected most of these accounts, the audience rarely challenged the veracity of tales even when it seemed they should have done so. Men are comfortable with the past the stories recall; the tales validate their lives and attitudes. The stories fit a politics-of-the-moment, often addressing a point.

Shortly after settling in ʿAmran, I heard the following representative account from an old man who had been a hostage under Imam Yahya (1904–1948) and later was Imam Ahmad's (1948–1962) agent in ʿAmran. Until I found some parts of the account in al-Wāsiʿī's history (1947:91), I viewed it as a legend or a direct attempt to "pull my leg" (not uncommon in the first months of fieldwork). The story was repeated for various audiences with some minor changes, and an occasional significant change.

> It was in the time of my grandfather. The town leaders climbed down the well next to where the Himyarite castle used to be. There were steps along the side of the well made from stone. At the bottom they found two bodies. They were men about ten feet tall. They stretched from here to there [pointing]. They were our ancestors, the Himyarites. See! Our ancestors were really men, not like we are.
>
> Their hands were huge but well proportioned. The nose was as long as from your wrist to your fingertip. The head was from your fingertip to your elbow. The legs were as long as a donkey's. They were just like us only bigger.
>
> Under them they found a door to a storeroom. Inside were casks made of animal skins. These were full and when they were opened a red liquid, like blood, spilled out. It flowed out and everyone was covered with it. Later it was learned that it flowed along an underground ditch under the wall and came out near a well about three kilometers away. It was for irrigation. See what kind of men our ancestors were! There was never anything like them!
>
> Our men also found gold statues of all the animals and people too. They were just like real animals only smaller. There were dogs, camels, rabbits, donkeys, giraffes, lions, birds, snakes, and many others. They were exact right down to the penis. When the imam heard about this he wanted everything sent to him. Everything was sent to Sanʿa except for one gold statue that _____ [a man of

low status] stole thinking the imam would not miss it. The imam said that the dead men were our ancestors. When he saw that a statue was missing he started an investigation and _____ was afraid. He sold the statue to a Jew who melted it and tried to sell the gold in Aden, but the imam's agents caught him and both men were sent to jail.

The account makes several points. The Himyarites, members of a political dynasty of the second to fifth centuries A.D., are to be regarded with awe. This attitude is commonly expressed when people describe the huge, carved stones believed to be remnants of Himyarite construction. Clearly ʿAmranis' ancestors had great technical expertise and were larger than life. This is an important point of contrast, for ʿAmranis often speak of themselves, half-heartedly, in deprecatory terms: "We were better in the past; then we were true Muslims. Then we were really men."

The imam is regarded both as the seat of knowledge, perhaps a reflection of the narrator's relationship to him, and as all powerful. That the imam could know of the theft and then successfully apprehend the culprits is merely a variation of the often expressed notion that the imam could and did catch those who evaded full payment of their taxes. Perhaps it also recalls a time when corruption is thought to have been rare. Although bribery is viewed as wrong, many believe it is common. People think that under an imam, a true Islamic leader, this would not be the case.

In one variation of this story, modern elements are added. Again there is a theft. This time, however, the guilty parties escape.

> The imam kept the statues in his palace in Marib. He had them lining the ledges that circled the room. When I visited Marib on business and stayed with the imam I saw them. They were of gold and were exactly like real people and animals. The statue of the man had fingernails and [laughing] a little penis.
> The Egyptians came to see the imam and saw the statues. They stole them, every one of them, and flew away in a helicopter. They took them directly to Cairo to present to [Gamal ʿAbd] al-Nasser. Al-Nasser put them in a museum along with other things they stole from us.
> "You saw them when you were in Cairo, didn't you, Salih?" [addressing a guest].

Here foreigners are condemned and al-Nasser is the target of indirect attack. He is implicated in the theft, but his influence upon the revolution (which included supporting the Republicans with 40,000 Egyptian soldiers) is really what is questioned.

THE ORIGIN OF SOCIAL DIFFERENCES

In the preceding narrative it is no accident that the thief is of low status or that he is abetted by a Jew. Accounts of the past, congruent with perceptions of the present, tend to link moral deficiency with certain ascriptive occupations. ʿAmran's social hierarchy[1] is based on the interrelated criteria of affiliation, occupation, and marriage (see discussion in Part II). These criteria compose the formal model of social status. Some of the elements of this formal, or ideal, hierarchy are evident in the following origin legend, known to a number of ʿAmranis. I first heard the account from the son of an innkeeper, one of the low status, *walad al-sūq*[2] or "children of the marketplace." He refers to his status group by the polite, but rarely used label, *bani al-khamis*.

> It was before the time of Jesus, son of Mary. At that time Asad al-Kamal [a Himyarite leader] wanted to lead an expedition to conquer lands beyond the "sea of darkness" [probably the Red Sea]. He called all the people together to go with him. Some expressed doubts about such a long and dangerous trip into an unknown area. They were sure they would become lost and never return to their families. Others were brave and anxious to see what they could bring back from such an expedition. Finally when they were ready to depart, those who were afraid decided to remain behind rather than risk being lost forever.
>
> Asad al-Kamal was very clever. He took a donkey with the expedition who had just foaled, but left the foal behind. He knew no matter how far they went the donkey would be able to find her way back to her foal. The group set off and was gone a long time, but eventually returned, led by the donkey who heard the cries of her foal. They brought with them many treasures gathered along the way.
>
> The men who had been afraid were looked upon as cowards, not fit for the work of "men." They were called the "tribe of one-fifth [*bani al-khamis*]" because that is how many refused to go with Asad al-Kamal. They were left to do the tasks in the market.

The legend accounts for a major social division, distinguishing between the *gabīlī*, the brave tribesman and follower of Asad al-Kamal, and the *walad al-sūq*, who was afraid. It also equates cowardice with those who engage in commercial or service trades in the marketplace, thus indirectly espousing the virtues of a warrior-agrarian lifestyle. Finally the narrative suggests a permanent connection between occupation and behavior, with the honor or stigma of the former being passed patrilineally.

The legend describes simple occupational divisions, linking the tribesman with soldiering and the *walad al-sūq* with commerce, but these distinctions, particularly among the latter, are drawn more precisely. The tribesman, whether a warrior or a cultivator, is a jack-of-all-trades and undertakes many and varied tasks, each of which he can perform for himself. By contrast, commercial and service tasks require specialists, and individual *walad al-sūq* families are associated with particular occupations. Although one informant suggested that occupational divisions originated with the Himyarites, ʿAmranis cannot explain the relation between ancestry and occupation. It is clear that whereas a person's "ancestral occupation" might be a barber or a butcher, he is not required to perform that type of work. The label "butcher," for example, merely describes his social position.

Occupational divisions are permanent and ranked. Although imprecise, generally three *walad al-sūq* substrata are recognized (see chapter 4). The lowest substratum is formed by the poetic messenger-town crier and the bleeder or cupper. The highest includes the "merchants" or *bayāʿīn*, who are sometimes regarded as former tribesmen (see chapter 3). The intermediate substratum includes the barber-circumciser, innkeeper, bath attendant, butcher, and greengrocer.

The legend discusses the *walad al-sūq* and the tribesman but makes no reference to the *sāda* or Zaydi elite. The *sāda*, it was explained, came to Yemen well after the time of Asad al-Kamal when the Imam al-Hadi Yahya ibn Hussayn was called to intervene in a dispute between warring tribes in the last years of the ninth century. He brought with him a few followers, also descendents of the Prophet Muhammad. At least a few ʿAmranis believe that as the imams expanded their sphere of influence, they augmented the ranks of the true descendents with appointees. They like to point out that a nearby all-*sayyid* village might have come into existence in this manner.

Even when ʿAmranis raise doubts about the ancestry of local *sāda*, they do not seriously challenge their descent. The *sāda* are recognized as men of religious skill, piety, and honor. Only a few informants could explain that the *sayyid* entered the social system at a later stage, but most ʿAmranis would find this information insignificant anyway. Although the *sayyid* stratum was, through conquest, imposed on the social structure, the *sayyid*'s superior position was assured because his vocation and moral supremacy were related to his descent in the same way that occupation and behavioral criteria defined the *gabīlī* and the *walad al-sūq*. The distinction in their origins is therefore relatively unimportant.

Before the revolution, social position was manifested by the dagger (*janbiyya*) worn by adult men. The *sāda* wore their daggers off the right hip, the scabbard tilted off the belt by about forty-five degrees. The *walad al-sūq* also wore their daggers at an oblique angle but hung across the stomach. The tribesmen's daggers hung perpendicularly across the stomach in line with the navel.

Since the revolution the upright scabbard of the tribesman has been adopted by all *walad al-sūq* and many *sāda*. This eliminates visual cues, but it has not altered the fact that ʿAmranis associate each substratum with specific characteristics that contribute to the definition of relationships. This has two aspects. First, the *gabīlī* and *sayyid* strata are each perceived as homogeneous, whereas the *walad al-sūq* stratum is subdivided into occupation-specific categories. As a result, although all tribesmen are brave and all *sāda* are honorable, the *walad al-sūq* may be differentiated by how much they deviate from the behavior of real "men." Second, being a tribesman obligates him to protect the weak; therefore the tribesman is responsible for the defense of the *sayyid* and the *walad al-sūq* since both strata stand outside the tribal system, a point formerly made clear by the attitudes in which their daggers were worn.

ʿAMRAN'S JEWISH POPULATION

The formal model of ʿAmran's social hierarchy only describes relations between Muslims. Until the founding of the state of Israel in 1948, ʿAmran, like many highland towns, had a rather large Jewish population. Its security, like that of the nontribal groups, the *sayyid* and the *walad al-sūq*, was the responsibility of ʿAmran tribesmen living in the town and in villages in the tribe's territory.

Even though the Jews occupied the lowest rung in the social system, ʿAmranis remember them with a curious mixture of disdain, respect, and enthusiasm. Characteristically, they regard the Jews from a politics-of-the-moment viewpoint. Commonly, mothers shout at a child, "*Ibn* (*bint*) *yahūdi* [son (daughter) of a Jew]," when the youngster is misbehaving. Men in the marketplace, when unable to strike a bargain, may accuse the vendor of being a Jew (*yahūdi ibn yahūdi*). When poking fun at another, one of my informants would say, "Look at him. His grandfather was a Jew. He wore earlocks. He converted at the hand of my grandfather, Muhammad. [Laughing.] Yes, by God, its true."

At other times people remember how well the Muslims and Jews got along. Stories of strife between the two groups were never told when I was present. Often men attributed the harmony to the good offices of the *shaykh* who ensured that the Jews would live peaceful, unmolested lives.

It is believed that about 300 years ago Jews from nearby villages came to ʿAmran seeking the protection of the *shaykh*. The *shaykh* agreed, arranged for the acquisition of a large plot of land next to the walled town, and gave it to the Jews. On this land they built their houses and synagogues, and dug wells.

The agreement under which the Jews settled was made with the *shaykh* who represented ʿAmran tribe. He allowed the Jews to settle and for a fee—reported to be the scattering of ashes from the public baths on his fields—provided them with protection. They were considered part of ʿAmran and guaranteed the same protection the tribe was bound to provide for the *walad al-sūq* and *sayyid*, a point emphasized in this account:

> Once, a long time ago, after the Jews had been here many years, two Jews went to Kahlan to see about some property they owned there. While they were there a fight broke out between the Jews and some Muslims. In the end, one man from Kahlan was killed. The Kahlanis wanted to kill the Jews. When word reached ʿAmran of the problem, the *shaykh* sent tribesmen to defend the Jews. They went to Kahlan and brought them back. Seven men from Kahlan were killed by our men, while we lost only two (cf. Goitein 1973:55).

In the ʿAmran area, a few Jews had large landholdings. Several owned tracts in other areas. Because of size and distance, some of these plots were sharecropped, both by Muslims and Jews.

Many Jews rented stalls in the market and several owned their own shops. Unlike other Jewish communities, ʿAmran's Jews are not remembered as skilled artisans or craftsmen. The occupations enumerated for them are few. Very likely, most have been forgotten. One literate man, too young to have known the Jews, stated that in addition to being plasterers, tanners, cushion-makers, and gold- and silversmiths, the Jews did many of the tasks today associated with the *walad al-sūq*.

ʿAmrani perceptions of Jewish piety were important. So devout were the Jews, ʿAmranis say, that from sundown Friday until sundown Saturday they could not talk; all would sit quietly in their houses praying. An innkeeper recalled going as a child to the Jewish quarter to light the Sabbath fires and getting paid one-fourth *bugsha* (forty *bugsha* equal one old riyal). Informants always noted that the

Jews could not eat any meat slaughtered according to Muslim tradition, or drink from any cups that might have had broth in them.

When the Jews left for Israel (ca. 1948 to 1951), there had been between five and six hundred of them living in the Jewish quarter in 121 houses. As was common practice the two synagogues were attached to, or were part of, private houses (cf. Goitein 1941:30). Although few ʿAmranis remember the Jews' actual departure, all seem to regard it with sadness. The imam's agent in ʿAmran recalled his role:

> When there was talk of the Jews leaving, the imam told them to stay and not to believe the stories of the foreigners who were traveling about visiting them. When they decided to leave, the imam said they had to sell everything. They couldn't take so much as a cup with them. The imam sent me a message ordering me to buy the houses and the land. I bought 121 houses and 10,000 *libna* [100 acres].[3] Then I sold the land and the houses to the Muslims.

Western scholars often state that the Jews did not receive full value for their property. Naturally ʿAmranis do not share this view; but some, after asserting that compensation was fair, say the Jews had no choice but to take what was offered. Prices paid for houses ranged from 30 to 80 Maria Theresa thalers[4] although a few sold for more than 100 MT. Land sold for 3 MT a *libna*. According to the imam's agent, houses in the *madīna* had cost 200 to 500 MT at the time but he noted, as have others, that the Muslims' houses were much larger.

> No one wanted to buy the synagogue. Finally, since everything had to be sold, I said I would buy it and gave the Jews 40 MT. Now it is a storeroom. What else could we do?
> Everyone wanted to buy the big houses by the gate. The imam bought the big one that now belongs to ʿAli and the one where Yahya lives. He paid 1,000 MT for both of them. The big one by the gate belonged to Sālim al-Garada. He was the richest Jew. He had land all over, some nearby but a lot by Kahlan and Jawb. The house where Yahya lives was the best house in the quarter.
> After they left, the Jews sent me a message over the radio. It came from Aden. [Laughing.] It said, "Greetings to _____ who bought all our houses and land for nothing." [More laughing.] What could I do, the imam said to buy everything down to the last cup.
> After they had been gone about one year I received a letter from one of the Jews. He was in Israel. He said that he had buried some money in his house. He had been afraid to take the money with him and wanted me to send it to him. I went to the house—that's where Hussayn lives today. We dug in the wall where the letter told us to dig and we found the money. Hussayn wanted to keep it, but I said the imam only ordered us to buy the houses and it didn't include what was in them. I sent the money to the Jew.

Today, there is scant evidence of the Jews having lived in ʿAmran. The Jewish quarter appears, except for being enclosed, as just one of many "suburban" areas that have sprung up outside the walled town since the revolution. Most of the houses have been converted to Muslim architecture, and many of their distinctive Jewish features were destroyed.

Many smaller homes were torn down to make room for larger ones, or in some cases, the foundations of two houses were combined to make one large house. Only a few houses remain two stories, and the open courtyards that characterized Jewish architecture have been covered over. Today there are only seventy-one residences. Those dwellings not converted or modified are considered, by ʿAmran standards, quite small.

From the ʿAmrani perspective, the Jewish exodus had a positive effect. It gave people access to new houses and property. From all indications, the last house built in the walled town was completed ten to twenty years before the Jews left. Informants often remark on the overcrowded conditions, suggesting that further building in the *madina* was not possible. Construction outside the walls was impossible because of lack of security. For this reason, ʿAmranis welcomed the opportunity to move into the enclosed Jewish quarter.

Although many families benefited from the acquisition of houses, the sale of land was not subject to such open distribution. (Neither were houses available to all; a few men bought more than one house and either resold them later or rented them.) In addition to a few shops in the market, ʿAmrani Jews owned 10,000 *libna* of farmland, most of which was held by a few wealthy men. Land was the traditional measure of wealth, and these Jews were then (and still would be) considered quite rich. Of these 10,000 *libna*, 3,000 were in ʿAmran district. The imam bought 5,000 *libna* for himself; the rest was sold to a few wealthy Muslim families.

THE WALL

With the Jews' departure, ʿAmranis acquired new houses, but the expansion separated the population. The Jewish quarter, like many highland villages, was built as a self-encircled, residential area. The exterior walls of abutting houses formed a perimeter barrier enclosing the community. All doors faced onto the interior streets and houses. The gate lay about 100 yards south of the High Gate of the *madina*.

The *madīna* is surrounded by a twenty-foot-high, freestanding, cut-stone wall. When the Jews left, there were two gates, the High Gate and the Low Gate, in the wall. The gates and eleven bastions are connected by an interior walkway about twelve feet above street level. The wall surrounds about 330 houses, a small market, three mosques with gardens, and a few open spaces, in an area at least eight times that of the Jewish quarter.

The wall is in disrepair; but it remains a symbol of ʿAmranis' mettle, since it is reputed to have been built during one Ramadhan. ʿAmranis also pride themselves in their resolution of the problem caused by the wall separating the town's population:

> There used to be only two gates to the *madīna* [cf. Rathjens's map (1953:26)]. After the Jews left, some people moved into the Jewish quarter. Women who wanted to visit their friends and relatives had to walk through the market to get out the High Gate or go out the Low Gate and walk around the wall to get to the Jewish quarter. The women didn't like to walk all the way around the outside of the wall and went through the market. Their husbands were afraid that the *walad al-sūq* would call the women names or cause them trouble and feared this would ruin their wives' honor. The men told the women they couldn't walk through the market, but since the women had many friends in the Jewish quarter and felt obligated to them, they didn't want to use the Low Gate. Every day women from the Jewish quarter and the *madīna* were walking through the market to attend women's parties. The men decided to open a new gate opposite the Jewish quarter's gate so the women could walk back and forth. This we call the Women's Gate.

This account portrays ʿAmranis' concerns with ascribed status, propriety, and the security of women's honor. An easy solution was found to this problem; but not all conflicts, particularly those with outsiders, could be so easily alleviated.

The wall was built for defense. Although they recognize that even other villages of their own tribe could and did attack the town (and vice versa), ʿAmranis prefer to view their enemies in terms of the major tribal alliances or confederations. Tribesmen like to describe themselves as independent, but their, and the tribe's, autonomy was partially undercut by alliances with other tribes. The Hashid tribes, including ʿAmran, recognize a paramount *shaykh* (*shaykh mashayikh*) as their titular leader.

All fourteen Hashid tribes stipulate descent, in a figurative sense, from Hashid. Although claiming a common ancestor (and one informant included Hashid in his genealogy), the relations between the various Hashid tribes are based on affiliation and mutual support rather than on actual descent. It is through putative kinship that obligations and relationships are defined, so claims of kinship mask the political basis of the alliance.

The Hashid tribal confederation stands in opposition to those tribes stipulating descent from Bakil, Hashid's brother. The Bakil tribes differ from the Hashid in that they do not have a paramount *shaykh*. The geographical distribution of Hashid and Bakil is such that each tribal unit is surrounded, at least in part, by an opposing group. At least a few ʿAmranis view this as more than a coincidence.

One informant expressed the nearly heretical notion, based on the accounts of the well-known tenth-century Yemeni historian, al-Hamdani,⁵ that ʿAmran had been a Bakil tribe until the reign of the first Zaydi imam. Regardless of the truth of this specific point, many ʿAmranis recognize that it is probably not accidental that their tribal territory is bordered on the northwest and southeast by Bakil tribes, but rather related to the imamate's control of the tribe, an arrangement used to inhibit uprisings against the imam's authority.

ʿAmranis pride themselves on their Hashid connections. Still, one's allies notwithstanding, the threat of attack was real, and protective measures had to be made on a local basis. In the past, guards were posted and the town gates were locked from dusk to dawn. Sometimes even these precautions were not sufficient. The following episode is said to have occurred somewhere between 125 and 250 years ago. Although the majority of men favored the latter date, this may have been an attempt to disassociate themselves from the incident.

> A man from the Dakka family killed a man from the Jabal (ʿAyal Sarih). The tribal leaders tried to reach a settlement but failed.
>
> The Sarihis came one night seeking revenge. They sent several camels loaded with sand to the Low Gate. It was locked. At first the guards refused to let them in, saying that they could not open the gate until dawn. The Sarihis said they had a load of sand for the *shaykh* and the guards opened the gate. Once the gate swung open and the camels started in, the Sarihis slit the sacks and sand poured out, blocking the gate open. Other Sarihi swarmed inside. They went first to the house of the murderer and killed him and all his household. Some of his relatives lived nearby and were awakened by the noise. They came to his defense, but they were killed as well. When the noise grew louder, everyone in town woke up. Most fled; a few stayed to fight. Later, some of those who had run away returned to fight. Seventy-one people were killed, including all the murderer's relatives.

ᶜAMRANI RELATIONS WITH THE TURKS

Tribal raiding was not the only threat ᶜAmranis faced. The Ottomans twice invaded and occupied portions of Yemen (ca. 1583 to 1630 and 1849 to 1918). It was during the latter period, sometime after 1872, that the Turks extended their control to ᶜAmran.

Older men, a handful of whom may have lived during the last years of Ottoman rule, are convinced that the wall antedates the town's conquest. Younger men, perhaps trying to associate themselves with the wall's construction or what is seen as the defeat of the Turks, suggest it was built as a defense against the Ottoman invaders. Harris (1893:106) notes that in 1892 the Ottomans took refuge inside the wall during a siege by local tribes: "Sanaᶜa at the end of October was still in a state of seige, the garrison and townspeople suffering greatly from hunger and disease, though in ᶜAmran the state of the inhabitants was more pitiable still."

All ᶜAmranis agree on several aspects of Ottoman rule. The Turks tore down the Himyarite castle in the town, carted the stones about a half-mile out of town, and built a fort. They dug a large well, also outside the walls, which is still referred to as the "Turkish well" even though it has been abandoned. The Ottoman governor's headquarters, built in the town, is today a private house. The Turks attempted formal, nonreligious education, the success of which, except for one aged man who could recite world capital cities, is unknown. They are also credited with the introduction of prickly pears.

ᶜAmranis recall Ottoman rule as harsh and oppressive. What role they played in instigating or defending against Turkish policies has been forgotten with the exception of one event. This account is so well known that it is, for ᶜAmranis, essentially summarized by the expression *"Shaykh* Hizam! Oh, what a man he was. There's never been anyone like him." This declaration is always uttered with a mixture of awe and reverence.

The object of this devotion was ᶜAmran's *shaykh* during the last years of the Ottoman occupation. ᶜAmranis believe the *shaykh* went to Istanbul seeking redress for the town's oppression. Baldry (1976: 174–80) argues that during the revolt by the imam against Ottoman rule (1905–7), the Turkish authorities co-opted a group of tribal leaders and sent them to Istanbul in 1907. The return of these leaders some months later created confusion among the rebelling tribes, causing a brief loss of momentum that squelched the imam's drive to unite the tribes and thwarted his campaign. Only one ʿAmrani indicated that the *shaykh*'s trip was anything but honorable. If others held this view they kept it to themselves.

The standard version of the event is as follows:

> The Turkish commander of the fort was Yusuf Pasha. He was the most cruel of men. He treated us badly. He let the soldiers steal from our crops. He put men in jail. Everything we did got us punished. It was terrible. Once he killed four men who caught the Turks stealing their grain. He cut off their heads and put them on stakes next to the government offices. He let his soldiers steal our property. He even set fire to our fields when we were about to harvest the grain. *Shaykh* Hizam went to the imam to stop this. The imam couldn't do anything so the *shaykh* went to Istanbul.
>
> He went to Istanbul by ship from Hodeida. When he came to Istanbul he said he wanted to see the Pasha. They refused, but when they learned he came from Yemen they quickly took him to see the Pasha. The Pasha heard our grievances and he said he would take care of everything. *Shaykh* Hizam stayed as the Pasha's guest for a while and they showed him their museums. When he was about to leave they asked him if he wanted money or other things. *Shaykh* Hizam said that thanks to Allah he had money but would take some household furnishings. These he brought back with him.
>
> When he came back a letter was sent to the commander in Sanʿa and Yusuf Pasha was taken there. The Turks cut off Yusuf Pasha's head. A new commander was sent to us.

In ʿAmrani eyes the trip to Istanbul is clearly the high point of their history for it reaffirms their claims to tribal autonomy, the importance of the *shaykh*, and the tribe's collective defeat of the Turks. There are other incidents from which ʿAmranis take some pride but none in which "good" and "evil" are defined so precisely. For example, twice men from ʿAmran were involved in plots to kill the imam. Neither attempt was successful and both men were beheaded for their trouble. One of these men is regarded as a martyr and a street has been named in his honor, but generally neither man's exploits are recalled. Perhaps this is because the imam, while oppressive and cruel, was also a spiritual leader.

Even though many accounts focus on ʿAmranis' exploits, it is striking that they tell almost no tales of the civil war years. Those I heard dealt with individual incidents—a young boy being run down by an armored car, a man losing a leg in a mine explosion, or a woman shot while on the roof of her house. ʿAmran tribe does not appear to have played a role in the fighting although it is well recalled that thirty-six men and two women were killed during the civil war.

Messick (1978:30) has suggested that this was a difficult period.

52 / ʿAmrani Views of the Past

Because ʿAmranis avoid talking about it, it appears to be a time they prefer not to recall. It may be that, in a sense, the war really demonstrated the weakness of the tribe or the *shaykh*'s inability to take action, for while ʿAmran, like many Hashid tribes, supported the revolution, it was not long before Egyptian troops were garrisoned in the former Turkish fort. More important, the revolution was a period that made clear the fragility of the social system.

LIFE BEFORE THE REVOLUTION

The preceding accounts emphasize the tribesman's role as a warrior. They provide no information on daily life and they tend to obscure the fact that agriculture was the dominant element in ʿAmranis' lives. Successful harvests were never certain and stories of the past focus on the many hardships ʿAmranis faced. In spite of the gloomy tone of most recollections, I think men reveled in the knowledge they had been strong enough to survive, an awareness of their strength made clear by the apparent ease of today's commerce-based economy.

The following is a tribesman's recollection. In many respects it is a typical expression of the fears and concerns ʿAmranis associate with the past. The tribesman also provides some indication of the importance of social position and the nature of social relationships.

> In the time of the imam everyone worked hard just to eke out a living. We were in constant fear of famine. Men worked in the fields from dawn to dusk. Land was scarce. Most people had only a few *libna*, enough so they didn't have to buy much food.[6] There were only a few big landowners. Often men and women worked together in the fields. In those days we ate our breakfast and lunch there. Women or children brought us our meals. We had to guard our crops from thieves. At harvest time we had to have guards twenty-four hours a day. Men used to sit in huts, or several would sit in the small room atop a watchtower guarding against theft.
>
> Even children had to work. When I was small I took dinner to my father when he was on guard. Many children shepherded sheep and goats. Now only a few people herd animals; then everyone had animals to care for.
>
> When the women weren't in the fields they were home grinding grain and carrying water from the wells. They had a lot of work and it was hard. They cooked meals, brought them to the men, and cared for the animals. Some women sewed the embroidered strips of cloth that are on the legs of women's pants. Only a few could do this work and they were well paid.

(Now, men only guard lucrative cash crops like *gāt*. The watchtowers are in disrepair and many threshing grounds are being overgrown by weeds. Men do not comment on the decline of agriculture, but they like to point out that until the advent of electric-powered milling machines women spent most of the day grinding grain. Such an emphasis is a way of stating that they produced what they ate. It is a matter of pride that their breads came from their grain; their meat, eggs, and milk products from their livestock.)

> Everyone was afraid of losing their land. Only a few people had cash to spend. We paid for our purchases with grain or took them on credit. When we needed money we sold grain in the *sūq*. If we needed grain later, the "merchants" [a *walad al-sūq* substratum] sold it back at a higher price. The "merchants" were always hoarding grain. If there was a drought, we had to borrow grain to eat. Sometimes we would borrow but once you had borrowed and couldn't repay, the "merchants" took your land. They could demand your land at any time. That's how they came to be rich. They stole our land because we had to have food to eat.

(As in the past, it remains a sore point for many tribesmen that they are not the only landowners. Whereas tribesmen would like to control all land, some *walad al-sūq* families, just like the Jews, have been landowners.)

> We had food, but we were afraid to eat too much because we feared famine. We hardly ever ate meat. Maybe once, sometimes twice a week was all the meat we could afford. In the worst times we hardly ate anything. Our fathers would decide how much grain we could use and it was rationed out over a month. When the rains didn't come, we ate less. Except for the *shaykh* and the government officials, only the sick and the new mothers ate meat every day. Often we ate a thin gruel.

(Although the diet had less meat than today, many men recall being in better health and having heartier appetites. It is common for men to remark on how much more they used to eat, a reference both to their hard work and their high quality local foods.)

> Those who didn't have land, and even those who did, had to do other work. Some were sharecroppers. For their labor they received one-half of the harvest. Sharecropping was common. Men from large families would work for others to get extra food.
> Not everyone worked in the fields. Water for irrigation and drinking came from wells. Each well had four workers. There was a man to lead the donkey that raised the skin bucket and the others dumped it. They were paid twice a year in grain. Those who worked at the well by the mosque received grain from *waqf* [the religious endowment]. The poor didn't have to pay for this water, but the rich did [through taxes].
> Some men were simply hired hands. They did all types of work, cleaning septic systems, digging wells, plastering, or re-mudding houses. They were paid very little, either one riyal [Maria Theresa thaler] a week or one-eighth *gadaḥ* [a measure] of grain.[7] They usually took the grain.

(Although wells are now mechanically pumped, many of these other trades are still practiced. Many men avoid these unskilled trades, however, despite substantial increases in fees and wages.)

> Only a few men didn't have to work. They were the *shaykh*, major government officials, big landowners, and a few "merchants." Everyone else worked from dawn to dusk.
> There was little in the market. Most items, like garlic, grain, and fruits were locally grown. There was some homemade clarified butter and *gishr* [coffee bean husks] came from nearby. Our firewood came from tamarisk, hardwood [possibly acacia] and chaff from grain. Only a few items were imported; kerosene, tea, and cloth. Cloth only came in two colors, black and white.
> There were only a few "merchants" and the *sūq* was not open every day. Today there are ten or fifteen butchers here. Then there were only two or three. Each had only a sheep. Most of the shops were inside the walls, a few outside near the gate where Hamid's restaurant is. There were only thirty shops but many were hardly ever open. Since men weren't supposed to spend time in the *sūq*, many shops were only open on market days. Even the "merchant" families had only one or two people in the market, the rest were in the fields.
> Those who weren't "merchants" [barbers, public messengers, etc.], but who worked in the *sūq*, "belonged" to the town. They were paid twice a year by their customers.

(The *walad al-sūq*, from the tribesman's perspective, "belonged" to the town in a sense—they were under tribal protection and some of them received their semiannual wages from the town's treasury. The Jews also "belonged" to ʿAmran.)

> We were all afraid of the imam. When he sent a soldier here we fed him and sent him on his way. We had to feed the donkey or camel, too. If a soldier [or soldiers] stayed the night, we gave them lodging and food. Those who housed the soldiers [usually the *walad al-sūq*] were paid on a semiannual basis from our taxes.

(Although men complain that there were inadequate food supplies, they note, almost with pride, that the area's taxes had kept the local storage facilities filled to the brim. Now, men point out that these warehouses are empty, neglecting to note that taxes are no longer paid in kind.)

> The imam could force men to be his soldiers. There were many men from ʿAmran who were in his army. Men could avoid service if they had money. Even when the imam had you in the army, he might confiscate your land. Everyone tried to avoid the army, but many were forced to join.
> The imam's soldiers reported to the *ʿāmil* [the imam's agent charged with overseeing the district]. All messages and mail went to him as well. The *ʿāmil* issued the imam's orders to the people.

(At least during the last years of the imam's power, the *shaykh*'s role was limited. There are few accounts of the *shaykh* engaged in anything but intertribal dispute resolution.)

> We all lived together in one house. Today everyone has his own house. Then we were all packed together. There were sometimes four or five families in one house. [These were usually nuclear sections of extended families, but occasionally included renters.] Everyone inherited a piece of the house and they all lived in their sections. We couldn't afford to move and there were no new houses. All the new houses outside the wall hadn't been built and it was dangerous to live alone.
>
> We didn't have nice furnishings like we have now. Then we had only a few woven mats and straw-filled back cushions. We used animal skins, tanned by the Jews, as blankets.

(With few consumer goods and limitations on expansion, there was a general facade of equality. Until recently virtually all houses had the same interior and exterior design. To be sure, some were larger, had more rooms, or stood taller than others, but these were not always indicators of wealth or social position. Only the interior furnishings that guests see may reflect a difference in financial status.)

> Only a few people were invited to weddings. We didn't invite everyone like we do now. This was to avoid expenses. Everyone knew the size of the gifts they had received from a family and they repaid you at your wedding. Then gifts weren't money. Usually people gave grain, but if they were close to you [friend or relative] they might give a sheep. We didn't give our brides gold. The brideprice was low. Then we paid only thirty to forty Maria Theresa thalers in brideprice.
>
> At weddings we chewed *gāt*. Only the rich could afford to chew every day. *Gāt* was cheap but we couldn't afford it. You could get enough *gāt* to chew all day for one-fourth *bugsha*.

(It is difficult to define the term *rich*, because many men who are known to be wealthy appear to be quite poor. In fact some of these men feel that to wear "fancy" clothes or to have particularly nice household furnishings is equivalent to putting on airs and contravenes the often stated, but hardly accurate, premise of equality within status groups.)

THE TOWN'S EXPANSION

Like many accounts of the past, the tribesman's narrative has an aura of timelessness. ʿAmranis tend to speak of the "past" and "present" as if they were discontinuous, a descriptive device partially due to the rapid change of pace that in a sense had helped make the past seem one-dimensional and immutable. This is misleading of course, for, although informants' accounts portray ᶜAmran as unchanged and so fraught with hardships as to be unappealing, the town in fact was attracting new residents and expanding for at least the last thirty years. Even though ᶜAmranis tend to overlook some aspects of this development, it indicates that well before the revolution the town was growing in importance.

According to informants' accounts and the report of Rathjens's (1953) visit to ᶜAmran in 1931, the town consisted of two enclosed residential areas until the Jews' departure. There also were two market zones, one inside and one outside the wall, and a mosque and public bath outside the wall.

After 1950, new shops were built in the area outside the High Gate. By the late 1950s there were around twenty to thirty new business locations in this area outside the wall, now referred to as the "old" *sūq*. These included a few assorted-goods shops or general stores as well as teashops, inns, and others specializing in the sale of *gāt*, grain measurement, and local craft items. Informants are unsure of the reasons for this expansion, but it seems likely that the town's market increased in its importance.

During this same period residential construction began outside the walled areas. Although the acquisition of the Jewish quarter had provided many new houses, population growth apparently necessitated further expansion. This may be evidence of ᶜAmran's increasing importance. It also indicates there was a general feeling of security. With a contingent of the imam's army garrisoned in the town, the risk of attack was reduced.

The development of the first residential quarter was begun by a wealthy *sayyid* who held a prominent position in the local government. He built a large house several hundred yards outside the High Gate, near a well. Shortly thereafter other new constructions began in the area, although it is probable that only a few were completed by the time of the 1962 coup d'etat.

Construction continued during the civil war, but development flourished in the postwar years. This rapid growth not only more than doubled the town's population but also converted farm land to commercial and residential use.

Many ᶜAmranis believe that this expansion is evidence of the decline of traditional values. One man explained the relationship between development and values by pointing out that before the revolution four major watercourses had carried the annual runoff from the surrounding mountains to the valley. Now, many of these waterways and their tributaries are blocked by new construction. In the past, rains sometimes caused flooding in the town; now, the light runoff is blamed on residential and commercial building.[8]

CONCLUSION

It of course has not been urban expansion that led to a shift away from agriculture but rather the growth of the commercial sector, spurred by promises of greater opportunity and security, that has changed the social landscape. Thus what ʿAmranis really question are not the physical alterations that are the obvious manifestations of the town's development, but the invisible or subtle way that these modifications have and are restructuring social relationships. Many ʿAmrani relationships, both intra- and intergroup, as well as intra- and interpersonal, are based on a formal ideology. The ambivalence ʿAmranis express about the nature of social change, as evidenced in their views of the past and present, represents a widening gap between perceived standards and actual behavior. Of course, this formal framework has only been an approximation of reality, and although the discrepancies between actual and real behaviors increase, many standards of assessment are still those embodied in the formal schemata. The emerging modifications in social relationships, or social structural change, are evident in terms of affiliation, occupation, and kinship and marriage.

PART II

Affiliation, Occupation, and Marriage and Kinship

3

Affiliation: Changing Bases of the Social Order

A national identity has been fostered by the central government in the post–civil-war years. Regionalism still remains important, however, and is most obvious in terms of tribal identity. Membership in or relations with a tribe are matters of different types of affiliation. Historically, the tribe was a central element in the social order, linking the different social strata. The importance of ʿAmran tribe has been declining, both as a result of the Turkish conquest and the imams' efforts to centralize the government as well as a result of recent economic development. This has led to a restructuring of the tribe's political role, a change most pronounced in a modification of alliances since both leadership and membership criteria have been altered.

WHO IS AN ʿAMRANI?

"Who is that man?" I asked a companion.

"He's _____ who lives in Hadaba [a new residential area]," came the reply.

"But *who* is he?" I persisted, trying to elicit some additional information.

"Don't worry about him, he's not one of us," my companion answered.

When ʿAmranis define their identity, they do so on several levels. In situations like the above, "us" in the response, "not one of us," can have a variety of meanings, noting one of the varied forms of affiliation men recognize. These different levels of integration reflect not only identification in terms of the central government's categories but also those of the tribal system.

ᶜAmran is an administrative district, a *nāḥiyya* in official government terms. When a person states that he is from ᶜAmran it means only that he lives somewhere within the boundaries of this zone or, rarely, the weekly market he attends. The assumption of the surname *al-ᶜAmrani* by men who have moved elsewhere is a statement of place of origin. Closer questioning will reveal whether a man actually lives in a village near ᶜAmran or in the town. A man who in Sanᶜa says he is from ᶜAmran, would, in ᶜAmran, say he is from Darb, one of the local villages.

Now, many ᶜAmran residents are recent arrivals from villages often well beyond the boundaries of the administrative district, and it is less clear what is meant when a person says he is an ᶜAmrani. In the past it meant affiliation with the ᶜAmran tribe. For long-term residents, affiliation is still conceived in a tribal idiom.

ᶜAmran's tribal territory includes eight villages in addition to the town. In tribal terms, to be an ᶜAmrani means living inside the clearly circumscribed boundaries of ᶜAmran district (*maktaba ᶜAmran*), a concept denoting the tribal area and an administrative district under the imam. ᶜAmranis prefer this designation over the official government term, *nāḥiyya*, because it reflects traditional identification and may imply autonomy from the national government. It is also a means of figuratively excluding outsiders, something ᶜAmranis do.

Affiliation is based on increasingly exclusive categories of membership. Thus while the tribe is a territorial entity, not all residents are members of the tribe. ᶜAmran contains nontribal peoples as well as tribespeople. Even though the former are outside the tribal structure, they are formally linked to it.

ᶜAmranis recognize a number of features distinguishing tribal from nontribal peoples. Most of these are thought to be rooted in the past, but some reflect how ᶜAmranis think things should have been rather than how they actually were. Among the criteria demarcating tribal from nontribal are residence (rural vs. urban), relation to commerce (independent vs. dependent), and alliance (allied vs. nonallied). Tribesmen might include all three criteria in abstract discussion, but in ᶜAmran these have not been absolute since most tribesmen-peasants lived in the town.

In the past, if tribesmen lived in the town, they maintained an ideologic separation between their residence and the adjacent marketplace, the latter being associated with nontribal peoples. The basis of the tribesman's disassociation lay in his self-image as a brave warrior, self-sufficient cultivator, and defender of those whose lack of formal alliances made them "weak." It is this last factor that is stressed when tribesmen set themselves apart from the nontribal peoples, indicating a set of relationships based on ancient customs, some elements of which may still be found.

THE CONNECTION BETWEEN TRIBAL AND NONTRIBAL PEOPLES

Historically, most tribes maintained "sacred enclaves-markets" (*hijra sūq*)[1] within their territories. In ᶜAmran this space is sometimes called *sūq mugaddas*, "holy market." The marketplace was a zone of tribal protection where residents of the marketplace were safeguarded and intertribal quarrels and feuds were not allowed. Within this zone, necessary services—both commercial transactions and religious teaching—could flourish free from the violence that threatened those outside its boundaries. Tribesmen protected the marketplace because they needed the services it provided (even if they would prefer to deny this aspect) and because they had formally guaranteed the security of some of its residents.

By custom, a tribe (*gabīla*) might agree to serve as the protector (*rafīq*) of individuals passing through or establishing residence in its territory. Those persons whose security was guaranteed (*jiwār*) required safeguarding because they were isolated, without allies. Normally it was the head of the tribe, the *shaykh*, who extended guarantees of safety, and it was his pledge that obligated his tribesmen followers to the same cause. It was precisely this sort of relationship under which the *shaykh* protected the Jews.

Soon after I came to ᶜAmran, an informant told me how to acquire a protected status, in case I might actually need it:

> If you kill a man, you can be sure that his relatives will come to kill you. How can you protect yourself? [I took this to mean that I had no relatives to fall back on.] If you are afraid, all you have to do is go to the *shaykh* or some other man of importance. Go to him, explain what you have done, hand over your dagger, and say to him, "My fate is in your hands." Then he has to protect you and no one can kill you.

Although I never had occasion to follow this advice, it helped me understand accounts of the establishment of protector-protected relationships. The implications of accepting protection are shown in the following account, one of many stories explaining how families came to be associated with the marketplace:

> You know *bayt* al-Warth [the Warth family], don't you? They used to be tribesmen. They are not from ʿAmran. They used to live near Huth. They were a small family then. They became involved in a dispute. I think it was about land [a common source of disagreements], but maybe it was something else. It was about two-hundred years ago and no one remembers for sure. A man was killed by the three al-Warth brothers. They were afraid to stay, being certain they would be killed. They fled. One brother went to Hamdan, one to Hajja, and one came to ʿAmran. When the brother who settled here sought work he had to become a "merchant" [*bayāʿ*]. He had no land and the only way he could make a living was in the market. They used to be tribesmen but now they are "merchants" [*bayāʿīn*]. The same thing happened to the other brothers. Now after many years they have lots of land [a reference to some of the descendents in ʿAmran] and are now a big family [both in numbers of individuals and in terms of wealth in some households].

In this account the establishment of a protected relationship is implicit in the dual meanings of *bayāʿ*. I have translated *bayāʿīn* as "merchants" both because of the occupational niche entered by al-Warth and because of the common Arabic association of *bayāʿ* with selling. The term has the equally important connotation of acceptance of, and obedience to, another's authority (Tyan 1960:1113). Thus, for ʿAmranis, accepting protection required al-Warth to associate with the marketplace; but his social position, while below that of tribesmen, remained above that of the other providers of service, the *walad al-sūq*, with whom the *bayāʿīn* are often classified.

Not all protected persons came to the marketplace as did al-Warth, nor did the two nontribal groups have comparable relationships with the tribe. Both conducted their activities in the same physical space, both relied on tribal protection, and both provided services. It was in the tribesman's polar views of these services that the two groups were distinguished. The *walad al-sūq* provided commercial services, the *sāda* offered religious instruction and mediation.

The marketplace provided the *walad al-sūq* a safe haven in which to engage in commerce, an activity despised by tribesmen but one necessary to daily life. At the same time it was an area where the *sāda* could provide religious services, an activity tribesmen respected highly. Just as the tribesman was dependent upon these services, the *walad al-sūq* and *sayyid* also benefited from each other.

ʿAmranis emphasize the need to safeguard the *walad al-sūq* and minimize their protection of the *sayyid*. This may be related to the *sayyid's* ancestry and social role. His descent from the Prophet Muhammad defined him as a man of religious expertise. Serjeant (1967) has suggested that the *sayyid* was also a mediator, like the first Zaydi imam, and that "sacred enclaves" were established in tribal territories so the *sayyid* could resolve disputes. As such the *sayyid* would have had to be free of alliances. Thus the entry of a *sayyid* into ᶜAmrani society would not be contingent on his acceptance of a lower, subservient status, as was the case with al-Warth, because the *sayyid's* role required him to be outside and independent of the tribe.

Unlike Gerholm (1977:123) I could find no evidence of an ideology of mediation attached to the *sāda*. It is not clear whether ᶜAmranis know of this role or overlook it. It is certain that if the *sayyid* was known once as a mediator, ᶜAmranis no longer recognize it. Rather, they view dispute resolution in terms of offices (some of which were occupied traditionally by a *sayyid*). But when they describe the neutrality of the marketplace they do so in terms of tribal law.

In the tribal idiom, the marketplace was an arena in which a man could make a public statement of his grievances. Following tribal law, it was, in theory, in the marketplace that men slaughtered bulls, either as an offer of apology to one they had offended or as a demand for assistance and retribution. By making his position known in a public display, the litigant was able to demand support for his position, and those who witnessed his statement, in a real or figurative sense, were obligated to assist in seeking a resolution. Actions of this sort are now rare, but the inviolate nature of the marketplace is still an ideal to be maintained and men will leap to intercede in a dispute to prevent bloodshed. Such a response is viewed by tribesmen as an expression of tribal standards.

In the past it was important to maintain tribal norms since failure to do so could bring disgrace. This point is clear in the following well-known accounts, which also describe how some families came to be *walad al-sūq*:

> *Bayt* al-Harish used to be tribesmen. Many years ago they killed four or five men. At that time they were living in ᶜAmran. They were punished and made "barbers" (muzayyin). In those days they had a different family name. Today only a few of them still identify themselves by that name.
>
> *Bayt* al-Gasabi was always an ᶜAmran tribal family. Years ago there was fighting between ᶜAmran [town] and al-Janat [a village of ᶜAmran tribe] over the murder of a "poetic messenger" [*dawshān*]. The men from al-Janat had killed the "messenger" when he went to deliver a proposal from ᶜAmran to end the

dispute. The men from ʿAmran went to punish them. When they were sneaking up on al-Janat, one man from *bayt* al-Gasabi came upon a Janati. Although he had his dagger drawn, he refused to kill the Janati. He said he was a man of peace. When everyone heard this, they went to the head of *bayt* al-Gasabi and said they had to punish the coward. They disowned him and made him a "barber" [*muzayyin*]. His name was changed. Since then his descendants have been "barbers."

The accounts suggest the importance of acting like a tribesman and make several other points. Tribal standards were not maintained in either case, but the resulting demotions were different. In the case of al-Harish, the crime was committed within the community. Since the murderer's kin did not prevent the multiple killings, the entire family lost status. In the case of al-Gasabi, refusing to kill the enemy seems to have been an individual rather than a collective failing. However, what may have been omitted from the accounts was the status of the families involved. At present, *bayt* al-Harish includes many men of importance; if this was also the situation in the past it might explain why the demotion was not extended to the coward's kinspeople. By contrast *bayt* al-Gasabi is now relatively unimportant. It is possible the family was no more important at the time of the incident, a factor that may have contributed to its members' collective loss of status.

THE KINSHIP BASIS OF AFFILIATION

The tribesman's stress on the differences between himself and the *sayyid* and *walad al-sūq* tends to overshadow basic similarities among all ʿAmranis. Regardless of social status, every individual has a network of kinship ties. The tribesman's emphasis on the elaborateness of his linkages (to be discussed shortly) creates the impression that the *walad al-sūq* and the *sayyid* are isolated persons. Being "unconnected" may be an appropriate depiction of those individuals who came to ʿAmran, like al-Warth (see above), but it was not, as will be shown in chapter 5, a permanent condition. Membership in the tribe is based on a patrilineal descent idiom and it is the descent group that is the primary mode of affiliation. While tribesmen use many "kinship" terms[2] to describe their networks of connections, those they use most commonly represent the same descent categories found among the *walad al-sūq* and the *sayyid* groups. The difference between tribal and nontribal peoples, then, lies in the sociopolitical meanings attached to kinship categories. Consequently it is through analysis of descent groups that alliances can be understood.

There are three progressively inclusive descent groups. Of these, the minimal agnatic group—the *asra*—is the smallest. Generally it is represented by the extended family and, in the past when families are said to have remained together in a single dwelling, was a residential group as well. Now the term is also applied to households of brothers who have divided inherited property and separate residences.

Those minimal agnatic groups that trace their ancestry to a common antecedent may be identified as a *ḥabl*. The *ḥabl* is similar to a lineage although it maintains collective ownership only of that property, such as family cemeteries, to which individual title cannot be given. Beyond this limited form of joint ownership, members of a *ḥabl* do not engage in any formalized collective activity.

The maximal agnatic group or *bayt* is composed of several *ḥabl*. The group is identified by a common surname but the genealogic connections between the groups' members may be remote and are often de-emphasized. The *bayt* resembles a clan since actual shared descent may not be demonstrable. In the few cases where informants attempted to detail their genealogies fully, it seemed probable that some generations, and lateral connections, were omitted.

Although these three categories exist, not all descent groups exhibit this extensive elaboration (see chart 1). Some descent groups are so small that a single *asra* is also the *ḥabl* and *bayt*. And there are a number of descent groups in ʿAmran large enough for *ḥabl* to be defined, but only a few of these enjoy such social and political prominence that the intermediate group is identified.

So far I have implied a certain discreteness to descent terms. Whereas this is true if one is speaking solely of kinship relationships, it is rarely the case that the terms for these categories are used only in their kinship sense. Kinship, particularly for tribesmen, is a basis of political action and, as I will show, is the idiom upon which alliances are built. In daily speech ʿAmranis use of terms is a mixture of political and kinship references. For example, "We are all one *asra*" is an expression used by men seeking to mediate or prevent disputes between related and unrelated individuals alike; it is a call for men to act as if they had some preestablished kinship obligations toward each other.

ʿAmranis' fluid use of descriptive and reference terms allows them to identify different groups in either inclusive or exclusive ways.[3] The variability of kinship usage can be illustrated with the term *bayt*, which has three different referents, each describing a level of kinship

68 / *Affiliation: Changing Bases of the Social Order*

CHART 1. VARIABLE EXPRESSIONS OF DESCENT AND AFFILIATION: THE KINSHIP MODEL

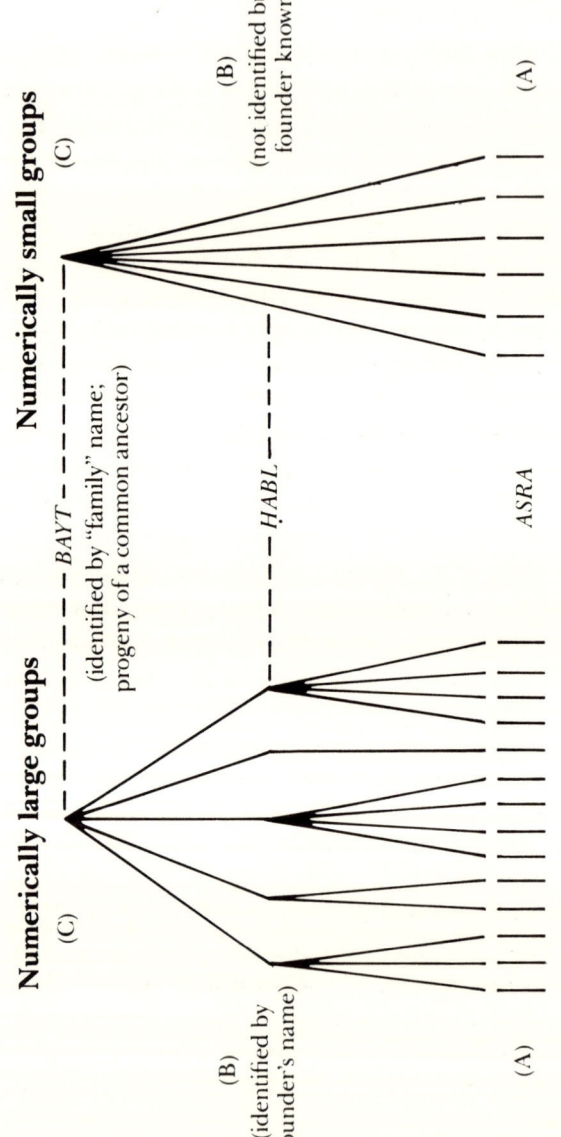

Note: This chart is not intended to demonstrate the depth of genealogic connections that are variable.

connection. (In the following, the letters preceding each example correspond to the categories in chart 1.)

(A) *Bayt* Jamil al-Jundi is the house or residence of Jamil al-Jundi. It may describe either the nuclear family or the minimal agnatic group (*asra*).

(B) *Bayt* Hamud (al-Jundi) refers to those minimal agnatic groups descended from Hamud al-Jundi and marks a point from which descent groups have branched. This reference is to the *ḥabl*, but since *ḥabl* is only used abstractly, it is identified by the descriptive term *bayt*.

(C) *Bayt* al-Jundi refers to all those bearing the surname al-Jundi.

The terms *bayt* and *asra* have variable referents. At least on the verbal level, descent groups are manipulated, allowing for the formation of groups of varying size but still bound by the types of obligations characteristic of the ideologic category used to describe them. Listeners, aware of the context and the terms' connotations, understand the implications of each form of usage.

This sort of fluidity does not surround the term *ḥabl* which is used almost exclusively to describe forms of political affiliation. As noted earlier, *ḥabl* as a kinship reference is applied only to divisions of descent groups that are both large and prominent. Furthermore, this kinship use is limited to the descent groups of tribesmen. It is here that tribesmen distinguish themselves, organizationally, from nontribal peoples. Occasionally *ḥabl* is used to describe the *sayyid* descent groups, but in this sense the meaning is limited to ancestry, and usually takes the form of depicting the *sāda* as (*ḥabl*) *bani hāsham*, a reference to the line of descent of the Prophet. *Ḥabl* is never used to describe *walad al-sūq* descent groups despite the fact that, like a few *sayyid* groups, some are large and prominent. To apply the term to the former group is inappropriate because it would imply that such groups have an organizational structure similar to that of the tribe.

FORMS OF ALLIANCE

An alliance is referred to as a *ḥabl*. Although related to the kinship category, as a political term (see charts 1, 2) it has two additional meanings, because membership in an alliance is defined and derived in two ways.

Those who are members of a maximal agnatic group (*bayt*) are affiliated with a *ḥabl* purely on the basis of the patrilineal connection, a tie implying oneness and carrying obligations to act in a unified manner. Thus as a descent or alliance reference term, *ḥabl* describes a group larger than any single lineage, because it includes all those minimal agnatic groups bearing the same patronym regardless of the closeness of their actual descent connections. In this case *ḥabl* refers to all those bearing a common surname, but assigns to this group, at least terminologically, behavior usually expected to exist between more closely related kinspeople. This supposed sense of communal responsibility is also inherent in the meaning of *ḥabl* as a cord or sinew (see chart 2).

The second meaning of *ḥabl* is an alliance between unrelated descent groups. There are many families in ʿAmran who originated elsewhere, moved to the town, and affiliated themselves with established alliances. Not all newcomers came to be part of the *walad al-sūq* category. Many resident ʿAmran descent groups also find it useful to ally themselves with larger or more prominent descent groups since such alliances are important both for mutual defense and as an access to political power (see chart 2).

As is the case with the kinship usage, the term *ḥabl* is only used abstractly to identify alliances. When I asked a man, "What is your *ḥabl*?" his response was "*Bayt* (surname)," not *ḥabl* (surname). Thus in addition to the three kinship usages of *bayt* described earlier, the term identifies allied, but unrelated, descent groups. The meaning of *bayt* is determined by context. When the meaning is clouded, the intent probably is to convey the impression of the largest possible group, even if this is not the actual referent in a specific instance.

Members of a descent group are allies almost by definition. For nonkin to ally with a descent group *cum* alliance (*ḥabl*) requires first (and of course with agreement of the parties) a formal document or declaration. The procedure for alliance formation, while not standardized, establishes the types of reciprocal obligations to which the parties agree. These may be seen in the following oath (*ragm*)[4] which is a means of extending to unrelated groups the same jural obligations or relationships that exist within a descent group (cf. LaFontaine 1973:39).

> As my signature attests, I have become, in debt and in arms, a member of (named group). To them I pledge what I have (property) and they are bound to meet my obligations. This oath is made to them. Bloodshed brings revenge. Allah is my witness.

The oath creates an alliance premised on kinlike responsibilities. The signatory agrees to fulfill the same obligations to his allies as he

CHART 2. THE TWO BASES FOR ALLIANCE MEMBERSHIP

In the abstract these related minimal descent groups are referred to as a *ḥabl*. In actual reference the group would be labelled *bayt (patronym)*.

Maximal agnatic group (*Bayt*)

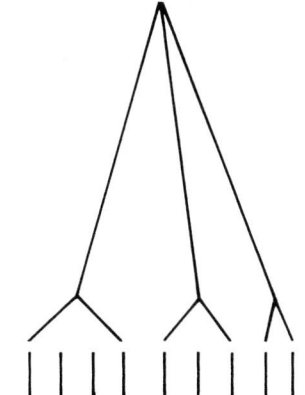

Minimal agnatic groups (*Asrāt*)

In the abstract the alliance between *Bayt* 'A' and *Bayt* 'B' is described as a *ḥabl*. In reference to a specific alliance the two groups are described as *bayt (patronym of the core group)*.

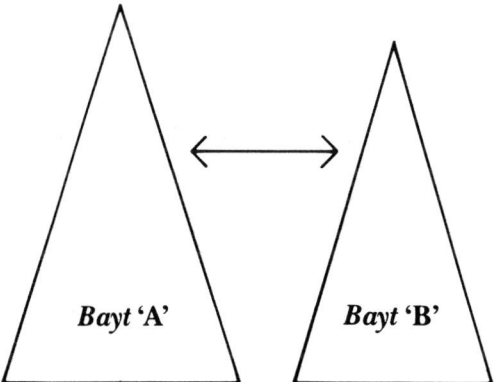

would for his actual, if distant, relatives. The relationship is reciprocal; his allies must also stand up for him as though he is kin. Since the agreement requires renunciation of prior ties, including real kinship connections, a man's loyalties are well defined in any conflict.

Additionally, the individual or group executing an oath is expected to substantiate its ability and willingness to fulfill these duties by arranging for the slaughter of a bull in the *sūq* as a show of assets and a public declaration of the change of allegiance. Some informants, perhaps with reference to the present, state that instead of having a bull slaughtered, a "poetic messenger" (*dawshān*) can be hired to announce the new affiliation.

In theory, the *ḥabl* is collectively responsible for the major public obligations of its members, an extension of its jural identity. These include debts (blood money, or *diyya*) in the event of murder, accidental death, or other major offenses. Informants never specified the latter. In addition, the *ḥabl* is supposed to support its members in disputes, to line up with them. This is the meaning of "in arms" in the oath. Sometimes men refer to the size and strength of their *ḥabl* in terms of the number of men they can muster.

Although men are obligated theoretically to pay the debts or support the actions of their *ḥabl* members, they cannot be forced to do so. I could find no evidence that failure to meet one's obligations resulted in any sanction stronger than a probable reduction in the group's support for the reneging individual.[5]

In part this may be a consequence of the rather imprecise nature of these obligations. As informants describe payment of blood money, it is the *shaykh* or the head of the involved *ḥabl* who determines if payments should be made, in what amount, and by whom. Thus one can be assessed because one's *ḥabl* is involved in a dispute or because the *shaykh* has decreed the entire town or tribe liable for a death. It is generally believed that ʿAmranis feel a strong obligation to contribute, but they are quick to point out, somewhat contradictorily, that in the final analysis it is the responsibility of the murderer and his immediate family to pay the blood money.

If a *ḥabl* receives payment from another *ḥabl*, the money is supposed to be distributed according to the principles of inheritance. I have no examples of blood money being distributed; but if the division of money follows inheritance, only a small segment of the victim's descent group collects.

Financial obligations may extend beyond blood money. When a

dispute between ʿAmran and a tribal village occurred, and one man was killed, a number of men were jailed. Their respective *ḥabl* met the costs of maintaining these men in jail, providing their food, *gāt*, and other expenses. Each side, ʿAmran and the village, also contributed 8,000 Yemeni riyals (U.S. $1,800) during the nearly six-month incarceration period. In ʿAmran, the *ḥabl* of each involved man contributed towards these costs, although some men suggest that the bulk of the expenses was paid by the men's immediate descent groups.

The support function of the *ḥabl* was graphically demonstrated early in my stay in ʿAmran. A report arrived that a resident, a member of a major *ḥabl*, had been killed in another town. The news spread and within a short time nine taxis and a few other vehicles, filled with over seventy armed men, left to claim the body. The body was retrieved, although it turned out not to be an ʿAmrani. The men who participated were almost entirely members or allies of the descent group (*ḥabl*) of the presumed dead man. A few local officials were also in attendance.

To be effective in political action, the *ḥabl* has to be large. Some large descent groups stand on their own, or are in ʿAmrani terms, cut off. This is not practical for small groups who tend to cluster together to increase their relative strength. Such a cluster may be viewed as a primary alliance. This type of relationship may be seen in the following hypothetical example (see chart 3 on following page):

> *Bayt* al-Fard, *bayt* al-Shakhs, and *bayt* al-Nafr are allied. The largest descent group in this alliance is *bayt* al-Fard (Core B), and members of the two smaller allied groups (B-1 and B-2) identify themselves as part of the al-Fard *ḥabl*.

This alliance may also have a connection with another alliance. The basis of this secondary alliance is seen in this continuation of the above example:

> Since *bayt* al-Fard is still not a particularly strong *ḥabl*, it generally follows the course of action adopted by the alliance of the *shaykh* (Core A). Because of this tendency to support a major alliance, and to increase its importance, at least in a figurative sense, members of the *bayt* al-Fard alliance may state they are with or part of this larger alliance (see chart 3).

Informants view the first affiliation as always to one's primary alliance group. When the number of allies increases, as by secondary alliance, the degree of commitment to these more "distant" allies

CHART 3. PATTERNS OF ALLIANCE FORMATION

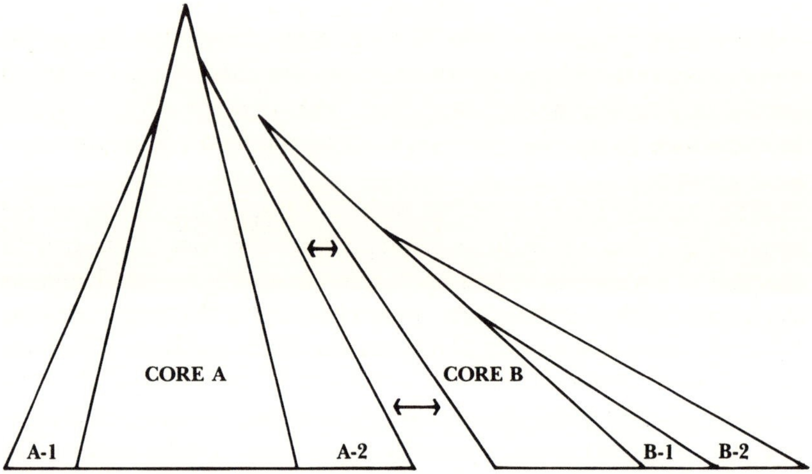

Core A is the basis of the alliance. Attached to this core are allied descent groups A-1 and A-2. Core B, including B-1 and B-2, is also allied to Core A. The relationship between Core A and Core B is a secondary alliance.

decreases. This approximates the way real kinship connections are ordered in terms of the closeness of the relationship.

When I was investigating alliance types, some men suggested the small alliances had been neighborhood associations, groups formed with the expressed purpose of mutual protection. Other informants argued vigorously that alliances extend beyond the bounds of neighborhood and cited respect for alliance leaders as the reason for *ḥabl* formation. Actually both views are probably correct. The smaller, primary alliances may have begun as neighborhood groups, founded on descent groups; and over time, with the formation of secondary connections, the disparate structure described by informants emerged.

ALLIANCE AND TRIBAL ORGANIZATION

Because alliances are the basis of the tribe, the dependence and autonomy of allies can be seen in tribal organization. ᶜAmran tribe is composed of the town, lying rather near the center of the tribal territory, and a number of peripheral villages situated near ᶜAmran's boundaries with other tribal areas. Until one village was ceded to a neighboring tribe, for refusal to pay blood money in the resolution of a dispute, there were nine tribal villages. Each village, like segments of the town, contains one or more primary alliances composed of resident descent groups. In the past at least it was uncommon for members of a descent group to be resident in more than one tribal village.

Although linked to the tribal center (the town), in terms of political affiliation, each tribal village has its own separate identity, contains both tribal and nontribal peoples, and is, in a sense, an independent entity. Like the tribe as a whole, this autonomy is symbolized by boundaries separating one village's lands from those of adjacent villages and those of the town.

Despite the fact that villages are allied to the town, tribal solidarity, although emphasized by informants, is hardly the rule. Now, as in the past, these differences are symbolically expressed in verbal duels held during the annual, postpilgrimage, holiday celebration. Each night ʿAmrani men gather to exchange insulting poems about each other. The attacks are sometimes harsh but lightened with humor. The objective is to poke fun at each other by pointing out foibles. Only a few men are the butt of these jokes, those who will take the insults in good spirit. On a few evenings, tribesmen from one of the tribal villages come to ʿAmran and exchange insults both as village versus town and on an individual level. The insults are viewed good-naturedly but may reflect existing antagonisms and the segmentary nature of tribal relations, and it is men of importance who are often attacked in these duels.

Each village, like the town, has its leader or leaders who represent one or more local constituency. Generally these men are the heads of descent groups and primary alliances. In theory all ʿAmran tribesmen are allies, and alliance heads and their followers recognize the *shaykh* of ʿAmran tribe as their head (see chart 4). The leaders of each of the allied groups form a consultative body that collectively determines the tribe's course of action. Although they may not, as individuals, agree with the decisions of the *shaykh*, their pledges of allegiance to him as tribal leader theoretically obligate them to follow and support the courses of action he chooses.

Ideally, heads of alliances are selected by consensus of their constituents, but it is typical for *ḥabl* leaders to come from the most prominent minimal agnatic group of the core descent group. In the earlier,

76 / *Affiliation: Changing Bases of the Social Order*

CHART 4. THE ALLIANCE RELATIONSHIPS BETWEEN VILLAGES AND THE TOWN

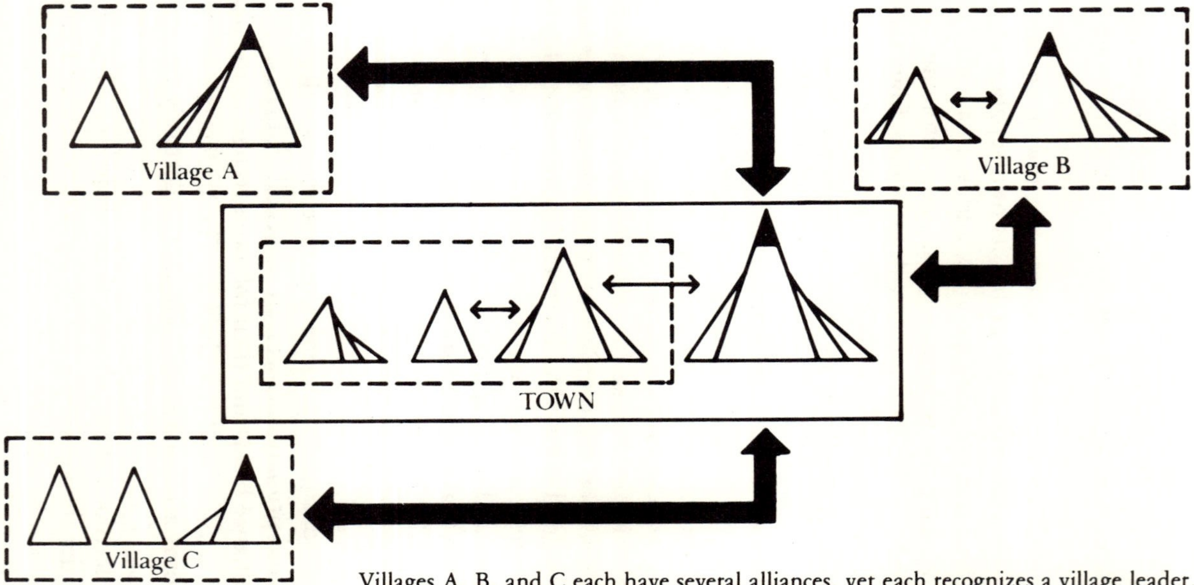

Villages A, B, and C each have several alliances, yet each recognizes a village leader, represented by the darkened triangles. In the town there are also a number of alliances, and the *shaykh* (darkened triangle) is regarded as the town leader. Villages A, B, and C are also tied to the *shaykh* in terms of tribal affiliation and because his power base is the largest in the tribal territory. Although village alliances may side with the *shaykh*, they are not counted generally as part of the *shaykh*'s core power base, which is centered in the town.

hypothetical example of the *bayt* al-Fard alliance, the *habl* leader would be expected to be a senior male of the most prestigious, usually the wealthiest, minimal agnatic group. Leaders of the two allied but unrelated maximal agnatic groups (*bayt* al-Shakhs and *bayt* al-Nafr) would be determined by similar criteria. These latter leaders would be consulted by the head of the larger, secondary alliance, although deference might be shown to the head of *bayt* al-Fard because of his personal importance as head of a primary alliance, a position contingent on the numerical strength of his descent group.

In theory, positions of authority may shift over time. In practice there is a clear tendency for these offices to remain in the same minimal agnatic groups. This is seen most clearly in the case of ʿAmran tribe's *shaykh* who, for at least the last four generations, has come from the descent line of one minimal agnatic group, the title passing from father to son.

Despite a premise of equality among all tribesmen,[6] descent groups are stratified, and access to political power is directly related to the control of resources, both property and men. The importance of these criteria can be seen by examining the maximal agnatic group of the *shaykh*. The *shaykh*'s descent group is numerically the largest in the ʿAmran area. Some minimal agnatic groups within the *bayt*, including the minimal agnatic group of the *shaykh*, control large tracts of land. This combination of wealth and manpower explains why a single minimal agnatic group has dominated political power and why town residents have held tribal leadership positions.

Because of its prominence, the *shaykh*'s descent group is the core of a major alliance in ʿAmran town. The *shaykh*'s personal stature is certainly related to the size of his alliance group, yet he is also supposed to be "disassociated" from it. No one seriously believes that the *shaykh*, by "selection" to his office, ever severed his connections with his descent group. However, since the *shaykh* ideally represents the entire tribe, the *habl* from which he was elected has as its head an influential man, but not the *shaykh* himself. In theory the *shaykh* can be seen as a disinterested party since he consults with the leaders of every *habl*, and he is not in the awkward position of trying to represent both the interests of his alliance and those of the tribe.

The *shaykh* cannot of course really stand apart from his *habl*. The power and influence of a leader is judged by the number of men he can muster, if only for display purposes. Informants state that in the past all *habl* were just patronymic groups. Each group stood on its own; it was cut off or not allied. However, when the size of a descent group (*bayt*) decreased due to migration, death, or failure to bear sons, the group had to join with larger groups, usually those whose leaders had access to political power. When ʿAmranis stress the fictive kinship aspect of these alliance relationships, they gloss over the differences in power. In reality, an alliance brings weak groups under the protection of a politically and/or numerically strong one. Thus while the *shaykh* has obligations to his allies, his prominence is contingent upon their remaining with him.

In the past the *shaykh* was the representative of his *ḥabl* in ʿAmran and also, as the central tribal leader, of those *ḥabl* in the tribal villages allied with him. His alliances were numerous and he was loyal to all of them, but the extent of his support was a function of distance and degree of connection. Because his own *ḥabl*, from which he was "disassociated," was his base of power, it was his primary focus. In this sense his position was not significantly different from that of other *ḥabl* leaders.

Although a few men tend to present the same idealized view of the *shaykh* Levy (1957:271) offers—of a great warrior, wise leader, and generous host who is popularly selected by his constituents—there is really no consensus on the role or importance of ʿAmran's *shaykh* in the past, and thus his position is variously described. There are those now opposed to the traditional leadership, who argue that the *shaykh* had little power before the revolution. He was, they say, merely the imam's agent and as such acted only on the orders of the imam's local representatives. They point out that the *shaykh* received a government subsidy.

Even those in support of the shaykh and who regard the office as important have difficulty defining his prerevolutionary role. To his supporters, the *shaykh* was a middleman or agent of the imam who attempted, usually unsuccessfully, to moderate the imam's demands. Concessions from the imam were hard to achieve, they say, regardless of the *shaykh*'s power. If he could not moderate the directives from Sanʿa, he could still fulfill his obligations to his followers. Most notably, the *shaykh* was responsible for the poor, for whom he made provisions from his stores, and for acting as host to guests. Even ʿAmranis with moderate land holdings recall looking to the size of the *shaykh*'s harvest as an indication of their ability to survive hard times and properly entertain visitors. The *shaykh*'s assets had a direct bearing on his relationship with his tribe, for they were indicative of his ability to provide for his followers.

Everyone agrees that the *shaykh*'s most important role was as a mediator. For his services he received payments, some of which he had to immediately spend in providing hospitality for the disputants and other guests. His net receipts as well as income from his lands and government subsidy made the *shaykh* a wealthy man. The more important tribal leaders, it is said, could be identified by their wealth. A *shaykh* with assets was respected since these were an indication of his success as a mediator. Some of ʿAmran's former leaders are remembered for their successful resolution of difficult issues.

Although the importance of mediation is not questioned, some ambivalence is expressed about mediators. The following joke was told to me several times, and the punch line was often used, out of context, to refer to decisions that had been made, although not necessarily, by the *shaykh*. In the versions I heard, the *shaykh* in question was never from ʿAmran; he was always from another tribe, usually one of ʿAmran's enemies. Of course, if this joke is told elsewhere, the *shaykh* would be from yet another group.

> The men of the town were worried that it would not rain and they feared their crops were going to die. They didn't know what to expect so they went to ask their *shaykh*. He was a well-respected man and they were sure that he would know the answer. They asked the *shaykh* if it was going to rain that day. He looked at the sky and replied, "It's going to rain today . . . or maybe not."

Informants explained that the *shaykh* in question, like all tribal leaders, has tried to give an answer that both satisfies his clients and, more important, cannot be found incorrect. The *shaykh* does not take a stand; he is a middleman, always working between the parties.

Although such a portrayal demeans the importance of the *shaykh*, it highlights only one facet of his office. In theory, it is the *shaykh* who commands power and can initiate military action. Informants, perhaps clinging to the tribal ethos, stress this point, but in ʿAmran such actions were probably infrequent. If the *shaykh*'s leadership is in question, and hence described imprecisely by informants, it is because the *shaykh*'s office was co-opted by the imam. If the tribal leader was more important than now, it is because his power was eroded by the imamate's skillful manipulation that turned the *shaykh* into a conduit of the theocracy.

It will be recalled that in 1907 the Ottomans manipulated ʿAmran's *shaykh*, along with other tribal leaders, into momentarily supporting the Turks against the imam, thwarting a tribal challenge to the Turk's occupation. In the 1930s the imam created his own army, drawing on the same manpower resources that served the *shaykh*. The army weakened the tribal military role and may have disrupted the tribal structure by complicating individual loyalties. Hostages were taken from the *shaykh*'s maximal agnatic group as another device for inhibiting tribal rebellion. Although he took political advantage of other tribal leaders, the imam did not take advantage of his position to replace ʿAmran's *shaykh* with a man of his own choosing, an indication that ʿAmran did not pose a serious problem to the imam's drive for centralized control.

The imam's tactics placed the *shaykh* in the unenviable position of enforcer of central government directives. Informants preferred to cite the above reasons for the *shaykh*'s diminished power and the tribe's loss of autonomy rather than suggest that the *shaykh* was a party in the process, although he must have been aware of his changing role. According to Salzman's (1974:203–4) theory of encapsulation which describes this process of co-opting independent tribal leaders into government agents, it is unimportant whether the *shaykh* was an active or passive participant. ʿAmranis tend to view the loss of tribal autonomy in terms of the imam's power, noting for example that the appearance of a messenger from Sanʿa brought momentary terror to their hearts. In this light, the *shaykh*'s actions may be described generously as an attempt to maintain some influence with the imam and not as an attempt to join the Sanʿa leadership. Even the most vocal critics of the *shaykh* never linked him with the government.

At the time of the coup d'etat, ʿAmran tribe was an important, if militarily inactive, member of the Hashid confederation. The presence of the local garrison of the imam's army and the imam's co-opting of the *shaykh* probably explain the absence of warfare and raiding in the tribe's recent history. Still there was unity within the tribe, particularly in terms of the importance attached to the *ḥabl*. Even though the *ḥabl* may not have had to defend against tribal attack, it was still essential in defense against the imam and as a means of resolving local disputes. Most important, all ʿAmranis were in support of the *shaykh*.

THE TRIBE IN THE POSTREVOLUTIONARY ERA

ᶜAmranis view the tribe as less unified now than in the past. It is common for men to refer to the greater solidarity they feel existed until about ten years ago. Men remark that before 1967 all ᶜAmran was one *ḥabl*, meaning at least that all tribesmen were followers of the *shaykh* and, perhaps, that all alliances were connected with the tribal leadership. These views are seen in the following account, a typical expression of how the tribe has changed:

> Before the revolution all ᶜAmran was one group. We all had the same *shaykh*. He was our leader. When orders came from the imam, it was the *shaykh* who told us what to do. If there was fighting, it was on orders from the *shaykh* and he was the one who paid us. When we were one *ḥabl*, we all joined together to fight our enemies. Then there was a split. Now we fight [bicker] with each other.

Alliances remain important and are discussed frequently by some individuals, but men find it difficult to express the nature of these ties. Informants often cited mutual defense, in both a physical and a financial sense, as the reason for alliances. However, the need for alliances may be on the wane. Government control has greatly reduced the threat of intertribal warfare and economic growth has increased the relative prosperity if not economic independence of most households.

Although informants like to emphasize the importance of alliances, it is not always clear who is allied with whom. To many this is an indication of change. However, informants' impression that allegiances were fixed in the past tends to overlook that alliances could be severed, obligations of allies to one another might be unfulfilled, and individuals were never bound to the decisions of their leaders. In terms of behavior, things might not have changed significantly; but, according to informants, there have been major transformations. These are not stated explicitly in the common lament of all tribesmen on the decline of the tribe, but the point being made is that relationships have changed.

When men referred to ᶜAmran as one *ḥabl*, they did so, it seems, in two senses. First, there was one leader, and tribesmen were supposed to follow him. Second, the *walad al-sūq* and *sayyid* were "followers" of the *shaykh* since at least the former "belonged" to the town. There was stability in social relationships, a point expressed in remarks that everyone had and knew his place in the scheme of things.

To the outsider the split in 1967 came when there were no external threats against which the tribe could coalesce. Either before or in the early years of the revolution, ᶜAmranis faced a common opponent, the imam. When the tribe split in two, the civil war had passed the ᶜAmran area and there were no external pressures necessitating internal cohesion.

ᶜAmranis do not accept this explanation. For them, the split was clearly the result of unique forces. They see the revolution as having created an atmosphere in which the social order could be challenged. The circumstances that precipitated the split originated with the 1962 change in the country's political structure. In ᶜAmran this amounted to the removal of the *sāda* from office and their replacement with tribesmen, usually members of the *shaykh*'s descent group. The *shaykh* became the government administrator; and while he was still connected with the central government, he was, at least initially, an active participant representing the tribe to the capital. The *shaykh*'s restoration of his traditional relationship with the government coincided with the latter's interest in maintaining tribal loyalty to the republican cause. At the outset of the civil war, then, the tribe was united with the government against the royalist forces of the imam, and it is in this light that I believe informants tend to see ᶜAmran as one *ḥabl*.

The incidents ᶜAmranis suggest led to the split center on the "weakness" of the *shaykh*. The first of these occurred during the postpilgrimage holiday celebrations in 1964 or 1965, when a dispute erupted between the *walad al-sūq* and the tribesmen:

> The problem was fomented by a minor altercation between two women—one from the *walad al-sūq*, the other a tribeswoman—over the use of a special holiday swing. The fighting between the women was stopped with the *walad al-sūq* woman apparently suffering the greater injury, but the dispute was rekindled the next day when a group of the tribeswoman's male relatives and friends attacked the husband of the *walad al-sūq* woman's maternal aunt. This conduct infuriated the related *walad al-sūq* families. They sought the counsel of the *walad al-sūq*'s recognized leader and spokesman, Ahmad al-Safunj, a *bayāᶜ* or "merchant" who functioned much like a *ḥabl* leader even though the *walad al-sūq* did not have alliances.
>
> Ahmad decided that since the *shaykh* was the local administrator it would be impossible to find an impartial mediator in the town, and he decided to take the case to the *shaykh* of a neighboring Bakil tribe who agreed to arbitrate and settle the dispute. On the appointed day the two parties met to settle the problem ac-

cording to tribal law.⁷ The final decision was for a penalty on ʿAmran tribe of twenty-one bulls for failure to meet their obligations to ensure the safety of the *walad al-sūq*. However, the tribeswoman's family received several bulls from the *walad al-sūq*. Finally each side was required to contribute an additional number of cattle, approximately twenty per side, and these were slaughtered on successive days and distributed to all ʿAmranis.

Although this resolved the central issue, another problem was brought for adjudication that indicates the level of tension and type of relationship that existed between the two groups. It had been normal for tribal soldiers as well as those of the imam's army to be billeted in ʿAmran houses when there was no room in the fort. These soldiers were always placed with the *walad al-sūq* who were compensated semiannually for these services; but they felt they were being exploited. The problem was exacerbated by the constant flow of soldiers passing through the town at the time. The resolution called for each group to house soldiers in the ratio of one-third by the *walad al-sūq* and two-thirds by the tribesmen.⁸

The incident is believed to have been both significant and unusual. Informants feel that it was the revolution's emphasis on equality that led to the tribe's being challenged. They overlook the fact that the *walad al-sūq* always had access to redress and that these options were within the parameters of tribal law even though the *walad al-sūq* were not part of the tribe.

The influence this incident had on the *shaykh*'s stature cannot be determined. It clearly had an impact on the *walad al-sūq* who, some informants suggest, were drawn together under one leader. In all probability, the event served only to solidify the political prominence of Ahmad al-Safunj. Apart from his ancestry, al-Safunj, as the head of a large descent group and a wealthy landowner, satisfied the same criteria for leadership as any *ḥabl* leader.

As tribesmen, the *shaykh* and other leaders could not be impartial in resolving the dispute and so the decision to seek outside mediation was not a challenge to their authority. The formation of a youth organization did confront the traditional leadership, however:

In 1966 or 1967 an informal youth organization emerged, encompassing most of the young men in the town. Some men argue that the group was inspired by the Iraqi Baʿath Party, but its concerns focused on two local problems: the escalation of the bride-price and the reception of returned pilgrims from Mecca.

Since the revolution, bride-price (*shart*) had escalated so rapidly that many men could not afford to get married. The men of the youth organization called a town meeting and ensured the attendance of the town elders by closing the town's gates and posting guards. With the elders in attendance, the young men demanded that a limit be placed on the bride-price. Eventually the elders agreed to enforce a limit of 400 YR. The youth also won concessions on the number of wedding gifts, meals to be served at weddings and a prohibition on shooting rifles or igniting firecrackers.

The young men were equally successful in changing the pattern for receiving returned pilgrims. Rifle fire was banned as were the costly receptions returned pilgrims had been expected to provide for well-wishing guests.

Although the primary aim of the youth organization was the stabilization of the bride-price, its formation was an expression of father-son conflict. Intergenerational conflict was not new, but was exacerbated by the types of changes that had occurred following the revolution. Most young men felt that their fathers and other senior men were out of step with the pace of life, and they saw themselves as best qualified to deal with modern contingencies. Probably correct in the belief that bride-price would only increase further if no action were taken, the young men chose to force a decision on the older generation. That the *shaykh* acquiesced to the demands is taken by some as a sign of weakness, but that view fails to note that without the support of others, enforcement would have been impossible. This episode was not the only evidence of the *shaykh*'s presumed inability to lead.

As early as 1963 or 1964, the *shaykh* had attempted to modernize the town through a cooperative association. This locally initiated program was largely unsuccessful. Some men attribute the plan's failure to the central government's intentions to regulate the rate of development. It is clear that from 1964 to 1967 development in and around ʿAmran was directed from Sanʿa. A road-building crew from the Peoples Republic of China was housed near the town and the construction of the Sanʿa-Saʿada road was underway. A clinic was begun and a school was under construction. The town's leadership participated only slightly in these projects; the decisions were made in the capital.

While some of the projects were completed after 1967, informants argue that it was the *shaykh*'s lack of influence with the government that weakened his position. The *shaykh* was not seriously consulted on the projects; and when there was a possibility of a major agricultural program being started near the town, he was unable to influence the decision. It is a widely held belief, but one for which there is no evidence, that had there been stronger connections with the Sanʿa regime, the town would have developed more quickly.

It is in this setting that the split occurred. There are two explanations of the rift, but neither is associated with a particular viewpoint or either of the factions that emerged. The better known, or commonly cited, account provides a rather simple explanation for the split.

The loss of the proposed agricultural project alienated many tribesmen, a group of whom were from one *habl*. They expressed their displeasure with the *shaykh* by electing a "new" *shaykh* from amongst themselves. The man chosen had held some minor government posts and had traveled in the Middle East, and it was believed his experience and connections would better serve the needs of the town.

At roughly the same time, Ahmad al-Safunj, the *walad al-sūq* leader, died. Ahmad's position was taken by Hamud al-Shajar, another wealthy "merchant." When he assumed leadership, Hamud was in partnership with several members of the "old" *shaykh*'s descent group, a relationship that ensured *walad al-sūq* "support" for the traditional leadership. However, not long after the split, Hamud and the "old" *shaykh*'s relatives had a falling out and the partnership was dissolved. So pronounced was this dispute that Hamud, and his following, chose to support the *ḥabl* of the "new" *shaykh*.

The other, less well-known account attributes the split to the actions of "foreign operatives," although it may be better characterized as a major misunderstanding. This version was mentioned less often because some men were reluctant to openly discuss the foreign influences they felt were at the core of the split:

> Some of the organizers of the youth organization were under Baʿath Party influence. At first this connection was unknown, but eventually it came to the attention of some men who drove the non-ʿAmrani Baʿath provocateur from the town. Labeling the youth organization's actions as revolutionary, some tribal leaders began to question the *shaykh*'s role in agreeing to enforce the bride-price demands. Thinking the *shaykh* was a Baʿath sympathizer, and fearing loss of their offices, some tribal leaders severed their affiliations to the *shaykh*. The first to renounce his allegiance was a highly respected leader of a tribal village and his action led to a chain reaction among other tribal leaders.
>
> Initially each newly nonaligned group stood as an independent entity, but shortly their stance was coordinated by a man who came eventually to be called a *shaykh*. A new *ḥabl* was formed around the "new" *shaykh*'s descent group.
>
> The isolation of the "old" *shaykh* did not last long, for shortly some of the village leaders realized that the "old" *shaykh* was not a revolutionary, and returned to his side. In the villages some *ḥabl* leaders chose not to realign with the *shaykh* and continued to support the "new" *shaykh*. This pattern has continued so that now each village has a representative of each major alliance.
>
> The split was not simply a local matter but had broader repercussions. The paramount Hashid *shaykh* spent roughly a month in an unsuccessful attempt to restore unity to ʿAmran tribe. Eventually many of the *shaykh*'s supporters did come back to his side and he has maintained his support of the Hashid confederation. The new alliance, based primarily on two descent groups, is not strongly tied to the confederation's leadership.

Although some ʿAmranis describe these two alliances as if they were comparable, there are some significant differences between them. The "new" *shaykh*'s core supporters reside neither in the town nor a village, but around a well adjacent to their lands. Many of their supporters, not counting those in villages, have lands in the same general area. This is similar to the neighborhood associations informants recalled as a starting point for alliances.

More important, perhaps, in contrast to the traditional tribal leadership, the leaders of the new alliance, representing two descent groups, have only moderate landholdings. The core group is numerically smaller and less wealthy than the "old" *shaykh*'s *ḥabl*. The new alliance is not without wealth, but the requisite commodities, cash and land, are held by important "merchant" (*bayāʿ*) families allied with the "new" *shaykh*. Further, many members of this alliance are not tribesmen.

The traditional leadership structure established the *shaykh* as the first among equals with his ability to make decisions based, in part, on his disinterested third-party status. The *shaykh* received a subsidy and was already wealthy. He had nothing to gain from his transactions. The "new" *shaykh*, lacking these "guarantors" of impartiality, is seen by his detractors as motivated by personal and ideologic concerns. Of course, many charges and counter-charges are leveled by both sides.

The split forced the "old" *shaykh* to resign in favor of his son, a man of recognized diplomatic skill who had served as government administrator in the postrevolution period. As a relatively young man (although I will continue to refer to him as the "old" *shaykh*), he was believed to be better equipped to deal with the government apparatus in the capital and better able to modify his office in accordance with the diminishing role of the tribe as a warrior group. In this he was partially successful; when the central government decided to formalize local cooperative associations in 1973, the *shaykh* was elected president and many of his allies gained seats on the governing board.

Although it seems the "old" *shaykh* could easily shift his role to deal with modern circumstances, he did so at the cost of residential tribal solidarity. In the prerevolutionary era, men settling in ʿAmran had to establish some sort of relationship with the tribe, either by joining a *ḥabl* or by accepting tribal protection. At least by the end of the civil war this custom had been abandoned. Many migrants settled in ʿAmran town but were not required to sever their ties to their natal villages. As a result they remained outsiders; and as the number of these unaffiliated residents has grown, the town's social structure has shifted away from the tribal system that still prevails in ʿAmran tribal villages where affiliation is mandatory. Practically, it would not have been possible for the *shaykh* to both maintain tribal solidarity and speed the pace of the town's development. As it was, neither was under his control.

With only a portion of the town affiliated in *ḥabl*, the importance of such groups may be questioned. For the older generation, the *ḥabl* defined those upon whom one could depend. Even though members of an alliance might not meet their obligations, it was still essential that an individual's affiliations be known. As one older informant remarked many times, "If there is a war with Bakil (or a Bakil group), who can you go to and say, 'I am your neighbor,' " a plea or demand for assistance rooted in the protector-protected relationship described earlier.[9] The point remains that affiliation depends on formalized relationships.

It is common for men to point to the split in leadership, as well as the failure to recruit newcomers, as evidence of the decline of the *ḥabl*. It is true that men are no longer sure of alliances and that both the "new" and "old" alliances include some "merchant" groups. More to the point, these modifications were underway before the civil war heightened tensions and created the unity men like to recall. Alliances require the participation of their members; and if individuals believe they are in a position to take care of their own needs, they often feel less inclined to fulfill their jural obligations. Some informants were in fact in a position to "look after themselves," and others were not, and it is not surprising that the role and continued viability of the contemporary *ḥabl* was variously described.

When informants attempted to demonstrate the fragility of the *ḥabl*, they often referred to the collapse of one group. The circumstances surrounding its breakup were unusual, however, and may well have been the undoing of a *ḥabl* even in prerepublican times:

> A dispute among members of *bayt* al-Shathab arose over some missing money. Jamal al-Shathab claimed money had been taken from, and rifle shots had been fired into, his shop. At a meeting called by the family to investigate these events, Jamal accused his father's brother's sons of both acts. The accusations led to heated words and Jamal is said to have threatened his cousins with an automatic rifle. They, in turn, grabbed him and stabbed him several times. Although there were witnesses, no one could single out the man who struck the fatal blow.
> With Jamal dead, the cousins and their father, the head of (*ḥabl*) *bayt* al-Shathab, fled. The next day many men gathered at the hospital and in homes to see what should be done. The incident drew such a response because many ʿAmran families are connected with *bayt* al-Shathab, a descent group that originated elsewhere but has many households and a long history in ʿAmran.

Before any local action could be taken, the murderers' father turned himself in to government authorities, and his sons were arrested soon after. The government took charge of the affair and, after several delays, two of the cousins were sentenced to prison terms and one to death.

During the months between the arrests and trials of the men, the *habl* slowly collapsed. It was clear that the leadership was ineffective, a point made obvious when charges against the assailants' father were dropped due to his "senility." However, rather than drawing upon their own members for a new *habl* head, the individual families sought alliances with other *habl*. As one former member put it, "*Bayt* al-Shathab is dead. Some of us are with this alliance, some with that alliance. What else could we do? When you fight among yourselves, there can't be a *habl*."

The actions of the al-Shathab descent group indicate the conflicting views of the *habl*. Even though in a sense the *habl* may not be necessary for defense and mutual support, there remains a felt need for *habl* connections. The advantages of *habl* affiliation might be difficult to articulate, but there is little doubt that affiliation is important.

For example, one of the al-Shathab murderers escaped and took refuge with kinsmen in a nearby village. These kinsmen tried to get the ʿAmran *shaykh* to intercede on the murderer's behalf. Although the *shaykh* could do nothing, the kinsmen's action was seen as typifying *habl* loyalty. When informants reflect on the role of the *habl*, they think of actions such as this in particular.

Of course such unified *habl* action occurs only in crisis situations. At most other times men prefer to remain independent. Recent economic and physical security has made it easier for men to avoid the obligations of *habl* affiliation, yet there are occasions when their potential vulnerability is accentuated. Strangers sometimes appear at weddings or on market days to ask ʿAmranis' help in paying blood money. ʿAmranis pity these men, because they have to lower themselves to beg for assistance. Seeing the depth to which an unsupported individual can fall, they cannot help but ponder what they risk with the decline of their own support groups.

CONCLUSION

The role of the *habl* has been shifting from one of mutual defense and support to that of the basis of political factions. Although a shift of emphasis, this role change has also involved a restructuring of some relationships. The *habl* once existed to distinguish tribal affiliation and the important protector role of the tribe, but major alliances now include nontribal low-status groups in their membership. The continuing importance of the *ḥabl* may be traced to its actual or potential political role, a factor that explains the active participation of wealthy men, but this shift is also seen as an indication of the decline of the tribe. Those who hold the latter view tend to be those who have been unsuccessful in their attempts to find new economic niches that would enable them, like those who have achieved economic security, to feel less reliant on the *ḥabl*.

4

Occupation: Ascription and Achievement

The formal model of the social system has provided a basis for ordering ʿAmrani interstrata relations. Since occupations were arranged according to status and ancestry, the model also fixed relations to the means of production. Even though the model suggests a certain rigidity to the distribution of economic niches among the different social strata, there was, given the rather limited nature of the prerevolutionary economy, a fair amount of occupational variation, some of which contradicted the ascriptive model.

Postrevolutionary economic growth has increased occupational opportunity and diversity. Stimulated by the greater financial security of commerce and buoyed with repatriated funds from emigrant labor, there has been a surge in mercantile activity and a decline in agriculture. This shift in economic emphasis indicates a change in some attitudes toward the marketplace and commerce, and has modified the traditional measures of status.

OCCUPATION AND STATUS

The following exchange is an old man reprimanding his grandson for not being home when he was needed:

"Where have you been?"

"In the *sūq*," comes the meek reply.

"What are you, a tribesman or a *walad al-sūq*?"

"A tribesman," the boy answers as he dodges the half-hearted swings of his grandfather's cane.

"Tribesmen don't spend time in the *sūq*. 'Men' don't go in the *sūq*. Do you want to be like the *walad al-sūq*?"

"But everyone hangs out in the *sūq*," whimpers the boy.

"Even so," says the old man, taking a final swipe at the boy as he scurries into the house.

Both in historical references and present-day transactions, social position is a recurring theme. For ᶜAmranis the marketplace has been and remains a locus for status differentiation. As we have seen, those who traditionally worked in the "sacred market" (see chapter 3) or were associated with a nonagrarian lifestyle were considered different from and under the protection of the warrior-peasant. Widespread and rapid economic growth fueled by monies repatriated from Saudi Arabia has not changed these attitudes. The post-1962 revolutionary constitution proclaimed the equality of all men and the universal right of individuals to undertake the work of their choosing (Yemen Arab Republic 1971:390–91). While this has "opened" the marketplace to those who once viewed commerce with disdain, it has not lessened the ambivalence felt toward those whose traditional occupations were connected with merchandising or provision of services. However, since traditional standards for assessing one's own and others' status were linked in part to occupation, the entry of tribesmen into the commercial sector has required a redefinition of the occupational categories in the formal hierarchy so as to preserve the barrier between social strata.

In ᶜAmran, social status is not based exclusively on relationship to the marketplace. There are two forms of status differentiation. The system usually considered by scholars as "traditional" is based on the principles of ancestry and occupation (cf. Gerholm 1977). For ᶜAmranis this is only the most obvious expression of social difference, a model whose broad outlines lay in the Asad al-Kamal legend. In this system, social difference was manifested by prescriptive rules for wearing the dagger, defined social position in terms of ascribed socioeconomic activity and behavioral characteristics.

Status is also based on wealth and attendant criteria such as social contacts, influence, and prestige. Some ᶜAmranis consider these less rigid, nonascriptive standards as new or emergent, yet the same individuals admit that achievement has always been a status determinant, although to a lesser degree than is now the case. The application of these status markers is most apparent, although no less imprecise, in the arrangement of marriages (see chapter 5).

Because social status is now more achievement-oriented, some ᶜAmranis perceive a shift in their social structure from one system of differentiation to another. Although the majority of ʿAmranis may not define the transformation in exactly these terms, they are acutely aware that social change is occurring; that it is the result of the revolution; and that they must try to make this transition with the least loss, if not greatest gain, in social position. The shift in standards of differentiation, then, represents a change in emphasis, not in kind.

THE ASCRIPTIVE SYSTEM

Ascriptive occupations are not unique to Yemen,[1] but the social divisions are more complex than those found outside the southwest corner of the Arabian Peninsula. Whereas the formal hierarchy has attracted considerable scholarly attention (see table 1), there is agreement only on the broad parameters of the model. Much of the confusion appears to arise from the fact that the data were gathered at different intervals and in a variety of locations. It is also probable that no single system ever existed. For all its apparent rigidity, the social hierarchy was variable, and occupational categories were defined as much by local circumstances as universal prescriptive rules.

The Yemeni concern with status, particularly the obvious occupation-related, stigmatized social positions, may be considered unusual. The Yemeni interpretation of Islam declares the equality of all believers; the Yemeni social system does not. This incongruity is not lost on some ʿAmranis, particularly the educated youth,[2] who generally have some secondary school education. They assert, in the revolutionary spirit, that all men are equal, but in a contradiction apparent to all, will, when pressed, explain that occupational divisions were imposed by the imam, the agent of Allah, that these became traditional, and cannot be violated. The students' descriptions are more a means of condemning the imam, and condoning their own nonegalitarian behavior, than an explanation of social differences. Less educated men take a simpler, more straightforward approach when they describe the hierarchy as the "decision of Allah," implying that it is pointless to question the system.

The foundations of the formal model were laid out in the Asad al-Kamal legend (chapter 2), from which it may be assumed that the tribesmen are superior to the *walad al-sūq* because they control the means of production and means of defense. The *walad al-sūq* provide services the tribesman cannot perform for himself, and in so doing are forced to accept a lower status and dependence because they are

Table 1. Sample of Hierarchies Described by Scholars

Rathjens (1951:175-77)

sāda
tribe (shaykh, ʿāgal)
service providers
  butcher
  water worker
  bath attendant
  grocer
  coffee seller
  bleeder
  barber
  executioner
  public crier
  minstrel
Jew
akhdām (1)

Bornstein (1974:11)

sāda (3)
shaykh
peasant
bayāʿ or salesman
butcher
barber
potter
weaver
innkeeper
bath attendant
public crier
akhdām (1)

Dostal (1974:3)

sāda (3)
tribesmen
low status
  butcher
  tanner
  weaver
  potter
  bleeder
  barber
  public crier

Chelhod (1970:63)

religious experts
peasants
merchants
craftsmen
ʿanadīl (including:
  barbers
  weavers
  public criers, etc.)
akhdām (1)

Glaser (1885:202-4)

sāda
shaykh & ʿāgal
tribesmen & ʿarab (2)
muzayyin
slave descendants
akhdām (1)

al-Attar (1964:103-6)

sāda
shaykh
merchants & craftsmen
peasants
slave descendants
akhdām (1)

---

(1) *Akhdām* are dark-skinned people from Tihama or coastal plains.
(2) *ʿArab* refers to merchants. Gerholm (1977:202) says it is used to refer to townsmen of tribal origin. The term is not used in ʿAmran.
(3) Neither Dostal nor Bornstein enumerate the *sāda* in their descriptions, but they refer to them elsewhere. Their placement reflects my interpretation of their position.

without the tools (land and arms) necessary to provide for some of their own basic needs. The *sāda*, who were late "entrants" into the system, must be viewed in a different light since their ascendency over the tribesman is a reflection of their noble ancestry and spiritual power.

Presented in these terms, the social categories appear monolithic, yet each is internally divided into ranked groups. This is most obvious among the *walad al-sūq*, where ranked groups are linked to narrow occupational niches; but status differences also exist, and may be viewed as "occupation related" among the tribesmen and *sāda*. Informants naturally preferred to deal with the broadest categories since to do so did not require them to elaborate on or to order substrata or to account for "anomalous" cases such as low-status men being large landholders or tribesmen being landless.

The hierarchical model, then, is based on ʿAmranis' selective use of status criteria. Overall rank is based on ancestry and occupation, but status within a stratum or substratum is determined by additional factors. Thus, even though the *walad al-sūq* "occupational" substrata are well delineated, their ordering requires knowledge of marriage patterns. The same use of multiple criteria can be found, if less precisely, among the tribesman and *sayyid* strata.

The model ʿAmranis describe, and use to make status assessments, represents a cultural ideal connected with the prerevolutionary era and thus is presented in the past tense even though many of its characteristics still obtain. Despite suggestions that change is only recent, it is probable that before the revolution the social system did not operate in as straightforward a manner as contemporary descriptions would lead us to believe. In presenting this model I have followed the general outline ʿAmranis use, but have accepted Peters's (1972) advice not to rely solely on informants' characterizations of social structure. I have therefore included variations within the scheme. This forces deviation "into" the model, but the result is a more accurate representation of the system with which ʿAmranis deal (see table 2). (For clarity, quotation marks are used to designate traditional occupational categories.)

THE HIERARCHY IN ʿAMRAN

ʿAmranis generally agree that the lowest *walad al-sūq* substratum was occupied by the "poetic messenger" or "public crier" (*daw-*

96 / Occupation: Ascription and Achievement

Table 2. Social Categories and Divisions Based on Defining Feature and Real Tasks

Title	Defining Occupation	Real Occupation	Social Category	Social Position
dawshān	public messenger	jiḥāz maker		lowest status
ḥajjām	bleeder	same[1]		
ḥammāmī	bath attendant	same[1]		
muzayyin	barber/circumciser	same[1]		
jazzār	butcher	same[1]		
gashshām	vegetable peddler	same[1]		
mugahwī	innkeeper	same[1]	bani al-khamis / walad al-sūq	
[sagāl][2]	polisher	same[1]		
— — —	— — —	— — —	— — —	— — —
ṣanaʿ[3]	weaver	same[1]		
— — —	— — —	— — —	— — —	— — —
maslāḥi	broker	same[1]		
kayāl[4]	grain measurer	same[1]		
— — —	— — —	— — —	— — —	— — —
bayāʿ	merchant	same[1]		highest status
— — —	— — —	— — —	— — —	— — —
		shāgī (day laborer)		lowest status
		sharīk (sharecropper)		
		peasant with sūq connection		
		landowning peasant	gabīli	
		ʿāgal		
gabīli	warrior-peasant	shaykh[5]		highest status

faqīh[5]	learned man	same
qāḍī[5,6]	legal expert	same
sayyid	peasant literate official imam	same teacher muhājir[7] sayyid

[1]This was the primary occupation. Not all men of the occupational group may have pursued this work.

[2]Sagāl, although now resident in ʿAmran, was not native to the town. Those who now work in ʿAmran are native to villages near Khamir where, informants state, all sagāl originated.

[3]Ṣanaʿ are a group characterized as weavers. There were not and are not now any sanaʿ families in ʿAmran. Ṣanaʿ live in villages close to the source of raw materials for their craft. Informants recognize them as a group, but are unsure where to rank them other than being sure that they are not gabīlī and that they have a lower status than the bayāʿīn, the highest status group of the walad al-sūq.

[4]This category is said to be unique to ʿAmran.

[5]The positions of the shaykh and qāḍī are often seen as being on the same level, probably because both have unique social positions and constituencies. In this scheme, the faqīh may actually be said to rank lower than the shaykh. However, individual variation is such that there is no absolute ranking. All of these men—shaykh, qāḍī, and faqīh—may be said to outrank low-ranked sayyid families.

Informants' presentations of the hierarchy do not account for individual variation. Instead they place all sāda in the highest ranked category. This conforms with a widely held view of status. Once when chewing gāt with the shaykh, a sayyid pointed out to the room that he was better than the shaykh because of his ancestry. The shaykh, who I felt was somewhat disturbed by the sayyid's claim to higher status, said nothing and nodded obligingly when I challenged the sayyid's claim.

[6]Guḍā' (s. gaḍī) who are of sayyid ancestry are referred to as gaḍī or by the title of their office. This distinguishes them from sāda without office or title. It is paradoxical that a man might achieve more respect through a title generally held to be below his natal rank. Such rank/status differences are characteristic of the upper echelons of Yemeni social structure.

[7]The term means a man of religious knowledge who receives gifts for Quranic readings; it is usually applied to a sayyid, but it is not specific to that group.

shān).³ Although a most despised individual, whose task it was to carry news and information to the villages visited by himself and his family, the "messenger" also had a number of important public functions. His "messenger's" falsetto voice and stylized phrases were essential elements to a number of occasions. These ranged from the rather simple greeting of visitors at events such as weddings or making announcements to men in the *sūq* on market days to the extremely important welcoming of intertribal guests at tribal affairs like dispute resolution or being the spokesman or "speaking man" for the tribe. In this latter role the "messenger" either stood at the head of the tribe with the *shaykh* and presented ʿAmran's point of view or carried information, under a white flag, between warring parties.

Under such circumstances he was a highly protected person whose murder, at these times if not always, was a serious breach of tribal honor. Like all protected people, the "messengers" enjoyed tribal protection, and, since they are said to have been landless, are seen to have "belonged" to the tribe on whom they relied for their support.

As their work was sporadic, "messengers" could not expect to subsist on the grain they were paid. Most were skilled in the custom carving of the dagger scabbard (*jihāz*) and encasing the wooden shell in leather. This craft afforded them ample opportunity to gather information as they travelled about making, repairing, or decorating scabbards.

Of roughly comparable low status was the "bleeder" (*ḥajjām*). The difficulty informants' have in determining the relative rank of each substratum is apparent in the trading of insults: a man called a "messenger" will call his opponent a "bleeder" and vice versa. Despite the implications of equivalence in this interplay, most men consider the "bleeder" somewhat less despicable than the "messenger."

The "bleeder," who used a vast array of blades, was reputed to have precise knowledge of where to make incisions, how to use cow horns to cup or suck off the offending blood, and how to alleviate bodily pains. According to a few men, including ʿAmran's only practitioner, this skill was in such high demand in the past that the "bleeder" was required to travel to villages as well as to attend the sick who came to him on market days. His only competition came from other, although non-stigmatized, traditional healers.

In addition to holding positions of low rank, the "messenger" and the "bleeder" are unique in ʿAmrani eyes because they are easily identified. Both have as their surnames their occupational titles. This is, no doubt, merely a variation of the standard practice of taking as one's name the place where one was born. Yet Muhammad Dawshan or Ahmad Hajjam are perceived as having personae directly linked to their status. This does not apply to most other segments of the *walad al-sūq* category.

When the generic label *muzayyin* was applied, it actually referred to a number of occupational groups whose members were of roughly equal low status but above that of the messenger or the "bleeder." The following occupations comprise the generic *muzayyin* category: innkeeper (*mugahwī*), barber-circumciser (*muzayyin*), vegetable peddler (*gashām*), bath attendant (*ḥammāmī*), butcher (*jazzār*), and polisher-cleaner-appraiser of daggers (*sāgāl*).

The "innkeeper" (*mugahwī*) operated teashops and restaurants for men shopping in the *sūq* or conducting other business in the town. Although he provided tea for men working in the market and government offices, the "innkeeper's" services were almost exclusively for travelers, since ʿAmranis, other than *walad al-sūq*, rarely spent much time in the marketplace. Inns were not much more than large unfurnished rooms where soldiers and travelers could find lodging for themselves and their animals. Prior to the revolution there were only two small inns in ʿAmran; and when large numbers of visitors, such as soldiers, came to town, they were lodged in the houses of other *muzayyin* families (see chapter 3).

The "vegetable peddler" (*gashām*) grew vegetables, primarily scallions, white radishes and onions, in mosque-owned (*waqf*) gardens and sold them either in the *sūq* or door to door. Some non-"vegetable peddlers" bought produce from mosque gardens and resold it in the market.

The "butcher" (*jazzār*) bought animals from livestock brokers or directly from villagers and kept them at his home until slaughtered for sale. Meat was expensive and demand was low. Only a few "butchers," in rotation, slaughtered each day; others traveled to regional markets since demand was highest on *sūq* days. "Butchers" also had special functions including the slaughtering of animals for religious holidays, rain-making ceremonies, and dispute resolution. For these tasks they received payment only for butchering and dressing, since the parties involved had purchased the animals from livestock traders.

The "bath attendant" (*ḥammāmī*) worked in public baths.

Aside from supervising bathers (fighting in the baths was commonplace) and scrubbing the backs of some for additional fees, the "attendant" built the fires, using discarded animal bones and wood, and kept the bathing area clean. The wives and sisters of the "bath attendants" worked in the baths on days that women bathed, but they did not lay the fires.[4]

From the ᶜAmrani point of view, the "dagger polisher-cleaner-appraiser" (*sagāl*) was an itinerant craftsman. Originally from villages near Khamir, these men pursued their craft at weekly markets and by visiting villages. They were noted both for their skill in polishing, sharpening, and repairing the steel blades of daggers and for their expertise in assessing the value of both the blades and the rhinoceros horn handles. They also sold daggers on a commission basis.

The "barber-circumciser" (*muzayyin*) was the most disparaged individual within the already despised *muzayyin* substratum. Aside from his cutting hair and circumcising male infants, the "barber-circumciser" was an essential performer in the marriage ritual. In fact both male and female members of this group may be said to hold the key to a number of ritual matters since they decided how ceremonies were to be performed.

At weddings the "barber-circumciser" was responsible for inviting guests, cooking the meat for the feast, purifying the room in which the bride and groom meet by smashing eggs to ward off devils, preparing the groom for the receipt of gifts, and announcing the gifts publicly. The importance of these tasks cannot be underestimated, because the manner in which the services were conducted reflected on the host family. Further, improper performance of purifications was felt to risk serious supernatural consequences and jeopardize the marriage since the bride and groom, as is now the case, were considered extremely vulnerable to magical attack. "Barber-circumciser" women were charged with similar responsibilities to the bride during the week-long wedding preparations.

Ideally the economic activities of individuals in the *muzayyin* group were dictated by their ancestry. Actually there were too many low-status men in ᶜAmran, at least in the *muzayyin* and "merchants" (*bayāᶜ*) groups (see below), for all to find work in their "ancestral" occupations. A few men were engaged in agricultural work, sometimes as day laborers or sharecroppers, sometimes on their own holdings. Others found work as "servants" (*khadām*) for wealthy families or government officials. Their responsibilities varied but included running errands, making purchases in the *sūq*, providing service to *gāt* chewers, cleaning offices, and watching shops when owners were away. One "innkeeper" family provided water to the "butchers" and, even fairly recently, received 200 YR a day for this service, made possible because of a family-owned well.

Ranking above the set of *muzayyin* subgroups were the "merchants" (*bayāʿ*, p. *bayāʿīn*). Although they were of low status in comparison to tribesmen, a recognizable social distance existed between the "merchants," many of whom claim to have once been tribesmen (see chapter 3) and other *walad al-sūq*. Some informants perceived the difference between commercial and service occupations as so great that "merchants" could never be categorized as *walad al-sūq*, but others implied they were only a special group of that stratum. "Merchants" quite naturally have viewed the distinction between themselves and other *walad-al-sūq* as very precise. If "merchants" were different from others of low status, they are never confused with tribesmen. Those tribesmen who now have shops identify themselves, when pressed, as businessmen (*tujjār*).

"Merchants" sold both imported and locally produced goods. In the prerevolutionary period, the number of products for sale seems to have been fairly small.[5] Some "merchants" were said to have exclusive ties to producers whose products, like honey and clarified butter, they sold. Often they were merely brokers between ʿAmran customers and villagers, Sanʿa merchants, or caravan operators.

The somewhat higher status accorded to the "merchants" allowed the most respected and wealthy to serve as informal leaders or spokesmen for the *walad al-sūq* (chapter 3), and it was to these men that those of lower status turned for protection and assistance. In spite of their "elevated" status, the "merchants'" ancestry seems no more unique than that of other low-status families, and their rank may be related to their control over the movement of goods.

Not enumerated in ʿAmranis' descriptions of the formal model were the "middlemen" (*maṣlaḥīn*), a substratum intermediate to the *muzayyin* and "merchant" substrata. Each "middleman" or his family specialized in a fixed inventory of items, some of which included grapes, firewood, *gishr*, salt, and *gāt*. The "middlemen" for these goods are still well known to informants. There were probably agents for items such as fruits, vegetables, nuts, and others.

There were also "measurers" (*kayālīn*), a well-defined variation of the "middlemen" whose primary economic activity was to facilitate trade in the market by providing an honest measure of grain for buying and selling. Considered impartial third parties, most "measurers" also bought and sold grain. Informants assert that in the past all grain deals required a "measurer" except for the collection of taxes (*zakāt*). There was a measurer for tax collection, but not from the "measurer" group.

Most, if not all, of the "measurers" were originally "barber-circumcisers" or "innkeepers." As this economic niche developed and its practitioners became a separate substratum, they assumed the responsibility of guarding the town, a task formerly shared by all *muzayyin* and paid for by town taxes. A few men slept in rooms adjacent to the gates, locking them at dusk and opening them again at dawn.

These are the stigmatized occupations of the *walad al-sūq* found in ʿAmran. Men in this category were considered deficient or defiled (*nāgiṣ*)[6] in the sense of being less than "real" men. It is this taint that set them apart from tribesmen.

In contrast to the *walad al-sūq* category, the tribesmen (*gabīlī*) stratum, lacking obvious divisions of labor, seems to display greater homogeneity. This superficial similarity is supported by the tribesman's association with food production, but there were many adaptations to the agrarian lifestyle. Informants tend to gloss over differences in access to the means of production, but are quick to note that, although all tribesmen supposedly came from the same mold, there are those whose casts are less than perfect.

Adaptations within the tribesman group may be divided into four loose occupational types (all of which ʿAmranis subsume under the warrior label). The first, the landowners, included those self-sufficient individuals or families with holdings of large enough size to be their sole source of income. The most prestigious tribesman families, including those of the *shaykh* and *ḥabl* leaders, are found in this group.

The second group are the sharecroppers (*shurakāʾ*, s. *sharīk*). Members of this set ranged from those who combined work on their own holdings with some labor on the land of large landowners to those who subsisted almost entirely from food produced on others' lands. Before the revolution, sharecroppers generally received about half of the harvest.

A third group included men who, in addition to farming, practiced some specialized skills. These trades included stonemasonry, well digging, carpentry, blacksmithing, leather tanning, and saddle making. None of these was considered a full-time occupation—such consideration might have been a tacit acknowledgement of a nontribal occupation—but informants indicated these trades were the primary work for some men.

This category also included "brokers" (*maṣlaḥīn*). Camel caravans had fixed contacts in towns with agents, who provided fresh animals and fed and cared for the drovers and livestock. *Gāt* marketing and brokering was an occasional occupation in which some tribesmen (and *walad al-sūq*) are engaged. There was at least one major livestock broker in this group.

Finally there were the day laborers or hired hands (*shugā'*, s. *shāgī*). These men earned their incomes through work on short-term projects such as digging wells, building houses, making mud bricks, re-mudding houses, plastering, and guarding and harvesting crops. In general, men who did odd jobs owned little or no land.

Beneath the pretense of equality, the tribesman stratum included a range of statuses. The *shaykh* stood at the apex of the stratum, his position related to his wealth, prestige, and alliances. Below the *shaykh* were other tribesmen holding progressively smaller increments of land and prestige.

The *sāda* formed the highest stratum. Although they were regarded as learned religious men and government officials, their skills represented the archetype of the *sayyid* stratum. Only a few *sāda*, those posted to ᶜAmran, served as judge (*ḥākam*), government administrator (*ᶜāmil*), controller of *waqf* (religious endowments or imamate lands), or collector of taxes. A few men held leadership positions in mosques, taught the Quran, or were "traditional" healers. Others were poor "religious" men who received donations for Quranic readings for the sick or deceased.

Although their tasks were characterized by religious or administrative skills, many *sāda* were illiterate. Those who could read and write often found work in other niches. Many *sāda* were tailors, a profession almost exclusive to this stratum. However, in the ᶜAmran area, the "occupation" of the largest number of *sāda* was farming. These *sāda* were peasants, distinguished from the tribesman's many adaptations to agriculture only by the angle of their daggers and the greater deference accorded them.

In addition to these ascribed status categories, there were two achieved status groups, the "legal experts" (*gaḍī*, p. *guḍā'*) and the "literate men" (*faqih*, p. *fuqahā'*). In social standing, ʿAmranis tend to place these two groups intermediate between the *sāda* and the tribesmen. As elsewhere in the hierarchy, ʿAmranis experience difficulty in these determinations, although the reasons are clearer. Among other considerations, both groups were quite small.

In some respects a "literate man" or a "legal expert" received no more respect than did the *shaykh*; often they were less important because they did not have the power of the *shaykh*. When informants made status determinations, I was often left with the impression they had chosen to place "legal experts" and "literate men" in an intermediate position more from a desire to end the encounter than because of a considered determination. The problem was, I think, the result of the statuses being achieved. A few men, from low-status families, had assumed paradoxically high positions through personal effort.

The defining element of both these statuses was possession of specialized knowledge. When informants ranked these men below the *sāda*, they did so in comparison to the "ideal" *sayyid* who had unique expertise. It might be said that it was the literacy and special training of these two achieved statuses that set them apart from their ancestral tribesmen or *walad al-sūq* origins, but some who held these titles were *sāda*.

This ʿAmrani interpretation of their social structure is based on an "ideal" division of labor and other defining criteria. As in any model it cannot account for deviation and, thus, ʿAmranis overlook the fact that within their proscriptive system there were too many individuals to fit into too few ascribed economic niches and these "extra" people had to devise new economic zones for themselves. Because it is an abstraction, the model is not representative of the present economic system and, by depicting the strata as mutually exclusive, it fails to deal with the reality of the past.

What ʿAmranis describe, then, is the prevailing *qabīlī-sayyid* conceptualization. Even in its abstract form informants have difficulty defining the strata. The extremes are relatively easy; it is in the middle group that problems arise. For example, the *shaykh* is a tribesman if one accepts that he is merely an elected official. He is something more if one considers his social, economic, and political roles. In this case he may be as prominent as a high-ranking *sayyid* in government office. Here is the dilemma of the model. In accepting the standard presentation, one must also accept, as Gerholm

(1977:viii) has stated, a *sayyid* sociology that dominates all social ideology. Some of the informants who provided data were from the *walad al-sūq* and their interpretations, however reluctantly given, coincide with the dominant ideology. ʿAmranis know implicitly that there are many problems with the hierarchy they describe, but have no means of reordering it in closer harmony with reality. Though times have changed, their focus is still on the marketplace.

THE SŪQ AND THE HIERARCHY

In addition to delineating economic spheres, the formal model establishes patterns of interaction. The ideal—the prohibition on tribesmen entering the marketplace—was a statement of self-sufficiency and independence from commerce. In practice, only a few wealthy tribesmen were in a position to absolutely avoid the commercial domain and then only by hiring someone to conduct business and make purchases on their behalf. For the rest, contact with the market was to be kept to a minimum. Thus, there was an ideologic barrier surrounding the *sūq* and separating the spheres of the "real" and "deficient" men, but it was easily crossed by many ʿAmranis.

This separation applied not only to daily intercourse but also to economic activity. As noted, not all tribesmen had the wherewithal to make a living in their "ancestral" niche. There were many reasons why a man might choose to enter the market on at least a semipermanent basis. The following excerpts are from tribesmen's life stories:

> Long before the revolution I was a peasant. We didn't have much land. We were only two, my brother and I. I decided to join the imam's army. He sent me to al-Bayda where I spent many years. I didn't get home often because it was far away and I didn't have a horse. After many years I became lame and had to quit the army. After returning to ʿAmran I became a broker of straw, sorghum stalks, and other farm products. I usually worked for Ahmad. After the revolution I became an alfalfa merchant, but I still do a little selling of other products that men bring me. We have little land and most of it is no good.

> Before the revolution I was a carpenter. Most of the people in my family were carpenters. We all made doors and windows. It wasn't a good living, under the imam we had little. Now there is a lot of money and everyone has work. I did a little farming too, but we didn't have much land. I sold some of it. Now I have about 40 *libna*.

There were a number of nonagricultural niches occupied by tribesmen. Aside from those enumerated earlier, some tribesmen worked as guards in the market, as employees of the police, as local employees of the army, or in government offices. Most of these men maintained some connection with agriculture even if this meant owning fallow land.

Not all men sought economic niches in ᶜAmran. Migration, particularly internal migration, was always an option. Men were forced to seek work because they had no opportunity at home; land was in short supply. Even families with some land were often poor and had to seek additional sources of income. Some men, no doubt, disliked the hard agricultural work. Aside from these obvious reasons for migrating, it also was a means of avoiding status loss. To engage in unacceptable work in one's own town was to risk, if not guarantee, censure; to do so elsewhere seems not to have carried any consequence. No doubt many men left ᶜAmran and were never heard from again. Some migrated, however, learned new skills and returned. Their accounts reveal that they were prepared to enter the marketplace and only needed the revolution to legitimize the process.

> Before the revolution I went to Taᶜiz to stay with my mother's brother. The trip took five days by horse. I was accustomed to riding since my father's brother had been a camel driver and I sometimes went with him on trips. My uncle in Taᶜiz was a pharmacist. [Today he is a successful drug wholesaler.]
>
> I went to school and learned to read. I worked in his shop. There wasn't much to being a pharmacist then. There were only a few pills that came from Aden. Still I learned most of the things you need to do. After the revolution I came back to ᶜAmran and opened a pharmacy here.

> I used to be a peasant. We had little land and most of the work was sharecropping. I learned how to make shoes. Then I decided to move to Sanᶜa. There I learned to be a brazier, making items from tin and other metals. After the revolution I moved back to ᶜAmran and opened a shop as a brazier.

The revolution, then, is a convenient marker announcing and justifying changing attitudes toward the marketplace. If there had been a vague ideologic barrier surrounding the *sūq*, the revolution made the boundary even more blurred and imprecise. As barriers have broken down, there has been a trend away from occupations based on ascription to those based on achievement and defined in nonstigmatized terms. As a result, where once there were reasons to avoid commerce, now connection with the market is prized by most and, except for the wealthy or die-hard traditionalist, unavoidable for the rest. New exigencies require new attitudes. A typical expression of these views is evident in a young tribesman's response to his rhetorical question, "Do you know what is good about the *sūq*?"

> It gives you a place to be. You never have to wander around. Look at the people who don't have a place. Sometimes they call us *walad al-sūq*, but they have

nothing to do. Now that I have a shop I always have work. I have a place to be. I can sit here and visit with friends and make money besides. In the past, when we could only farm, we were poor and alone. Now we see people all the time. Some people say its wrong for a tribesman to be in the *sūq*, but look how many tribesmen have shops. That's because it's a good place to be. Men without a place wander around like children.

The traditional system, whether in terms of its formal model or actual operation, was restrictive, constrained by the modest level of economic development and limited since acceptable niches were status oriented. Although the expansion of the economy and the acceptability of tribesmen engaging in commerce have eliminated these restraints, for many of them a connection with agriculture remains important. Even though many tribesmen now spend their days in their shops, there are noticeable absences during planting and harvesting seasons. If some men feel obligated to appear aloof from the market through nominal agriculture, it is not because of a serious question about the increased importance of the marketplace. The ambivalence that has accompanied the move to commerce is expressed in the following:

> I went to school up to the first year of intermediate school; then I quit. In those days we had to go to San'a to live in order to continue school. I went to work with my brothers on our land. We have a lot of land. I spent six years "riding the cow" [may be interpreted as fucking the cow, an assessment of farming]. Then I went to Saudi Arabia. I worked for a year, came back for a while, and since I wanted to get married I went back for another five months. I came back, got married, and opened this shop. I make a lot of money. Farming wasn't bad, my brothers still farm. It just wasn't the life for me.

While the revolution is often cited as the reason for ʿAmran's rapid economic expansion, repatriated funds from Saudi Arabia have been a major catalyst, hastening the growth of a money economy and stimulating the consumer goods sector. Most ʿAmranis recognize that Saudi Arabia's economic growth has had a profound impact on their national, as well as local, economy; but as they tend to dislike Saudi hegemony, they prefer to define economic stimulation in terms of the efforts of the revolutionary government. A few tradition-minded men, opposed to the republican regime, state with contempt that it was Saudi Arabia that put men in the *sūq*. Although this is a condemnation of the most obvious Saudi influence, in truth Saudi Arabia only accelerated social change:

> Before the revolution I went to Saudi Arabia. I spent many years there working in a shop. I made good money, and when I came back I decided to open a shop

here. It was just before the revolution and although I am a tribesman [in fact, a distant relative of the *shaykh*] I opened a shop near the new mosque. I had learned that being a farmer was too tiring and that life in the market was better. I was the first tribesman to open a retail shop.

SAUDI ARABIA, MIGRATION, AND THE DECLINE OF AGRICULTURE

Saudi Arabia's economic growth has influenced the Yemeni economy in a number of ways.[7] First, it has offered work to many in need of employment. In addition to receiving relatively high wages for unskilled and semiskilled labor, expatriate work enabled Yemeni to break out of the grasp of a stagnant economy at home. Second, many Yemeni have learned new trades. Often these were skills not yet needed in Yemen, such as pouring reinforced concrete, but they now have become essential elements in the country's rapid development. Saudi Arabia, usually through expatriate firms, has become a training ground for many Yemeni. Third, upon returning to Yemen, the migrants have been able to use their new skills and earnings. Thus Saudi Arabia has contributed to the acquisition of the capital, experience, and skills necessary for Yemen's development.

Yemeni men have a long history of migration (Swanson 1979). In the ʿAmran area, prerevolution migration was not as important as in southern regions, but men are known to have gone off in search of new opportunities. Many of these have not been heard from. A few, like one man who spent twenty-five years in Saudi Arabia or another who spent roughly thirty years in Ethiopia, have returned and resettled in ʿAmran.

These are isolated cases. The sharp rise in the number of migrants coincided with Saudi Arabia's oil-revenue-sparked development and dates to the late 1960s. These early migrants, like those who followed them, probably shared a number of characteristics. It seems likely they were from families of moderate financial standing and, particularly when the age gap was large, they were either the eldest or youngest son. The Swiss demographic survey (Central Planning Office 1978:pt. 1, 30) supports the first point, noting that poor families seem limited to internal migration. The cases of a number of former migrants, and the circumstances that led to their leaving, support the second point. Whereas informants do not recall who went first to Saudi Arabia, it appears that it was those who lacked sufficient work:

sharecroppers and those who mixed cultivation with part-time craft work. Also, migration was stimulated by the drought in the late 1960s and early 1970s.

Saudi Arabia's economic growth may be viewed as contributing to the decline in agriculture but it was not the sole influence.

The ʿAmran area has had relatively poor rainfall for a number of years. In 1978, after the winter harvest, a few men indicated that the year's production had been down between 50 and 60 percent from the previous year. Weather is not the only cause of production declines. Sharecropping is unpopular. Some men farm because they enjoy it or see it as the "right" way to make a living. Many simply do not look forward to the hard work. Since the revolution, sharecroppers' distribution shares have increased from one-half to two-thirds of the harvest if they provide the seed and labor for harvesting. Other share arrangements have also increased but some large landowners complain they cannot find men to work in the fields. Larger shares, and owners paying for major costs, like plowing with tractors, have not been attractive enough to offset the difficulty of selling one's surplus.

Whether men farm themselves or contract with others, Yemeni agricultural methods are labor intensive. In the past, most landowners paid for additional harvest labor with several large bundles of unthreshed grain. Today field workers receive 50 YR a day (almost the cost of 100 kilograms of imported wheat). To avoid high labor costs, many small-scale farmers have turned to cash crops that require fewer laborers. Tomatoes, potatoes, and alfalfa are increasingly important crops. As one man remarked one afternoon while we were chewing *gāt*,

> If I was to become a farmer again, I would grow tomatoes [then heavily promoted by the government]. You can make a good living and the work isn't that hard. Every day you can pick your money. A few crates taken to the market and you have made some good money.

High labor costs contribute to the high cost of local produce. Since most major crops are imported at prices consistently below the cost of local produce, demand is low. ʿAmranis believe their local produce is better quality, but few are willing to spend the extra sum to obtain it. Men with land suitable for growing *gāt* (land that is relatively scarce in the ʿAmran area) have turned to this more lucrative crop. Fields that once held fruit trees now sprout *gāt*. By using fertilizers, pesticides, and irrigation, growers enjoy bumper crops. As a capital intensive crop, *gāt* prices have kept pace with inflation.

Inflation has been an unforeseen import from Saudi Arabia. In the late 1970s the World Bank (1979:55) estimated the annual inflation rate at nearly 40 percent although official Yemeni government figures were somewhat lower. ʿAmranis do not attribute the obvious rise in prices to Saudi Arabia, but they do feel that, with the increased cost of living, migration is the only way one can accumulate the capital necessary to start a business or acquire the increasing array of consumer goods that are becoming necessities.

Nowhere is the combined impact of inflation, low agricultural production, and the changing relation to the means of production more evident than in the sale of topsoil. Status was traditionally linked to land ownership and the ability to produce one's own food. As yields have declined and land values have not kept pace with inflation, it has been popular to sell topsoil for construction projects. Dirt is needed to make mud bricks and to fill the lower levels of houses or shops to raise the floors to the level of the tarmac roadway. A landowner receives about 20 YR for each truckload of dirt removed. This is an obvious expression of land's current devaluation, and a hedge against its future value. It is also an indication of the trend toward the marketplace.

RETURNED MIGRANTS AND NEW MODES OF ADAPTATION

In ʿAmran, as elsewhere in Yemen, most families have had a husband, son, or brother working in Saudi Arabia. Upon their return these men generally arrange a marriage, and then either establish a sole proprietorship business or take up one-man operations like driving a taxi or being a stonemason. Any additional monies are invested in gold, rifles, or daggers, each of which tends to appreciate and is a hedge against inflation.

Until the middle 1970s the process of migration, return, and business formation was relatively simple since there were many niches to be filled. For most men the easiest business to start has been a "general store" (see table 3). This requires little prior experience; having been exposed to a market provides most of the requisite knowledge.

Opening a shop has been made easy by a communal spirit that still exists at least in the older sections of the market. Everyone helps each other. For example, a man started his first business by buying the inventory of the previous owner. When customers asked him for prices, he turned to his neighbors for assistance. A few men related that this was how they too had started.

While the cooperative spirit continues, at least now, it has become increasingly difficult to establish a viable business. Several factors contribute to this problem. First, although ᶜAmran's population has increased dramatically in both new residents and transient laborers, the number of unspecialized shops are too numerous to provide all owners with an adequate income. This is true even for those shops, now almost all, that do not close during the afternoon *gāt* chewing hours. Second, since most shops offer the same goods at comparable prices and with little intershop competition, business survival depends on the development of a good clientele. For many shopkeepers the weekly market has become the time to collect debts and extend further credit, often to people barely known to the proprietor. Third, inflation has become a serious handicap for many attempting to set up and maintain a business. Whereas men return from Saudi Arabia with substantial amounts of capital, the costs of provisioning a shop have also increased rapidly. Since a large share of repatriated funds must be spent to arrange a marriage and provide gifts to friends and relatives, many men can only afford to open a shop selling one or two items and hope to expand on the revenues the sale of these goods generates.

The most common solution to these problems has been to seek a competitive advantage. Frozen, imported chickens are popular items and have made freezers a necessity. Costs of purchasing and operating a freezer are high but the products attract customers and help provide a high turn-over rate on invested funds. Not all shopkeepers can afford the 6,000 to 15,000 YR cost of a freezer unit, but even men operating businesses from "shacks" have found it advantageous to squeeze a freezer inside.

Although freezers are important, not all "general stores" have them. In fact innovations seem to be linked to newcomers to the market, either new settlers or returned ᶜAmranis. Perhaps the traditional "merchant" (*bayāᶜīn*) families have felt less pressure to experiment and take chances. Most freezers, for example, are owned by tribesman and *sayyid* businessmen. Comparatively few "merchants" have units (see table 4). Similarly, all but one electric generator is

112 / *Occupation: Ascription and Achievement*

Table 3. Distribution of Shop Use

Type/User	Sayyid	Gabilī	Bayāʿ	Walad al-Sūq	non-ʿAmrānis[1]	Undetermined	Total Operators by "Trade"[,2]	Total Shops[2]
Merchandise	8	47	28	4	63	21	171	171
Carpenter	2	9	–	–	5	1	17	36
Tea Shop	–	1	3	4	2	1	11	12
Hotel	–	–	–	1	3	5	9	20
Restaurant	–	–	1	3	2	4	10	15
Pharmacy	–	2	3	1	2	–	8	10
Building Materials	–	5	10	8	5	1	29	34
Grain	–	2	4	6	2	–	14	14
Storeroom (Warehouse)	–	16	23	9	13	5	66	66
Salt	–	–	–	3	–	1	4	6
Cloth	1	–	3	5	11	–	20	20
Lumber/Steel	–	2	–	–	1	2	5	12
Wholesale[3]	–	5	2	–	–	–	7	9
Barber	–	–	–	3	3	–	6	6
Tailor	5	2	–	–	3	–	10	10
Stereo tapes	–	–	3	–	1	–	4	4
Leather goods	–	2	–	–	–	–	2	2
Residence	–	–	–	–	2	7	9	9
Office	–	2	–	1	1	–	4	4
Watch/TV/Radio repair	1	1	–	–	–	–	2	2
Welding/Brazing	2	–	1	–	2	–	5	5
Garage/Mechanic	1	–	–	1	1	–	3	5
Steel doors	–	–	1	–	1	3	5	13

							439	502
Kerosene	—	2	—	1	—	1	5	4
Fruit	—	—	—	2	—	—	9	9
Blacksmith	—	—	—	—	4	—	4	4
Total operators by social category	20	98	85	57	127	52	439	502

Note: Not included are those shops where only one is in operation. These include: laundry, glass, tannery, kiln, wool carder, car parts, pots, cold storage, bakery, sewing machines, electrical appliances, local cloth, fruit-drink shop, beanery, cars and trucks, sponge rubber, battery charging, generator plant, goldsmith, plaster, household mats. Also excluded are those shops whose owners or renters rarely use them and instead vend their wares from open areas in the market. These include butchers (nine); *gāt* (nine); guns and ammunition (five). There are also four mills around the town.

[1] Non-ʿAmranis are those recent settlers who reside in the town but do not participate in local affairs. Generally these are from Bakil villages.

[2] The total of the shops often exceeds the number of men practicing the "trade" since some establishments actually use more than one shop, generally defined as having a set of doors. In enumerating the shops, each set of doors was counted as a shop. Thus one carpenter has eight shops in use. He is counted in the carpenter column only once, but the eight shops appear in the total. As a result the totals are given twice, first for total operators by "trade," second for total shops.

[3] In categorizing shops, I relied on informants' accountings. Thus, in the total of merchandisers are some who might best be called wholesalers; but since they operate as wholesalers only from warehouses and conduct ordinary retail sales from their "primary" shops, they are labeled retailers. Wholesalers are defined as men who operate from a warehouse in which goods are displayed.

Table 4. Ownership of Freezer Units in General Merchandise Shops

	Sayyid	Gabīlī	Bayāʿ	Walad al-Sūq	non-ʿAmranis	Totals
Freezer	3	19	6	0	35	63
No freezer	4	24	22	4	19	73
Totals	7	43	28	4	54	136

Note: The totals do not include thirty-five shops that were not surveyed but do include twenty shacks from which general merchandise was sold. Of these only two had freezers. The remaining eighteen are too small to admit more than the merchant and a few goods.

operated by a *sayyid* or tribesman family.[8] However, most generators provide electricity for carpenters' tools or tailors' sewing machines, and *walad al-sūq* families are not associated with these professions.

Newcomers have brought ideas with them. Some, like cement-block "factories" are successful. Others, like a photography studio and an automobile seat-cover shop have failed. These adaptations are not limited to newcomers. Some ʿAmranis have also taken risks to develop new businesses:

> Fuad was a taxi driver. He, his brother, and his son took turns driving to the capital and elsewhere. When the taxi cooperative (see below) was formed, he found he was not able to make as much money. He sold his two cars and purchased a small truck and had a tank mounted on it. Initially he hauled water to remote houses and construction sites. Later he expanded to three trucks and hired a part-time driver. They work from dawn to near midnight hauling water.

A commercial enterprise is attractive to many returned migrants, but there are some risks. Even men with venture capital have difficulty finding suitable outlets in a largely undiversified economy. The decreasing economic importance of stigmatized, ascriptive occupations has not been accompanied by an increase in new economic opportunities. The following related cases indicate the extent of these problems:

> Hassan went to Saudi Arabia and worked there for about two and a half years, returning in 1978. He had migrated with the intention of amassing enough money to marry and have enough left over to set himself up in business. Of the money he brought home, some was used to finance his marriage, some for construction of a new family home, and the rest to buy a half-share in a used Mercedes truck. His share cost 85,000 YR. He used the truck to haul salt from Salif, near Hodeida, while his partners sold it in ʿAmran. Later he and his partners decided to expand to hauling any load available in Hodeida. Hassan found the work too tiring, the driving too dangerous, and his share of the profits too small, so he sold his share of the truck.

Hussayn left ʿAmran at about age sixteen. He went to Sanʿa where he worked in a variety of jobs for about six years. Most of the time he worked in a bakery. Then he went to Saudi Arabia. He spent seven years there, finally becoming a foreman of a rock-crushing crew with an expatriate road-building company. He came home to get married, but could not agree on the bride-price and left again after two months. He spent the next three years in Saudi Arabia at his old job. On his way back to ʿAmran he bought a bus. He thought that he could use the bus to take people to the nearby weekly markets. After several unsuccessful months he sold the bus. He then joined with Muhammad in building and operating a brick-baking kiln. Again, after a number of months and a heavy financial loss, he sold his half-share. He was ready to return to Saudi Arabia when he joined with Hizam in a general goods shop. Hizam owned the shop, but, since he had been in jail for six months, it was in decline and he was heavily in debt. After about a month, Hussayn bought out Hizam. The shop, including a freezer but almost no inventory, sold for 30,000 YR (including the lease). The losses in Hussayn's two failed ventures were figured at 200,000 YR. Finding himself with many ideas for expanding the shop, but lacking literacy, he joined with Hassan (see preceding case) in a joint venture. Together they bought a pickup truck to haul provisions from Sanʿa.

Most returned migrants have filled unskilled niches, generally in retailing, but a few have learned skilled trades. ʿAmran's private-sector economy, excluding agriculture, has only three components: retailing and wholesaling, construction, and transportation. The first, as noted, has been open to virtually anyone. The latter two are emerging as skilled occupations. Although there is a construction boom, and only a few men are skilled in building reinforced concrete buildings, there is little job security.

The labor surplus is most noticeable among the taxi drivers. Although many men know how to drive, driving is a skill. Drivers are supposed to understand both basic vehicle operation and maintenance. Even though it is a skilled profession and one of the few niches filled by men from all social strata, the number of taxi drivers is huge. For a time, the seemingly endless supply of taxis insured that drivers were constantly arguing over the right to carry passengers, a process that forced men to hang about the taxi stand for hours waiting their turn. This was unproductive and disruptive. A car is a major asset; but, until attempts were made to regulate drivers' activities, some men were unable to make a living.

The taxi cooperative was formed to coordinate and direct the movement of taxis. A controller was hired. Each driver contributed to his salary and to a pool to be used to pay blood money in the event of an accident. Although the cooperative regulated work and evenly distributed trips, drivers, feeling that revenues were too low, soon began to find ways to circumvent the association's rules. The movement of cars into Sanᶜa was supervised, but the return of cars from the capital was not. In the end, the only effect the cooperative had was to discourage the entry of new drivers into the overcrowded drivers' pool.

THE NONMIGRANTS

For the majority of migrants, work in Saudi Arabia has been a means of entry into new, generally nonstigmatized occupations. In the late 1960s migration was advantageous, providing training, and, more important, the capital to start a business. In effect this put returnees ahead of their contemporaries and allowed many to become established businessmen before the surge in migration. Today migration has become a necessity; yet when they return, men no longer have an easy time finding work. Where the early migrants could make their own decisions about the type of enterprise to enter, today's market pressures dictate men's actions. Increasingly, men of all statuses have entered those service-oriented occupations once considered suitable only for those of low status. Others have avoided what is seen as unacceptable work, but in so doing have been forced to accept peripheral positions, as day laborers or occasional *gāt* sellers. Many of these men see returning to Saudi Arabia as their only alternative.

As might be expected, those who have not migrated experience serious difficulty adjusting to the changing economy. Migrants have capital to risk, but nonmigrants often do not.

A young tribesman, lamenting the course of social change and the barriers preventing him and his brothers from establishing themselves, remarked:

> It's disgraceful not to have work. Look at us. We used to be a big [wealthy, important] family. Now everyone has a shop. Even the little [poor] families have shops and are making money. Yesterday al-Husni [a man regarded as extremely poor] bought land to build a shop. He is only an "innkeeper." What do we have? Nothing! All we do is farm, and when we have no farm work we just hang around. We wanted to open a shop like the others, but my father wouldn't let us. He says it's wrong to be in the *sūq*. We didn't want to sell general merchandise, just wholesale, like cement, flour, and rice. Now we don't have anything to do.

Like this young man, nonmigrants have remained in their traditional occupations. For many this has meant a decline in available work and may be a forerunner of status loss. The first condition is most obvious among the *walad al-sūq* who seem less likely to migrate.

With scabbards being imported, the "public messengers'" craft has been reduced to elaborate decoration of the leather scabbard covers. Only a few men earn money in this work; the rest have sought new positions, including several who operate hotels for transient construction workers.

The "bleeder" is surely the last such practitioner in ᶜAmran. Competition from the government clinic and pharmacies as well as other, traditional nonstigmatized healers, has almost eliminated the "bleeder's" clientele. His son has become a butcher.

While these occupations are waning, those tasks associated with the "innkeeper" are thriving; but it is not the "innkeeper" families who are enjoying this boom. Tea shops and restaurants are often owned or operated by tribesmen or *walad al-sūq* from other substrata. Traditional members of this status group have found work as aides in government offices and as vendors of boiled potatoes and eggs. A few have developed skills learned in Saudi Arabia.

Some men continue to work as "assistants" to government officials. As the number of government offices has increased, so have available positions. Being unskilled, these occupations are often equated with "servant" positions, but many men in these jobs enjoy an aide-de-camp status. Some men have been able to enhance their social standing through association with officials even though their direct monetary rewards, in terms of government salaries, are modest.

The most strikingly successful group are the "butchers." With ample funds in circulation and a prevailing belief that only the poor do not eat meat every day, "butchers" do a thriving business. Most have new homes outside the walls of the town with large enclosures for animals. At least ten "butchers" sell meat daily and perhaps twice that number on market days.

Migration may have been more common among the "merchant" (*bayāᶜīn*) families, but here too there are many who have not left ᶜAmran. Some of these are families with established businesses and the necessary connections with merchants in Sanᶜa and elsewhere. One *bayāᶜ* family derives a good income from selling medicinal herbs to villagers. They have no problem attracting customers. Others, who appear nearly lost in virtually empty shops, have warehouses full of items for sale to other shopkeepers. In the past, the "middlemen" were well known. Now, many men are brokers for a variety of items and even the seemingly simple shopkeeper is likely to have a storeroom full of case lots.

The central government has provided many jobs to those who have not migrated. Government salaries, particularly for those in the military, are low and men in the public sector have little prospect of amassing capital directly from their occupations.

A number of menial to semiskilled positions are found in the municipality, the office of supply and price control, the clinic, schools, and the local development board. The development association employs handymen, assessors, pipe fitters, and pump operators, in addition to the elected staff of officers.

Other openings exist for men with skills. School administrators and teachers come increasingly from among the citizenry. The overseers of many projects are local men. These positions are often part-time and men find additional work to supplement their incomes.

LAND AND STATUS

Changing attitudes toward commerce and the development of new economic sectors have been accompanied by shifting evaluations of land. Wealth, traditionally measured in units of land, has been a key determinant of status. Status is still linked to property, but increasingly the emphasis is on rental units rather than on lands used for agricultural production. This change in attitude is not new. Most of the shops in the older sections of the market were owned by a few related families who derived some of their wealth from rents (see table 5).

Sites on the tarmac road are highly prized and rents are often high. A substantial portion of these roadside lands were inherited by a single tribesman descent group whose male members (seven individuals) have built forty-five shops. A few of these shops are operated by their owners, who are wholesalers, but the rest are available for rent at an annual rate of 6,000 to 8,000 YR. Having been landowners, these families were able to sell less valuable land elsewhere to finance the construction of their shops. Several family members have supplemented land sales with rental incomes from completed shops to underwrite expansion costs.

Of course not all shop owners were wealthy. Many used monies earned in Saudi Arabia or their local businesses to build shops. Although well-placed shops are likely to be good revenue producers,

Table 5. Ownership of Shops

	Sayyid	Gabīlī	Bayāʿ	Walad al-Sūq	Waqf	Totals
In use	60	191	75	48	34	408
Closed, use unknown[1]	7	96	63	9	9	184
Unfinished[2]	10	55	24	6	4	99
Totals	77	342	162	63	47	691

Note: There were 1,168 shops surveyed. In addition to those enumerated above, 131 were known to be owned by men who have recently moved to ʿAmran. There are 346 shops, many in the unfinished group, for which ownership could not be ascertained. Of the 346, 168 lie in areas no longer heavily trafficked and in which many, certainly the majority of shops, are owned by *waqf* or an important *gabīlī* family.

[1]Some of these shops may be warehouses for goods.

[2]The unfinished category includes some properties that have only the outlines of shops, but which show no outward sign of heading toward completion. Several examples of this are well known. However, most of these shops are in the process of being completed.

there has been an overproduction of stores. Virtually every new house, even those far removed from the most prized locations, has provisions for one or more shops. Despite the widely held view that having a shop is a good, secure source of income and that rents are a hedge against inflation, a belief aided by the continued financial success of the major land and shop owners, most shops will only be used as storerooms.

Rental income is an easy way to make a living and a way of emulating the wealthy. Clearly, owning a few shops is not equivalent to the multiple-income sources available to the town's more prominent men, but being a landlord is a way to increase one's status. The importance of land ownership can be estimated through those rents which are known. In the older part of the market, the highest rent, about 3,000 YR a year, is for those shops owned by the religious endowments (*waqf*). Many feel these charges are too high since the location is considered poor, but others feel that since it is *waqf* property, and cheap compared to other areas, it is not excessive. In the same area, privately owned shops rent from as little as 200 YR a year, but often these are part of long-term arrangements.

These figures are the exception. Most rental charges are based both on the shop location and the leasing merchant's business history. For example, when a successful cloth dealer expanded his operation to an additional shop in the center of the "new" *sūq*, his rent was fixed at 24,000 YR. Although this is an extreme case, it is not uncommon for shops to rent for 8,000 to 15,000 YR.

With rents high, land values in desirable locations have risen. Land that ten years ago sold for 800 YR a *libna* now sells for 10,000 YR. In a celebrated sale, a plot of land on the main road sold for nearly 118,000 YR a *libna*. By contrast, land that can only be used for agriculture remains priced at 200 to 300 YR a *libna*.

Perhaps the most striking aspect of this change has been a shift in the evaluation of property. Before the revolution land was essential and was a status marker, particularly for the tribesmen. Now, with many plots lying fallow and activity focused in the market, it seems clear that land is losing its importance as an undifferentiated measure of status.

CONCLUSION

ᶜAmranis characterize the postrevolutionary era as one of increased economic opportunity with the majority of economic niches free from the stigma of the traditional ascriptive system. The revolution actually legitimized trends spawned by declining agricultural revenues, opportunities for wage labor in Saudi Arabia, and the growth of a market economy. As the economy has moved away from agriculture toward commerce, men moving into the formerly prohibited marketplace have attempted to define their economic activity in terms different from those associated with stigmatized occupations. For example, they have made a distinction between "merchant" and "businessman."

Economic growth has afforded opportunities for personal gain and loss. Generally those quick to enter the marketplace have prospered while those who entered only recently, and often less as a result of personal choice than of necessity, have fared less well. In terms of wealth it is easy to see who has gained and lost in the race to acquire a suitable niche, but this cannot be so easily translated into status change.

The process of economic change has widened the gap between ancestry and actual occupation, but this too was a trend long evident in ᶜAmran. In the past only the wealthy were in a position to "live up to" social standards regarding contact with the marketplace; now the wealthy tribesmen are the only ones able to minimize the gap between their occupation and ancestry.

Control of property remains an important objective, but there is less concern with numbers of *libna* than with the location and use of plots. Older men cling to the idea that any plot is valuable. Younger men are concerned with holding plots that may provide rents. Whereas in the past, land holdings influenced a man's status, now this is less likely to be the case. More significant is how one has manipulated his holdings. A few descent groups with modest, but strategically located, holdings have been able to enhance their financial positions; others, with huge holdings in less favorable areas, have lost status. The continued importance of some wealthy groups is largely a result of their careful buying and selling of property and converting relatively unimportant plots to valuable, or potentially valuable, land for future exploitation.

Despite these changes, many of the formal model's status criteria continue to influence status determination. Simply having gained wealth or assets is not a guarantee of improved or enhanced status, but it may contribute to one's marriage alliances, an important indicator of status.

5

Marriage: Individual Connections and Status Assessment

Changes in the political and economic structure of ʿAmran have reduced occupational stigmatization and restrictions on participation in alliances. These social structural modifications have contributed to a partial blurring of the formal bases of interstrata relations. However, formalized personal relations continue to be determined by ancestry and relative standing in an individual's descent group.

Marriage, itself a form of status assessment and declaration, is a major factor in the preservation or enhancement of status. While obligations to one's in-laws are not as strong as those to kin, it is affines, who may also be kin, who are important status determiners. Marriage patterns reveal intrastrata and intradescent-group status differences. With rapidly escalating bride-prices and individuals seeking to solidify status gains through marriage, ʿAmranis see affinal ties as threatened by the possible shift from relations based on respect and social equality to those based only on monetary concerns.

RELATIONS WITHIN AND BETWEEN KIN GROUPS

Early on the first morning of the holiday (periods following the Ramadhan fast and the pilgrimage to Mecca (in the middle of the month of Dhū al-Hijja), Amin, dressed in bright new clothes, set off for his round of obligatory visits. Later in the day, I asked where he had gone.

"I visited my relatives," he said.

"Whose house did you go to?"

"I went to my father's brother (ʿamm) and my mother's brother (khāl), and I visited the al-Safarjal house because my mother's sister (khāla) is married there. I also went to the al-Junud house because another of my mother's sisters is married there. I went to my father's sister's (ᶜ*amma*) house."

"Is that all?" I asked.

"Oh no! There were many others. I also visited Magbal al-Shaᶜir. He isn't a relative but his daughter-in-law is like a sister to my mother. Then I went to see some houses in Sharara [a nearby village]."

"I didn't know you had relatives there," I said.

"I don't, but years ago when Hizam al-Haddad's father came here he married a woman who was close to us. Hizam's sisters married to that village and I visit them. Then on the way back I stopped at ᶜAli al-Gasib. He isn't a relative either, but we have ties to him from when his family first settled here."

Every ᶜAmrani is bound by reciprocal obligations premised on kinship and pseudo-kinship ties. Many of these duties are formalized, as in visiting patterns. Others, particularly relations with distant relatives, are less structured and left to individual choice.

As in other Arab Muslim countries, kinship relations are based on a patrilineal descent ideology. This is apparent in the application of names. A man or woman bears not only his or her given name but also names of male antecedents, which are part of his or her identity. In those families that maintain lengthy genealogies, the degree of kinship connection can be traced; and obligations, as in disputes, may be specified.

Descent groups are composed of individuals who share a patrilineal ancestor. While in theory there are obligations to all relatives, in practice, the pressure to fulfill these duties decreases as the genealogic distance increases. The clearest application of the agnatic principle is in the household unit where descent is the basis of relationships. Patrilineality describes the statuses and roles of the household head, his sons, and grandsons. Combined with the ideal practice of patrilocal residence, well-demarcated social roles are established. Informants state that in the past these were necessary for the coordination of the household's joint enterprise on corporately held lands.

Within the household, whether nuclear or extended, there is a series of unequal relationships. The senior male is usually the decision-maker. His sons are expected to follow his directives. Nowhere is this more obvious, or a more serious point of conflict, than in the matter of property management. Although referred to as if collectively owned, property is controlled and its disposition directed by the patriarch in whose name title rests.

While the superior position of a father is to be expected, the principle of seniority also obtains among sons, with precedence being given to the eldest. Age, at least in the ideal, defines a man's position and relative authority within the household, and a hierarchical arrangement of statuses exists.[1] Where brothers have divided inherited property (the equal division of which is mandated by Islam) and established separate households, deference may still be accorded the eldest despite the fact that each sibling is in control of his own holdings. Of course, with time and as each brother becomes the patriarch of a household or minimal agnatic group, relations become more equal. However, the spokesman for the minimal agnatic group or several related minimal agnatic groups is often the senior male, whether he is the head of a nuclear household or the patriarch of an extended one.[2] Preeminence is not defined absolutely on the basis of age since prestige and personality are also relevant factors. For example, in a kin group, when a younger brother gains ascendency over an elder, the younger brother's sons are likely to "inherit" the advantage over their father's brother's sons (*'ayāl 'amm*). Seniority, then, is important, but other factors may contribute to rank within a descent group.

Whereas full brothers inherit equally, over succeeding generations, if not sooner, the relative equivalence of their sons and grandsons may wane as family size, inheritance, and success or failure in property management alter each household's assets. Although succeeding minimal agnatic groups have a common ancestor, they will not have comparable status. In each patronymic descent group, the minimal agnatic groups will each hold dissimilar assets, and individuals within these groups will enjoy varying amounts of other socially relevant, intangible assets. In effect, the rank of each household in a descent group is fixed for only a short period. The minimal agnatic segments of a descent group may be visualized as stretched along a continuum from high to low status.

Despite claims of equality within descent groups each maximal agnatic group is internally ranked. Rank is asymmetrical (see chart 5) and is similar to the structure of Kirchoff's (1955) "conical clan" and Ripinsky's (1968) "vertical clan."[3] This resemblance is found only among large, diversified descent groups. That some senior men of the most important minimal agnatic groups achieve leadership positions within their descent groups, and serve as headmen of political alliances (*ḥabl*) (which are based on the same kinship structure), is an expression of this asymmetry. Of course, there are some patronymic groups whose minimal segments are equally poor and whose internal ordering is unclear.

CHART 5. HYPOTHETICAL DEPICTION OF INTERNALLY RANKED DESCENT GROUPS

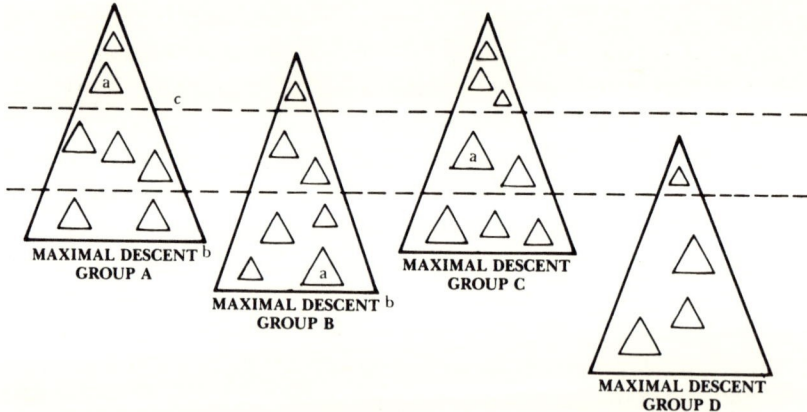

[a] Small triangles in each descent group represent the hierarchical structure of patriarchal households.
[b] Maximal descent groups are represented by triangles both because all descent groups are extensions of the basic household structure and because the arrangement of households in descent groups is asymmetric. The actual "shape" of any descent group depends on the distribution of households in the various rank categories.
[c] Dashed lines indicate divisions between high, medium, and low ranking households.

Rank has always been important. When informants contend (but cannot substantiate) that kinship ties were stronger in the past, I believe they are emphasizing that intradescent-group rank differences were less apparent before the efflorescence of a money-based economy. Further, in the past there were stronger perceived needs for descent group, and *ḥabl*, unity. It is clear that now descent groups rarely function as units, but this freedom of individual choice of action stems not so much from recent change as from the loose nature of descent groups. It is also an indication that even within descent groups the extent of one's obligations is variable just as are one's duties to participate in the activities of the kinship-based, political alliance (*ḥabl*).

As would be expected, ongoing ties are strongest between those who are closely related; they decline as genealogic distance, and perhaps social rank, increases; and they sometimes plummet after serious disputes. More important, at present, if not in the past, men tend to emphasize relatedness only to those of their remoter kinspeople from whom something can be gained. Even though it is obligatory for men to pay formal visits to prescribed relatives, real, ongoing connections are optional and are much more likely to exist between kinsmen of roughly equal economic status. Despite an ideology of equality among kin and within each of the major strata, there are vast differences in wealth and prestige even within many minimal agnatic groups. These are manifested in marriage alliances.

MARRIAGE PATTERNS

"Whom can you marry?" I asked an informant, a tribesman.

"Anyone from a good family. I can marry my daughter to any man who is religious, a hard worker, a man of good character."

"Would you marry your daughter to the son of a low status man?"

"Of course I could; there is nothing wrong with marrying anyone of good character. But everyone would disapprove. It would be a violation of our customs. The customs are not Islamic, but that is how we have always made marriages. If you don't follow the custom, then people will disapprove of you."

Marriage in Islam is subject to the principle of *kafā'a*, which stipulates that marriage partners be social equals and, specifically, that women do not marry below their status (Linant de Bellefonds 1978:404). Thus, in the Shi'ite interpretation, all Muslims are equals and therefore any Muslim may marry another, and a Muslim man may marry a non-Muslim (al-Ati 1977:84–97). Among Sunni Muslims, the Hanafi legal school, many of whose codes are similar to Zaydi law, stipulates that equivalence between affines extends beyond their being Muslims to their being of comparable social standing and morality and engaged in equally honorable professions (Linant de Bellefonds 1978:404).

In 'Amran it may be said that both interpretations have currency. The stated ideal, perhaps influenced more by the revolution than by Islam, holds that Muslims are equal; in reality, marriage partners should be equal in more than religion, at least if they do not wish to challenge tradition. Thus, even though informants express the ideal, none seriously considers marrying anyone of lower status.

The principle of equality finds its most obvious expression in stratum endogamy. As a general rule, members of the *walad al-sūq*, tribesman, and *sayyid* categories take wives from within their own strata. The only exceptions to this endogamous pattern are hypergamous marriages between *sayyid* men and tribal women; and in these instances the woman addresses her husband as "my grandfather," a reference serving to emphasize her non-*sayyid*, inferior, ancestry. Usually when informants asserted that they could marry anyone, they referred to the supposed equality of all members of their stratum and were not suggesting they could or would marry outside their group of presumed equals.

As informants describe the general marriage pattern, equivalence refers merely to stratum endogamy, a practice supporting images of intrastratum equality. Freedom of choice may be the ideal, but marriages within each stratum are further restricted. This is most easily discerned within some segments of the *walad al-sūq* where the occupation-related substrata are explicitly ranked. As mentioned earlier, there are basically three ranked groups in this stratum: "poetic messenger" (*dawshān*), the generic *muzayyin* category, and the "merchants" (*bayāʿin*). Marriages within the three substrata reveal social nonequivalence. The "messenger" substratum is said, by its members and others, to be rigidly endogamous. This fits well with the general view of the "messenger" as the lowest status. The only descent groups with equivalent status are other "messenger" groups, a fact forcing stratum endogamy. Since the "messenger" is so poorly regarded, those outside this substratum avoid status loss by refusing to intermarry with them. I know of only one case of substratum exogamy for this group.

Informants could easily detail the reasons for the "messengers' " endogamy, but they were less willing or able to describe the basis for marital alliances within other strata. This is because there are no rigid rules to determine equivalence, and many factors are taken into account in the establishment of alliances. These include the availability of marriageable females in families of roughly similar status, the previous marital alliances and overall reputation of these families, concerns about property control, and the felt need to expand those ties that are status enhancing or maintaining.

Whom one selects as a marriage partner makes an important

statement about one's social standing. When two or more substrata intermarry consistently, both substrata tend to be perceived as roughly equivalent. Informants often sketched the town's social hierarchy in terms of who had married whom. Assertions, for example, that "innkeeper" and "vegetable peddler" groups are close in status were supported by examples of specific marriages between members of the two occupationally defined groups. However, numerically small substrata, such as the "bleeder" and "bath attendant" groups, are to an extent forced to be exogamous by the limited number of potential partners within each stratum.

Marriages, whether stratum endogamous or descent-group exogamous or endogamous, are reflections of the status of the parties involved. Minimal agnatic groups that become connected through marriage tend to see each other roughly as equals, and outsiders usually adopt the same view. The "merchants" (*bayāʿīn*) emphasize their social distance from, and reinforce their superiority over, the other *walad al-sūq* substrata by selecting marriage partners from within their own stratum. This practice also stresses that a person's status is determined as much by his alliances as it is by his own family's position.

Before the revolution (see chapter 4) some men migrated to Sanʿa in search of work. Although some of them were of tribal ancestry, the jobs these men took were in the marketplace. Had they settled permanently in the capital, they probably would have become associated with the status of their occupation, a connection that would, I suspect, have been reinforced by the status of the women they would have married. This was the case for some men who settled in ʿAmran:

> The al-Zunji family was founded by one man who came here only recently, about 100 years ago. He had no relatives here and did not have any property. He went to work in the market even though he was a tribesman. He began to work for the grandfather of Salih al-Bagri, a "measurer," whose family had been "barber-circumcisers" in the past. After many years of working together, Salih's grandfather married his daughter to al-Zunji. Now the al-Zunji family are "measurers" just like the al-Bagri family.
>
> When Nassar al-Barguk came to ʿAmran he was "all right" (meaning he was a tribesman). Later he married into the *sūq* (*tanasab al-sūq*, specifically into a "merchant" family). Now all his descendants are "merchants."

It can be deduced from these examples that once a man relinquished his status by marrying a woman of lower status, his descendants must select spouses from that lower stratum. As a general rule, equivalence, once established, tends to be perpetuated in subsequent marriages. Many families continue to intermarry generation after generation. This reinforces each family's social position and reflects tacit agreement that families who were once equals continue to be so.

Whereas marriage can lower status by the injudicious choice of a spouse—a factor that may account for some of the marriages to women from outside ʿAmran or the occasional marriage to a parallel cousin (whose status may, or must, be assumed the same by outsiders)—there are some instances in which marriage can raise social stature. This is seen in the "measurer" substratum whose relatively new, ambiguous niche in the hierarchy lies between the "merchants" (*bayāʿīn*) and the generic *muzayyin* group. By ancestry they were *muzayyin* who, through specialization, created a new occupational category. Many of the "measurer" marriages are substratum endogamous, but the exogamous connections are more revealing. Some marriages are with *muzayyin* families (particularly in one rather large descent group, some of whose members are "measurers," the others "barber-circumcisers") and stem from past connections. Others are with poor "merchant" groups; these are all recent associations.

Aside from demonstrating how marriages can enhance social position (a point I deduce from the obvious difficulty informants encountered whenever they tried to define the social standing of the "measurers"), these marriages also underscore economic differences within a stratum. Because of intradescent-group rank differences and the importance of finding a spouse from a comparable group, mate selection is not a casual process. Social rank and marital choice within a single descent group is illustrated in the following examples from a "merchant" descent group:

> Jamil ʿAli Ahmad al-Hawsh is the son of the head of the al-Hawsh descent group. ʿAli was highly regarded within the community and was often sought out by the *walad al-sūq* for his counsel. Jamil married his father's brother's daughter (*bint ʿamm*, here used figuratively to refer to a genealogically close relative). His was an exchange or *badl* marriage. Jamil's sister was married to Jamil's bride's brother.

> Sadiq al-Hawsh is a man of moderate means today, who informants say was never very well off financially. Nonetheless Sadiq took two wives. His first wife was from another large "merchant" family (whose standing is unclear). His second wife was the daughter of a "measurer" (*kayāl*). Like his father, Salih Sadiq, whose mother was the "measurer's" daughter, also married twice. One wife is from a fairly poor and quite small "merchant" family; the second is from the al-Hawsh descent group. The second wife's family was quite poor, although their

their position has improved since the revolution. Despite being from the al-Hawsh descent group, the wife's genealogic connection to Salih is quite remote.

Mansur and Rashid al-Hawsh are the sons of a "merchant" woman. Their deceased father, like his brothers, had always been poor. Today his sons jointly operate a shop in the market that attracts a moderate clientele. Although Mansur is in his middle to late thirties, and Rashid is about ten years his junior, they have never married. Everyone, including the brothers, states that the high cost of getting married has been the reason for their delay in taking wives. Similar problems, lack of opportunity and lack of land, are said to have led one of their cousins to move to another town where he has opened a hotel and restaurant and recently married.

Each of these examples reveals some factors involved in marital alliance formation. Jamil's father was a man of importance, perhaps the most highly regarded man in the *walad al-sūq* community, and he could have jeopardized his position by marrying his children outside his descent group since, by doing so, he would have acknowledged the equal status of another. Instead, he chose to marry his son and daughter to high-status close relatives. It can be assumed, on the basis of patterns found among other important families, that had there been a real patrilateral parallel cousin available (and no dispute between the parties), Jamil's spouse would have been genealogically closer, and thus a more obviously equal mate (see below).

Sadiq was a man whose social position was at best moderate. That he took two wives certainly indicates that he had some wealth, but polygyny is not necessarily indicative of great assets. The first wife's status is unclear. The second wife's position is complicated by her family's ambiguous status (since some "measurer" marital alliances are with *muzayyin*). From the point of view of the "measurers," this would have been an important marriage. More interesting, it does not seem to have had any effect on Salih Sadiq's status. Both his marriages were to "merchant" families, neither of which was financially well off. Moreover, the fact that Salih's mother was the daughter of a "measurer" appears to have had no impact on her son's status or restricted his range of marriage partners. Sadiq's daughters were married to non-ᶜAmranis whose standing, then and now, is the subject of lively debate.

In the final example, the most obvious point is that poverty prevented the brothers from marrying. Bride-price has never been insignificant, but at least in the past it was not exorbitant. Thus, when informants refer to the brothers as "humble" or "pitiable" (*masākīn*), a description suggesting that, like their cousin, they were too poor to marry, it is possible that the men were, or thought they were, impotent (a condition often cited as the reason men do not marry). Some informants suggest that with their improved financial status, the brothers may be able to find wives.

The tendency for status equals to intermarry (illustrated in the above examples) is evident in tribesmen's marriages. The tribesman category lacks the clear occupational-status ranking of the *walad al-sūq*, but marriages with equivalent households or minimal agnatic groups is still the general, if understated, rule. If tribesmen who accepted work in the marketplace lost status by marrying down (as was the case of Nassar al-Barguk, above), the same threat holds for any tribesman who marries beneath himself, even if he marries a woman from a tribal descent group.

Although there are clear differences between tribesman households or minimal agnatic groups, informants were reluctant to describe their social rank. This reticence seems traceable to two factors. First, ordering extended families or nuclear households of a descent group conflicted sharply with the ideology of equality among all tribesmen. Many informants, perhaps for my benefit, stressed the common features of tribesmen rather than differences between them. Second, while the relative status of a household may be understood generally, such factors as wealth can only be estimated. As with the *walad al-sūq*, informants' assessment of social standing was based as much on marriage ties as it was on actual knowledge of assets. Further, ranking is not a simple matter of arranging the different surnames. Within each patronymic descent group, differences in wealth and prestige are likely to place the minimal agnatic groups in a number of status categories (see chart 5). Such complications are, no doubt, not merely problems encountered by the anthropologist; ⁽Amranis must also attempt to weigh the relative merits of an alliance on the basis of incomplete information.

PATRILATERAL PARALLEL COUSIN MARRIAGE

As in most Middle Eastern Muslim societies, the ideal Yemeni marriage alliance is with one's patrilateral parallel cousin.[4] In ⁽Amran, informants often suggest this is the most suitable marriage because the close connections between the families protects the bride's honor. Men are not obligated to marry their daughters to their brother's sons, but it is considered good form to consult them before completing a marriage arrangement. While patrilateral parallel cousin marriage is the recognized ideal, Chelhod's (1973) survey in Sanʿa and Khamir indicates these marriages account for roughly 10 percent of all alliances. In ʿAmran these marriages are often seen as a form of property (or status) control. This point was made by a man who had fairly close descent ties to the *shaykh's* minimal agnatic group.

> Our family marries our father's brother's children (*ʿayāl ʿamm*) because it keeps the property within the family. Some people say it is an important custom to marry your father's brother's daughter, but really it is land that is important. If you marry someone outside your family, then your property gets lost. Women retain their rights to inherited property [unlike elsewhere in the Middle East]; and if you haven't been careful in your marriages, they can take it away from you. But if you marry from your family, then you [as a group] retain control. That is why our patronymic group always marries itself. We are a wealthy family and an important one because we have land.

Despite the informant's emphasis on patrilateral connections, his descent group has many alliances with other ʿAmran families. This suggests there is more than one consideration in marriage alliances.

Parallel cousin marriage is not only a means of controlling property, it is also a statement about the position of the individuals involved. ʿAmranis generally view close endogamous marriage as significant not merely because it is an ideal alliance but also because it indicates power or pretensions of power. When a wealthy "merchant" arranged an exchange (*badl*) marriage with the son and daughter of his brother, most informants suggested that they were trying to emulate the marriages of the *shaykh's* minimal agnatic group.

The marriages of members of the *shaykh's* minimal agnatic group illustrate several elements of that group's property control and preservation of political prominence (see chart 6). Over several generations (genealogies were gathered from men and women), the number of children reaching adulthood was fairly small, and most of these were male. In fact, until the latest generation, the *shaykh's* minimal agnatic group was almost exclusively male. Since property control was a central concern, the few women who might have alienated it were married endogamously, while the remaining men married exogamously. The importance of internal links, and the practice of never marrying women outside the group, is accentuated by both levirate and sororate marriages by members of the minimal agnatic group.

134 / *Marriage: Individual Connections and Status Assessment*

CHART 6. MARRIAGES OF THE *SHAYKH*'S HOUSEHOLD

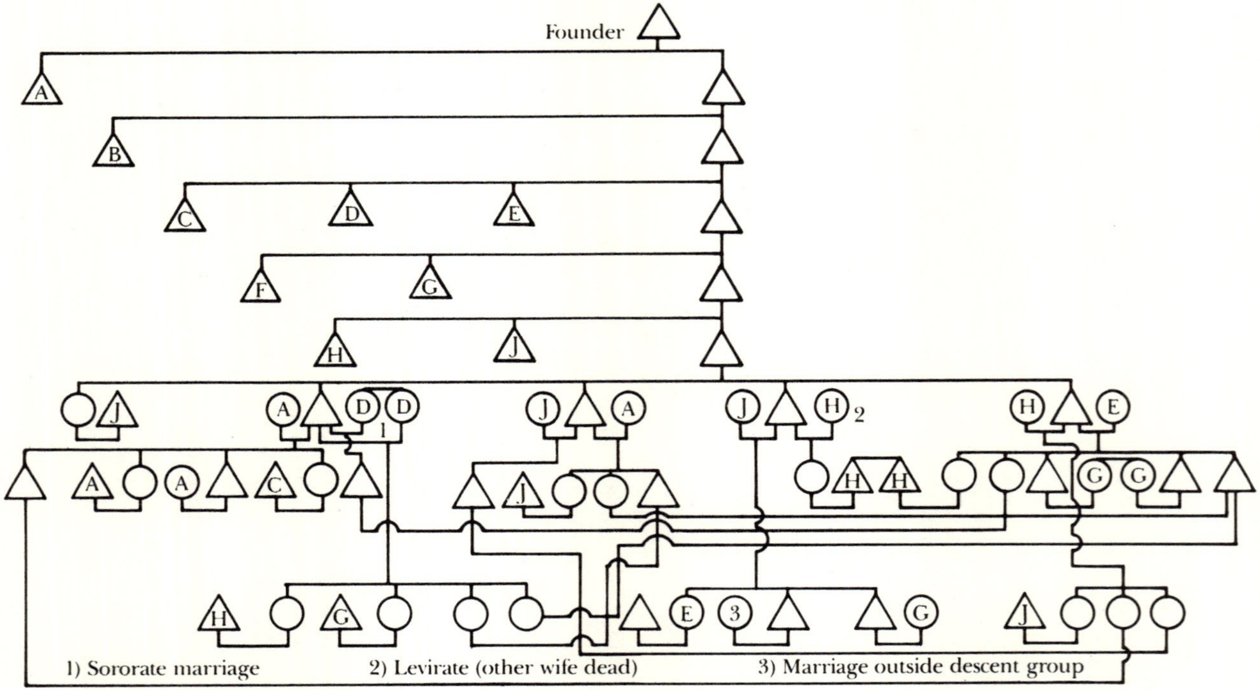

1) Sororate marriage   2) Levirate (other wife dead)   3) Marriage outside descent group

Note: In the upper half of the genealogy, letters are used to designate descent line founders. In the lower half, the same letters refer to living members of those lines married into the *shaykh*'s minimal agnatic group.

A central consideration of any high-status minimal agnatic group is the development of significant alliances. In the jockeying for power or preeminence, some minimal agnatic groups may have been denied endogamous marriages either intentionally or because there was a shortage of women. At least in part because of its unequal sex ratio, the *shaykh*'s minimal agnatic group could maintain both its internal cohesiveness while still effecting important ties with other descent groups.

Now this situation has changed. Virtually all marriages have become close endogamous links, many being patrilateral parallel cousin alliances. This may be explained by two factors. The first is demographic. The numbers of offspring of both sexes are numerous and marriages tend to reflect the ideal practice, thus insuring property is not alienated. This also serves to solidify property gains from previous exogamous alliances. Second, during the period of the marriages, the political structure and military role of the tribe changed. In the past, powerful families may have used exogamous marriages to cement political alliances with supporters; but after the imam became instrumental in appointing and supporting tribal leaders who did not challenge the central government, exogamic connections may have become less critical to the maintenance of a power base.

Whether by demographic chance, by careful manipulation, or both, the *shaykh*'s minimal agnatic group followed a pattern of marriage characterized by the simultaneous expansion and contraction of connections. Two factors contribute to that group's ability to form exogamous alliances with nonequivalent descent groups. First, the *shaykh*'s descent group controlled many resources and was in a secure status and power position. While other descent groups may have benefited from their momentary connection to that of the *shaykh* (some informants went to great lengths to note alliances with even obscure households of the *shaykh*'s maximal descent group), they were probably not true social equals. Second, the *shaykh*'s minimal agnatic group only took women from outsiders. In this respect they were following the pattern of *sayyid* men who may marry hypergamously from within the tribesman stratum but do not give women to men of the lower stratum.

Although I believe many ᶜAmranis regard the *shaykh*'s descent group's marriage patterns as the ideal, it is impossible for any but a few to actually emulate them. These marriages are unique, the product of special circumstances, including demographic chance. Further, the powerful social position of the descent group could not be jeopardized by its ties.

MARRIAGES FOR OTHER TRIBESMEN AND SAYYID FAMILIES

Strategic alliances are not limited to high-ranked families. Preservation of social position is important for all minimal agnatic groups. Under some pressure informants divided the tribal stratum into three types of minimal agnatic group: high, medium, and low. Their renderings were always imprecise (in part because the criteria were intangible) since each minimal agnatic segment of a patronymic group may have a different rank, and because the alliances made by a particular minimal group sometimes blur rather than clarify the status of the parties. I was often surprised by a marriage between minimal groups which had been defined differently. Of these, some were hypergamous (marrying up in status from the woman's point of view) and I suspect did not involve potential status loss to the wife takers. There were, however, some hypogamous marriages (marrying down in status from the woman's point of view). If my informants could set out general patterns, they could not or would not attempt to explain the reasons behind a particular alliance.

In ʿAmran, and surely elsewhere, there are deviations from the ideal norms for spouse selection. Often these result from rather ordinary, but often unnoted, unpredictable factors. A shortage of eligible women may force a man to look for a wife outside his status group. If women are available, their physical and mental character has to be suitable. The bride-price demanded may be too high, perhaps intentionally raised to "politely" refuse a proposed alliance. A woman may refuse a marriage and her father may comply with her decision. Thus an "irregular" marriage may not be an absolute statement of status change (although it is the circumstances that surround a marriage, rather than the connection, that are forgotten over time). One informant explained the events surrounding his marriage.

> When I returned from Saudi Arabia I wanted to get married. I had a chance to marry Ahmad's [a man of considerable prestige] daughter, but he said that she was too young and that I could marry her if I waited a year. I didn't want to wait and told my father to find me another woman. That's how I came to marry Kamal's [a man of somewhat less stature] daughter.

Most medium-rank descent groups are not as large as the *shaykh*'s patronymic group (some of whose members are of medium rank).

Marriage: Individual Connections and Status Assessment / 137

CHART 7. MARRIAGES OF A MEDIUM-LEVEL MINIMAL AGNATIC GROUP

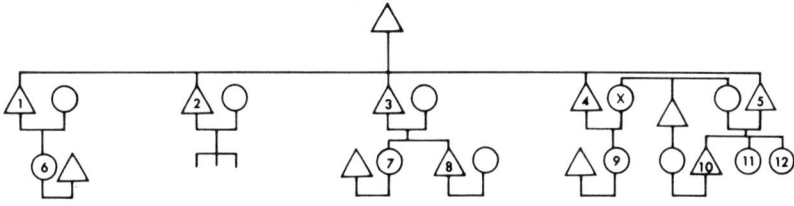

1. Married into a non-ʿAmran descent group, status unknown.
2, 8. Married into ʿAmran descent group "B," most of whom are of medium status.
3. Married into ʿAmran descent group "C," most of whom are of medium status.
4, 5, 10. Each married into the same medium status, minimal agnatic group of ʿAmran descent group "A."
6. Married into her mother's minimal agnatic group, delayed exchange marriage.
7. Married within her maximal descent group, distant relative.
9. Married into the same maximal ʿAmran descent group "D" as her mother had in her first marriage.
11. Married a man previously divorced from her mother's sister (X), now divorced.
12. Married into ʿAmran descent group "E," most of whom are medium status, now widowed.

The alliance pattern within these descent groups varies somewhat because of their limited size (see chart 7). Patrilateral connections are less frequent and there is a wider range of external connections. These ties are important. There are many instances of enduring marriage ties; sons are likely to take wives from the same patronymic group, if not the same minimal agnatic segment, as did their fathers. External links of the *shaykh*'s minimal group appear momentary, but among medium-rank families they are continuous. Except for occasional links to outsiders, in which property is concerned, most medium-level descent groups tend toward town endogamy but rarely to patrilateral endogamy. Connections within the community may be important to property control and to definition of status by marriage to those whose status is also well known.

The importance of property control was made quite clear in an unusual marriage:

> A man argued with his brother over use of some family lands and, in the heat of the moment, killed him. Their father, an elderly man with no other children, let the matter drop and after several years in hiding (at work in Saudi Arabia) the murderer returned. His brother's widow had been given a house and some land in their natal village. Soon the murderer arranged to marry his brother's

138 / *Marriage: Individual Connections and Status Assessment*

widow. Men said he did this not because of any sense of contrition but because the property was valuable and he wanted to regain control of it.

Most families appear to hold properties in a variety of areas, usually defined as rain-watered or irrigated plots. Older men, who still value land highly, feel it is important to have diversified holdings in the event drought, for example, should prevent a harvest in any one area. One way of increasing future security is through marriage alliances with families who have properties in other areas. In fact, shifts in property ownership are often attributed to lands being lost through marriage. Moreover, many families that have intermarried hold property in the same areas. An informant said that marriage and property were unrelated but that families with lands in the same locales were often good friends, and it was on this latter basis that they might intermarry. If property is not the most important influence on alliances, I believe it is a consideration that partially accounts for the broad range of alliances of medium-level families.

The low-ranking tribal descent groups also marry among themselves (see chart 8). Many of their alliances are town exogamous.

CHART 8. MARRIAGES OF A LOW-LEVEL MINIMAL AGNATIC GROUP

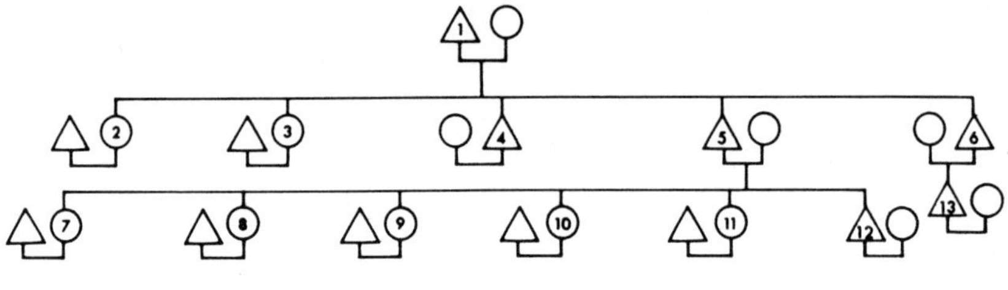

1, 2, 3, 6. Each married into a different, obscure, currently one household, ʿAmran descent group.
4, 9, 10, 12. Each married into a non-ʿAmran descent group, status unknown.
5. Married into an ʿAmran descent group "F," status unknown.
7, 8. Each married into the maximal descent group of her mother.
11. Married into ʿAmran descent group "E," most of whom are medium status.
13. Married into a non-ʿAmran descent group, low status.

There appear to be two reasons for these ties. First, these alliances may be an attempt to mask one's real social position. Second, they may be seen as a means of gaining access to additional property, gains the parties may view as important, but which are minimal in comparison to those of higher-status descent groups.

Among the low-ranking descent groups, parallel cousin marriages seem to be rare. This may be related to status. If equivalence is determined by marriage, then to marry someone of one's own descent group, whose position is known, only reinforces and does not enhance status. Thus parallel cousin marriages seem to be used by medium-rank families to avoid loss, but they are avoided by low-rank families because they emphasize low social position. For low-rank groups there is little to be gained by patrilateral ties.

The *sayyid* descent groups are also internally stratified. Some *sāda* were connected with the theoracy in Sanᶜa; others were merely peasants. However, the unique position of the *sāda*, vis-à-vis other groups, gave them an economic advantage. By being able to select wives from tribal descent groups, they could acquire control of property. Since they could not marry their women outside their stratum,[5] they could not lose control of assets. This practice assured many *sāda* of having local connections while allowing them to maintain a degree of social distance.

In ᶜAmran, two types of *sayyid* marriages are practiced. Those few individuals with important positions have tended toward stratum endogamy, often marrying with *sayyid* groups elsewhere in Yemen. In many of these marriages the status of the parties is unclear. Few ᶜAmranis have an awareness of the importance or status of specific *sayyid* minimal descent segments located in other areas. Likewise, *sayyid* descent groups in ᶜAmran have lands elsewhere, the extent and value of which might be unknown. Links formed with non-ᶜAmrani *sayyid* groups definitely reinforced the local stature of some *sayyid* families.

Many *sayyid* descent groups were engaged in agriculture and formed ties with local tribesman families. These alliances are, I think, also connected to status and economic position. In such marriages, the *sayyid* has generally taken women from medium-rank tribal groups. Hypergamy does not account for all marriages, however. As with medium-level tribal groups, *sayyid* marriages display a range of alliances. Unlike native ᶜAmranis, many of the *sayyid* stratum are relatively recent arrivals, a fact reflected in their marriages. *Sayyid* families often return to their natal villages to find spouses. The extent of the varied connections, especially those ties to *sayyid* groups outside ᶜAmran, tend to cloud the status of many *sayyid* families. Such blurring of status may have benefitted the *sayyid*'s unique position in the community.

BRIDE-PRICE

Just as social ranking and stratum endogamy are considered contrary to Muslim ideology, bride-price[6] (*shart*) is defined as improper. Informants often told me that bride-price was wrong, but most who complained about it also conceded that the practice was of such long standing that it was not likely to change.

Payment of a bride-price is not only a form of reciprocal exchange, it is also a statement of social importance. To accept a bride-price significantly below the standard sometimes indicates "weakness" within the involved descent groups. As such, bride-prices are reported, generally, to be the same for all marriages, irrespective of social position or status. This has the effect of placing all individuals on roughly the same level, a concession to the general idea of equality or at least an effort to avoid being marked as of unusual status. Since all men exchange roughly the same amounts, in effect there is little to distinguish one marriage from another; the "butcher's" marriage to an "innkeeper" family is, in terms of the bride-price, as important a transaction as a marriage between tribesman descent groups.

The sums of money involved in the bride-price have never been insignificant. Under the imam, bride-prices were in the range of 25 to 40 Maria Theresa thalers. There was some escalation of bride-price during these years, but compared to the current bride-price these increases were extremely modest. Older men regaled me with tales of how "little" they had paid for the rights to their wives, often noting that the high figures now being demanded and paid were "unlawful" (*ḥarām*). Of course, at the time these informants were themselves young men, bride-prices also may have seemed high or outrageous. When I sought to place current figures in some sort of perspective, informants could not, or would not, make comparisons. From their points of view, the 50,000 to 60,000 YR (U.S. $11,100 to $13,300) now being exchanged was so far removed from those 25 to 40 MT they had exchanged that no comparison of relative value or purchasing power could be made.

In the past, not all men were able to amass the necessary funds for a bride-price. Then, as now, some sought exchange (*badl*) marriages. A man would arrange to exchange his daughter for another's. Such marriages, while obviating the need for substantial funds, were and are not without difficulties. Since the exchange was purely in terms of women, if one marriage failed, or if disputes temporarily split a married couple, the other half of the exchange was also expected to separate until, or if, the problem could be resolved. Although exchange marriages seem a convenient means of arranging a marriage, and one method of hiding the financial insecurity of the parties involved, informants generally consider this a poor alliance since it is subject to greater than normal stresses and if one marriage dissolves the other is likely to take the same course if only to satisfy the needs of each household to maintain some sort of balance between them.

Bride-price may be lower among families who regularly exchange women. This is often the case of those, like the *shaykh*'s minimal agnatic group, who regularly practice patrilateral parallel cousin marriage. Such preferential treatment may be seen as an inducement to make an alliance or to renew prior ties between close kin. Even in these cases, which are often variations of the exchange arrangement (with the full exchange being deferred until a later period when children have grown), informants suggest that there should be some monies involved so that in the event of disputes or division of properties among brothers the marriages will not be affected.

In the early postrevolutionary period, the bride-price began to rise. This may have been due, in part, to the conversion from the silver Maria Theresa thaler to the riyal. By 1966 or 1967 the bride-price was about 1,000 YR. At this point the youth protested, formed an organization and demanded and received a guaranteed bride-price of 400 YR (see chapter 3). This figure prevailed for a number of years and then was increased to 600 YR. During this period, a great number of young men, estimated to include most ᶜAmranis now in their middle to late twenties, married. When the youth organization was still influential, those found exchanging more than the stipulated bride-price were fined 2,000 YR (an assessment collected by the *shaykh* and put in the town's treasury). However, as soon as most of the young men had married, they became inattentive, the youth organization disappeared, and the bride-price began to rise.

Information gathered on 1976 marriages, perhaps slightly exaggerated, put the bride-price between 8,000 and 10,000 YR. In March 1978 the figure was estimated to be 30,000 YR. Before each impending marriage, figures were circulated widely. Although having no concrete evidence for denying the validity of stated sums, informants were convinced that many figures were exaggerated, usually by 5,000 YR, and the truth of many claims was called into question. In July

1979, the bride-price was between 50,000 and 60,000 YR. These levels represent a 600 percent increase in about three years but are low in comparison to levels in many villages where the bride-price is reported to be slightly in excess of 200,000 YR exclusive of wedding expenses. Some ʿAmranis joke, only half-heartedly and with a full awareness of similarities in their own behavior, that fathers are exchanging their daughters for Mercedes trucks.

The rapid increase in marriage costs, including many additional expenses beyond the bride-price (often stated to be roughly 20,000 to 40,000 depending on the size of the wedding meals), has been a burden on virtually all families. Naturally, concern with the ever-increasing bride-price and related expenses was a subject of lively debate particularly among the younger men, many of whom at times despaired of arranging a marriage. In September 1978, a number of young men attempted to emulate the success of the former youth organization by holding meetings aimed at reaching an agreement to limit marriage expenses.

The young men were moved to action by the problems one of them, Nassar, had in arranging a marriage at a reasonable bride-price. While in Saudi Arabia, Nassar had arranged to marry the sister of his co-worker and fellow ʿAmrani, Ghalib, for a bride-price of 15,000 YR. When they returned to ʿAmran, Ghalib found that each family he contacted for his own marriage plans stipulated that the marriage be in exchange for his sister. Eventually Ghalib backed out of his agreement with Nassar and went forward with a sister exchange marriage. Despite some initial outrage at Ghalib's reneging, this soon cooled and some months later Nassar married for a bride-price estimated at 55,000 YR.

This affair, and its implications about changes in affinal ties, prompted a group of young men to meet with some of the town's politically important men. The youths proposed a bride-price limit of 15,000 YR. Although they were supported by the "judge" (*ḥakam*) and the commander of the local military garrison, the youths' efforts to limit the bride-price, or impose specific levels on the many additional wedding expenses, were unsuccessful. The commander, whom the group hoped would enforce the limit, declined because it was a local issue. While his agreement might have furthered the young men's cause, most men believe that as long as the decision was in the hands of men with marriageable daughters, no limits would be set. Although it is the *shaykh* who would have enforced this decision, he would have been powerless without the support of other alliance leaders, many of whom either had daughters or disagreed with the proposal. In fact, older men worried about the cost of arranging a son's marriage but were also concerned with loss of status if, under the proposed rules, they did not receive adequate compensation for their daughters.

By taking no action, fathers continued to face the necessity of concluding all marriage transactions as quickly as possible. To delay a marriage, when one has the money available, risks an almost certain increase in costs. At present, if a man concludes his daughter's marriage agreement for 60,000 YR and does not "convert" that into a wife for a son, he may find that the money received will be inadequate for arranging a marriage later. Of course, men can use the money for a shop or other investment, and they must weigh the comparative value of each sort of opportunity.

Informants avoided discussion of the bride-price transfer other than stating that the entire sum was supposed to be exchanged when the wedding contract was signed. There may be variations to how, when, or in what proportions the bride-price is exchanged, but it is clearly the case that some men made major investments, nearly totaling the reported bride-price, soon after their daughters were married.

Because of economic considerations, and in line with a tendency among medium- and low-rank tribal families to spread their ties with other families, a number of exogamous exchange marriages took place while I was in ʿAmran. These arrangements were so complex (see charts 9, 10, next pages) that informants had difficulty keeping straight who had married whom, although they were acutely aware of the reported bride-price (which was the same for each individual marriage). With a number of parties involved, status considerations may have been less important than simply orchestrating a marriage. It is possible that some subtle status manipulations underlay these arrangements and were obscured by the intricacy of the connections. If the exchange marriage does not affect status, it may still solidify relations with affines. Since in effect little or no cash is transferred in the exchange marriage, a man can avoid the almost obligatory years in Saudi Arabia and his affines will not be accused of avarice.

THE BROTHER-IN-LAW RELATIONSHIP

Informants place a great deal of emphasis on good relations with one's *nasab* (literally brother-in-law, but often extended to other

CHART 9. MULTIPLE EXCHANGE MARRIAGES AMONG MEDIUM-LEVEL FAMILIES

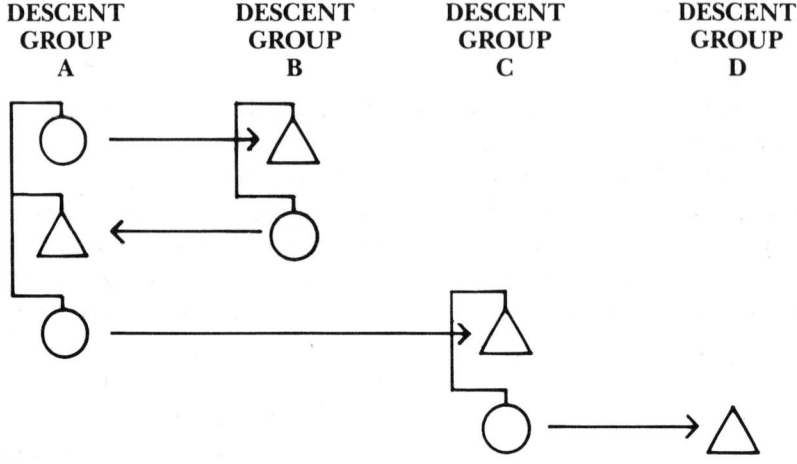

All marriages were between non-kin-related tribesman descent groups.
All marriage celebrations were conducted on 24 March 1978.

male affines including, in a general sense, the father-in-law who is called respectfully *ʿamm*). The growth of these relations was apparent in several marriages. Once a marriage agreement had been reached the parties often spent time together, particularly chewing *gāt* in the afternoons or visiting each other's place of business. One young man, soon to marry, suddenly became extremely concerned about the deportment of his future brother-in-law. Although the brother-in-law was also a close kinsman, the young man had taken no interest in his behavior until he felt it would reflect on himself.

The young men who tried to form a new youth organization to limit marriage costs argued that the important in-law relationship was being jeopardized because the exorbitant bride-price was a potential source of conflict between alliance partners. Fathers (or brothers), they said, were really selling their daughters (sisters) to the highest bidder. This type of accusation was leveled often at fathers (brothers) in general, particularly those outside ʿAmran, but it was never addressed to any specific person. How, the young men questioned rhe-

CHART 10. MULTIPLE EXCHANGE MARRIAGES AMONG LOW-LEVEL FAMILIES

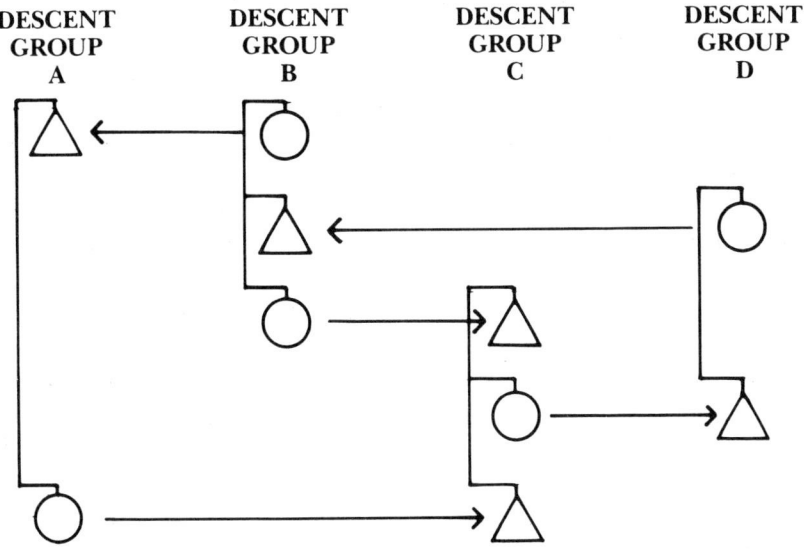

All marriages between non-kin-related tribesman descent groups.
All marriages celebrated on the same day in December 1978.
Bride-price reported to be 60,000 YR for all marriages.

torically, could a man have respect for his in-laws if the latter were so irreligious as to sell their daughters or sisters. Often a man who had arranged his daughter's marriage felt the need to make some sort of public statement about his action, usually pointing out that he had to do like everyone else or his behavior would be seen as inappropriate, an argument with some validity. Finally, the young men asked, could amicable relations exist if a man felt his brother-in-law had been interested in his money rather than the formation of a link between families? Instead of drawing men together through marriage, the bride-price was forcing them apart.

Although there are fixed obligations to one's brother-in-law, especially the formalized holiday visitations, there are those who claim that some in-laws make demands beyond those dictated by custom. This problem was treated with biting humor in a Yemeni-produced television series titled "Yā Nasabī" (Oh, Brother-in-Law). Each of the several episodes showed a hard-working man plagued by demands for jobs, marital counseling, and so forth from his brother-in-law, who was portrayed as both conniving and bungling. Relationships with one's brother-in-law seem strongest shortly after a marriage and wane with time. However, the importance of the connection may be demonstrated by the high incidence of repeat marriages to families with whom one has prior alliances.

At least in ʿAmran, ties to one's brother-in-law are only one important link. Among tribesmen, a man and his brother-in-law may have different political affiliations, each belonging to a different *ḥabl*. Questioned about the degree of obligation they had to their brothers-in-law, men stated they were bound to them as kin. However, when questioned further, and setting aside those men whose brothers-in-law were actual kin, informants answered somewhat differently. This can be seen through a hypothetical situation presented to informants. Although the responses may represent the ideal behavior, they also establish the relative importance of the *ḥabl* and affinal connections.

An informant was asked what he would do in the following instance:

> Your *ḥabl* is "X" and your wife is from a minimal agnatic group allied with *ḥabl* "Z." If someone from "Z" kills a man from "X," with whom do you side?

Invariably informants sided with *ḥabl* "X", although to do so would require standing against, and perhaps fighting and killing, their brother-in-law. Even when the situation was more specific, such as one's brother-in-law being the murderer, informants still said they would side with their *ḥabl*, rather than show support for their affine. In reality, of course, how a man would respond to a situation may be very different from what he said he would do in theory, for there is a great deal of fluidity in all situations. Actions are influenced by many factors, including noncontractual obligations to friends. When the exercise became tedious, some informants ended the questioning by pointing out that if a man had married properly, with his kin, then there could not be such potentially conflicting loyalties.

The importance of brother-in-law connections may be exaggerated by some informants. Now, as in the past, some men take wives from outside ʿAmran. This is most obvious among the *sāda* who have connections to *sāda* in other towns, but it is also found within other strata. In some of these cases, affines are rarely encountered beyond obligatory visits.

With the bride-price out of reach of some men, a few are "importing" Egyptian wives. The costs are considered minimal compared to those of marrying locally. There are only three or four Egyptian women in ʿAmran, but men often talk about going abroad in search of a wife. Some men point to the importation of "cheap" wives as a sign of the man's "weakness," but it also shows that affinal ties are becoming less important, a change that may have been revealed in the unsuccessful attempts to regulate the bride-price. It may also mean that men no longer believe their status is dependent on their marital alliances and that, as in other spheres, they can achieve a status on their own.

MOBILITY AND THE ARRANGEMENT OF MARRIAGES

The men who married Egyptians arranged their own marriages. Generally a man's marriage, at least his first, is arranged by his father or, if his father is dead, by some close kinsman. A son has the option to reject a potential wife, but it is important to realize that his range of choice is under his father's control. Potential spouses are matched according to the status of their fathers, which is determined by both the men's social position and that of the women they have married. Before the growth of the market economy, sons did not have a status of their own. Men married at an early age, were members of their fathers' households both in residential and labor matters, and had not established their own identity. To a degree this continues to be the case, but soaring bride-prices have forced men to delay marriage and to work in Saudi Arabia; and by the time they arrange marriages, their character is better known.

Because a man's status, defined by whom he marries, results from his father's status, alteration of social position is delayed or obscured. A man can only demonstrate a new status when he arranges marriages for his children. Coupled with the common practice of repeat alliances, social status can only change in small increments and then only over a period of time.[7]

Current marriage patterns appear to be much the same as in the past. Genealogies reveal marriages to roughly the same descent groups generation after generation. Since there is a delay in status change, the effects of rapid economic growth will not be manifest until the next generation marries. This point was made clear by an informant who explained the apparent lack of mobility of one descent group owning a number of shops along the main road and thriving in the new economy:

> The al-Habhab family doesn't marry the high-rank families because they are a low-rank family. It's true that today they have a lot of property and have some money, but they used to be low rank and they still only marry similar families. But look at Sirhan Farhan. He married a medium-level family because the al-Dayar family is of medium rank. It doesn't matter that today his father is poor and has to struggle to find work. Before the revolution he had some property; and when everyone was a farmer, he was better off than today.

Mobility may involve change upwards and downwards. Naturally informants who have improved their status would be reluctant to discuss this; it would acknowledge their former weak position. There are, no doubt, some instances of upward mobility. Several informants told me that a volume of al-Hamdani's work (ca. ninth century and hardly likely to reflect recent changes) listed the names and statuses of Yemeni families. When I sought this work, it was always unavailable, particularly when I explained my interest in its contents. As one man told me:

> No one will show you the book. If I had it, which I don't, I wouldn't show you either. No one would want it known that they used to be *muzayyin* and today are people of importance.

Of course, there are the cases of descent groups having higher status in the past. Men of these groups were anxious to explain their status loss in contrast to the reverse situation. There are also some cases in which status change is ongoing. Informants might be willing to discuss whom others had married, but they were very reluctant to consider the following case:

> The al-Rumi family were "middlemen" (*maṣlaḥīn*) for a number of items sold in the market. They were from the *walad al-sūq* stratum. The last male of this descent group died about ten years ago. His sister had married into a tribal descent group of at least moderate means. It was suggested that they were neighbors and friends and this was how the marriage occurred.

When I questioned men about the status of the tribesman descent group, particularly how such a marriage had occurred, most acted as if they had no idea the connection existed. No informant would comment on the status of the families involved. When presented with a hypothetical instance, ʿAmranis all agreed that status loss would result, but in the actual case they were noncommittal. The status of the parties may be demonstrated when the children marry, as in this similar example:

A tribesman "fell in love" with and married the "bleeder's" sister. They had three children, two of whom have married. The son married a tribeswoman from a village, and the daughter married a non-native ʿAmrani "innkeeper" who held a post in the local government.[8]

CONCLUSION

The combined effects of rapid changes in individual wealth, modified views of land as a status indicator, new means of access to political power, and the development of nonstigmatized occupations have had little impact on the formation of marriage alliances. Although these changes have laid the groundwork for new, modified bases of status determination, ʿAmranis still use marriage, a reflection of all status indicators, as an expression of social standing. Marriage is basic to the definition of relationships and has been a tool for maintaining or enhancing significant connections. While it is important to marry a social equal, the bases of equivalence are sufficiently vague that, in the near term, it is difficult to measure whether an alliance contributes to status loss or gain. Since a man's status is not fully defined until he arranges his children's marriages, and because, until recently, opportunities for dramatic status modification have been limited, those changes defined by marital alliance have generally been small movements.

The stability that surrounded marriage arrangements has been "threatened" by the escalation of the bride-price, increases made necessary by a man's need to arrange an alliance for a son or to amass the capital to enter a new business. Sons must take an active role in financing and arranging an alliance. This has raised concern that men may no longer form permanent, sometimes multigenerational relationships with their affines, but will seek only to "sell" their daughters. What is seen as a diminished ability to forge marital alliances according to traditional patterns carries with it the possibility of low-ranking men using recently acquired wealth to marry into higher-standing families. Equally alarming is the prospect that many interstrata marriages may occur, a circumstance that would seriously challenge the formal model. Even if these dramatic shifts are not likely to occur in the near future, the fact that some men no longer place emphasis on affinal ties or marriage as a status indicator suggests that the bases ʿAmranis have used for their relationships are changing.

6

ʿAmrani Perceptions of Social Change: Acceptance and Denial

Tradition-oriented ʿAmranis (a category that at least occasionally includes all long-term ʿAmran residents) often assert that in the past they were "better." By this they mean that they adhered more closely to the social rules, as they choose to define them. When comparing the past and the present, they stress that men used to know their places in the scheme of things but that some no longer hold to those traditional patterns. Occasionally men of all ages lament that everyone has become a *shaykh*, that everyone acts as if he were important. What they describe are shifts in social position, generally upward mobility, a process accentuated by the magnitude and speed of recent events that, according to ʿAmranis' formal depiction of status relationships, should not have been possible. Contemporary modifications are seen as linked to the revolution, yet generally they have not been part of a major social upheaval. In fact, even though there is much ambivalence, many changes have been accepted easily, if sometimes grudgingly, by most men, a receptivity that may confirm that these transformations are an extension of a long-term, ongoing process.

Deviations from the formal model are not new. Still, how do ʿAmranis perceive these recent changes? On what basis do they choose to accept or reject status modifications? I do not believe that ʿAmranis have any absolute grounds for their assessments. I do think, however, there are two factors that contribute both to the acceptance of some cases of upward mobility with relative ease and at the same time to the rejection of others. First, what are seen as formal status-determining criteria have taken on less precise definitions. Thus some status gains are acceptable because they are in accord with the precepts of the formal model, whereas others are accepted because they are seen as totally unrelated to the traditional hierarchy. Second, in spite of the overriding emphasis on status-based relationships, there are pseudo-kinship connections that cross all status boundaries. These informal links always have enabled individuals to demonstrate appropriate, and respected, moral and behavioral qualities and to achieve prestige, regardless of the characteristics attributed to them by the hierarchy.

FLEXIBLE BASES OF STATUS ASSESSMENT

Abdalla Bujra (1971) has studied social stratification in Hureidah, a South Yemeni town similar in some respects to ʿAmran. He notes that while the ideology surrounding social position defined social categories as discrete, nonmutable groups, there were always some opportunities for social mobility. In achieving a new status a group had to alter its former position and adopt qualities that were appropriate to the role it was assuming. Yet, as a group attempted to restructure its social position, other groups, threatened by this change, would seek to thwart these efforts by redefining the criteria for group membership.

Since there was some social mobility in Hureidah, Bujra concluded that the stasis portrayed in the formal model was illusory. He argued that although the social order was premised on a descent ideology, and should therefore be unchanging, in real terms descent elements were constantly being manipulated so as to account for individual shifts in social position. Modifications of the system were subtle when Hureidah was an isolated community but expanded when contact with the outside world increased. Social mobility became more pronounced with the development of new, nonstigmatized, achievable roles and occupations.

As we have seen, ʿAmranis, like Bujra's informants, describe the social structure as static. They offer an idealized presentation serving as much to preserve their own status as to diminish the gains made by others. This point can be seen in the variable definitions of the political alliance or *ḥabl*. If, as I believe, the *ḥabl* as a political action group in the traditional, military or defense, sense is on the wane, there are still those who are attempting to enter into *ḥabl* relationships precisely because of the status enhancement affiliation conveys. When some of the *walad al-sūq*, notably the "merchants" (*bayāʿīn*), became allied with the "new" *shaykh*, they began to alter their traditional relationship to the tribe and to overcome their ascribed "deficiency." *Ḥabl* affiliation is based on the kinship idiom. Even if tribesmen claim not to recognize *walad al-sūq* as kin in any sense, accepting them in a *ḥabl* nonetheless establishes the types of obligations presumed to obtain only among kinsmen. Some men rejected the idea that "merchants" were allied in a *ḥabl*, some dismissed the new alliance in its entirety, but others were less sure.

Some time after the 1967 split into two factions, a rift occurred among the "merchants." Some "merchant" descent groups chose to realign themselves with the "old" leadership. In the past they had sided with the *shaykh* as part of the protector-protected relationship; now they were seen in a new light. Sometimes unwilling to accord the "merchants" full affiliation, tribesmen allied in *ḥabl* still agreed that their alliances included some "merchant" descent groups, if in an appended state different from that of the past. Occasionally, when pressured to define their size and strength, some men would enumerate those "merchant" descent groups pledged to their *ḥabl*.

The "new" *shaykh* chose to define his followers in a nontraditional way. He preferred to see them as allies, defined the *ḥabl* only as an association, and avoided kinship references. This is precisely the restructuring of positions Bujra describes. Also, it indicates the decline of the tribe. Munson (1981) has argued that a tribe can exist only as long as it is kinship-based and autonomous. The "new" *ḥabl* is not conceived as a kinship group and its formation was in part influenced by ʿAmran tribe's increasing subservience to the central government.

Modification of the bases of *ḥabl* affiliation represents group transformation, but individual mobility is both more common and more fundamental. The patrilateral parallel-cousin exchange marriage by a wealthy "merchant" (see chapter 5) is an example of an attempt to demonstrate a new status. Informants were convinced that this alliance was made largely to mimic the marriage practices of the *shaykh*'s minimal agnatic group. As additional proof of this contention, informants cited the two brothers' new house, which was larger and better appointed than the *shaykh*'s.

When a *sayyid* married his sons to daughters of a well-known *sayyid* family in the capital, men were convinced this was a significant alliance, one demonstrating the *sayyid*'s prominence. However, few ʿAmrani men could state the basis of the ʿAmran *sayyid*'s importance. While most tribesmen, and some others, were unwilling to acknowledge the gains of the "merchant" whose local stature was known, they were, with far less information, willing to accord status gain to the *sayyid*. This is because they viewed an improvement in the status of the "merchant," whom most men disliked, as threatening; but they regarded the elevation of the well-liked *sayyid*'s position as derived from his ancestry and therefore acceptable.

Whereas some men have used marital alliances to solidify and dramatize status gain, others are experiencing difficulty maintaining their status. There may be many such cases, but the variables surrounding marriage arrangements are so numerous that isolating primary causes is difficult. In one case, however, a man of former importance had trouble finding a wife for one of his sons. The youth was without schooling, worked generally as a farmer on the family's vast holdings, and was one of many younger men who had not found any suitable niche. His father had made a number of unsuccessful attempts to arrange a marriage. In the present view, including that of the family itself, they were not keeping up. The son's marriage, when arranged, may well reveal the family's loss of status.

A number of factors contribute to each individual family's actual or potential economic improvement since the revolution. These include the location and use of their land; the opportunity and willingness to enter the mercantile sector; the acquisition of scarce, valued skills such as welding, driving, and construction; secular education; and judicious, forward-looking management of capital. In short, households or minimal agnatic groups have varied widely in their economic gains and losses. Clearly the deck has been shuffled. Still, in ʿAmrani perceptions, their social hierarchy, even if somewhat realigned, has not been substantially altered.

One reason for the endurance of old perceptions is that some aspects of the revised system, like new occupations, are outside the traditional framework. This separation of old and new has minimized conflicting values. Only those tasks directly linked to the traditional market have retained a tainted image. In spite of occasional derogatory remarks, tribesmen who have become shopkeepers have been able to define their livelihood as a form of buying and selling with the emphasis on terms apart from those linked to traditional standards. Some men stress the variety of "imported" goods they sell or the extremely modern Sanʿa-style design and layout of their shops as an indication that they are not *walad al-sūq* peddling locally produced items.

New positions are achievable. A number of young men (see chapter 4, note 2) have completed secondary school and some of them will enter government service. Others have attended military college (a secondary school) and are now officers in the Yemeni Army. Although their salaries are not generally on a level with those in commerce, as government officials they are considered men of actual or potential importance.

Some ʿAmranis measure change in terms of those who have not kept pace. There are men who have not found a suitable niche. They may temporarily retain their former status by selling assets (described as eating one's property), but this practice is seen as a short-term and inadequate solution.

My informants could not only state that before the revolution they were poorer, they were also aware of where each individual stood on a financial continuum. This is still the case, although the precision of modern estimates may be less accurate than in the past. Compared to prerevolution ʿAmran, it is clear that virtually everyone has benefited in a material way. Most important, ʿAmranis believe this to be the case, and can cite examples. Men often told me how much worse things had been under the imamate. In an absolute sense, most families enjoy greater holdings now than they had before the revolution. However, the gaps between individuals have become greater. The wealthy have had many more opportunities to augment their holdings (although some landowners have not diversified their capital); the poor have had relatively fewer chances and their gains have been considerably smaller.

When ʿAmranis discuss the improvements brought on by the revolution, they concentrate on wealth.[1] Money abounds; most people have some form of savings and many have acquired new, tangible assets. Since wealth is an obvious contributor to social position, it might be assumed that it has become the primary means through which upward mobility is achieved.

Actually, although my informants often measured men by their apparent wealth, and such factors as the money they spent on $g\bar{a}t$,[2] they also evinced an uncertainty about who had been really successful in the marketplace. Inflation and the slow movement of some men into new occupations may account for the difficulty in assessing gain. However, when I asked for examples of men who had gotten ahead, they preferred, except in the most obvious cases, to cite successful newcomers. In those instances, wealth alone proved high status. By contrast, when ʿAmran families were discussed, there were always veiled references to other variables (most often related to past marital alliances, political affiliations, or other circumstances) as contributing to social status. Wealth alone was an acceptable measure only for those deemed outside the ʿAmran social system, and was an inaccurate scale for assessing each other. Each informant evaluated the intangibles somewhat differently; and when I sought to corroborate a man's position, there was always someone who did not agree with the assessment others had presented.

A few men suggested that a new class system was developing, and that it was replacing the older, ascriptive hierarchy. In this respect they would agree with Béteille (1965:191):

> In traditional (Indian) society, . . . there was much greater constancy between the class system and the caste structure. One can even say, with some risk of oversimplification, that the class system was largely subsumed under the caste structure. This means, in effect, that ownership and nonownership of land, and relations with the system of production, were to a much greater extent associated with caste than is the case today.

ʿAmran, like traditional India, always had a class system that coexisted with, but in ʿAmrani eyes was largely obscured by, the more readily apparent ascriptive hierarchy. The social hierarchy in Yemen may appear similar to the Indian caste system, but it differs in several respects. Social mobility, particularly downward mobility, has always been possible and in fact individual statuses were generally in a state of minor change. Further, and perhaps more important, there were no ritual restrictions surrounding any strata. Under Islamic doctrine and local practice, all men were equal in religious affairs and some men of modest status held important religious positions in the community.

I have followed Bujra (1971) and Gerholm (1977), both of whom see little point to the argument over class versus caste. If labels are needed, it is, I think, more practical to regard the strata and substrata of the formal hierarchy as approximating closed classes, with the caveat that even in this formalized scheme there were great internal social differences.

Each ascriptive stratum is internally stratified. There were always wealthy and influential men from the *walad al-sūq* and many poor, unnoticed tribesmen and *sāda*. Yet, even now, wealth is insufficient for overcoming the tribesman's or *sayyid*'s prejudice toward those of "deficient" ancestry. The following examples portray men of low ascribed status who have been able to use their wealth to maintain a high standard of living (and perhaps to evoke feelings of envy or resentment from poor tribesmen and *sāda*). They continue, however, to interact primarily with those of their own ascriptive status and are likely to marry their children endogamously unless there are dramatic changes.

> Nassar is a "barber-circumciser." He has been in ʿAmran for about six years, having moved from a nearby village. He has been successful in his occupation, doing those tasks traditionally assigned to "barber-circumcisers." He has chosen to continue this work, almost to the point of flaunting his status, and he has been well rewarded. His skill at managing weddings is well known. He has a successful barber shop and has used his profits to build several shops for rental income."

> Naʿif is a "barber-circumciser." He still lives in a nearby village but has a successful pharmacy business in ʿAmran. He has training both from the Yemeni government and practical experience gained in Saudi Arabia and the Gulf. He is in demand with many of the newly arrived families and also has a large village clientele who regularly consult him. With his profits he is building a new house, which will also have space for three shops.

Both men have been successful but through different strategies. Despite their economic gains, neither enjoys a noticeable status improvement except within his immediate circle of associates, most of whom are also of low ascribed status. This is not surprising: others by acceptance of the new statuses would endanger their own social standing.

When asked to measure other ʿAmranis' status, informants tended to do so in formal terms, applying one of the following three variables: wealth, ancestry, or affiliation. Which criterion they choose is related to the desire, put simply, to make themselves look good. That is, a poor tribesman, when asked about a wealthy "merchant," is likely to make his assessment in terms of the descent factor rather than the economic one. Similarly, the wealthy "merchant" can be expected to evaluate the poor tribesman on the basis of wealth rather than ancestry. This, of course, does not mean that ʿAmranis are blind to the complex interactions of the three variables. More important, even though they may choose to isolate these factors in unrestricted situations, there are other, nonhierarchically based criteria that influence status. Many of these informal status determinants are achievable.

PSEUDO-KINSHIP RELATIONS

The image conveyed by the hierarchical model is one of separate spheres with very limited and specific types of interstrata interaction. It is important to understand that most transactions were largely free of the patterns dictated by the formal system. This is most clearly the case in economic dealings. Commercial links are necessary and they result in connections that join all members of society both as individuals and social categories. In the past interstrata and intrastratum interactions were typical in relationships between producers and marketeers or landowners and land users. Some of these transactions were the foundation for patron-client relationships. Others were informal, based on long-term associations. This explains why the rents on some shops have not risen in years, or how some tribesmen's entry into commerce has been supported financially by some "merchant" families.

An individual's relationships were not solely based on the formal model. Although one's status and obligations were fixed by formal alliances, other less formal duties cut across the hierarchy, stressing affiliation of community in the broadest sense. Because many of these ties were defined in pseudo-kinship terms, they provided opportunities for men to demonstrate status on the personal level and to achieve (at least within the confines of the system) a status based on individual merit. This may be seen most clearly in neighborhood interactions.

An informant explained the ideal relationship between neighbors as follows:

> Do you know who your neighbors are? Your neighbors are all those who live forty houses to the east of you, forty houses to your west, forty houses to the south, and forty houses to the north. Those are your neighbors and you have to be concerned about them. If they are in trouble, you have to help them. If someone is sick, you must visit them; and if they are poor, you have to help them find someone to cure them. If they are without food, you must cook for them. If they need help, you have to offer assistance. That is what it means to be a neighbor.

To be sure, I saw no evidence of this principle being carried to the extent described by my informant. Obviously in a town like ʿAmran, forty houses in any direction could include virtually the entire community. Clearly, as in agnatic groups where support is related directly to genealogic distance, neighbor relations are linked to physical proximity. Despite the obvious social implications in being of *sayyid*, tribesman, or *walad al-sūq* ancestry, such differences tend to be minimized when dealing with obligations to neighbors, regardless of how humble or lofty their origins. That is, duties to those in nearby houses are viewed as obligatory irrespective of the status of the inhabitants.

Neighbors (the term is situationally applied but always includes immediate houses) are expected to assist each other. A tribesman has obligations to his *ḥabl*, but everyone has ties to his neighbors. Ideally a neighbor's request cannot be denied, a precept symbolized in the expression "I am your neighbor," used as a demand for action, assistance, and protection.

The most striking examples of neighborliness occur when major events take place. Wedding feasts and the many parties surrounding a marriage celebration require both group labor and group emotional support. The same applies to funerals and wakes and gatherings to greet returned migrants and pilgrims from Mecca. In these events, neighbors not only contribute active support to the success of celebrations but also may provide limited financial assistance. It is as if, like kin, they can be shamed by not having provided suitable support. It is considered at least improper, more often "sinful," to avoid these obligations, and absences are noted. For men the fulfillment of their duties is easy; it is women who must provide the physical and emotional support.

Naturally, there are exceptions to and alterations in these patterns, which contribute to the ambivalence surrounding social change. Now many of one's neighbors may be recent arrivals and relatively unknown. A few men complain about their obligations. At a funeral, a man addressed the room as a whole and said, "Today men flee from weddings and wakes," a comment that brought a nodding of heads in assent among those who felt their attendance was costing them time and money.

The pseudo-kin concept extends beyond the limits of the neighborhood. This is seen most clearly in the use of kinship terms of reference and address where older men are called "uncle" and older women, "mother." Many families also maintain significant ties with others, and these become regularized into the kinship framework. The formal nature of these extra-neighborhood connections is most pronounced during the two annual holiday celebrations during which visits are made to consanguines and affines as well as to those with whom kinshiplike ties exist. Here are two examples:

Jamal was on his way to Mecca for the pilgrimage but was unable to continue and settled in ʿAmran. His own village was quite distant. He was taken in by a man of some importance who provided him with a room. When it became apparent that he would not return to his natal village, his protector arranged his marriage to a young divorcee. Jamal regularly visits his mentor's household during the holidays.

Hamid and his sister are *walad al-sūq*. They are from a nearby village. When Hamid decided to move to ʿAmran, he and his sister stayed for a number of years in the house of a poor tribal family. Now both Hamid and his sister have ample assets, but continue to visit the still poor tribal family not only during the holidays but also throughout the year.

Amidst the multiple levels of pseudo-kinship relations between neighbors and others, social status is often minimized if not totally overlooked. This creates the impression of a vague equality among individuals whose obligations are to their communities without reference to status. This is only a surface reflection. It would be inappropriate to emphasize social rank in the context of neighborhood, but this does not make status less of a concern. However, in these relationships men can achieve (or lose) status on their own merits. Fulfilling societal or religious standards of behavior can earn ʿAmranis a reputation for good works that may in many situations be stressed far more than ascribed character traits.

THE COOPERATIVE ELECTION

One way to get a fuller and more realistic sense of ʿAmranis' evaluations of each other is to review the outcome of the election to the local development board advisory council. The results suggest that while traditional measures of high status endure, there are other, sometimes new, routes to prestige and influence.

The ʿAmran cooperative development board serves the entire administrative district, with regionally elected committees organizing projects in their local areas.[3] The advisory board for the region has seventy members, twenty four from ʿAmran town. Elections were held in each community in the district.

The second election of the cooperative was held in December 1978. The election, although not its exact date, was announced in a variety of posters prominently displayed throughout the town. These government-produced, nationally distributed signs encouraged participation in the election and in the cooperative as well. Most of the slogans sought to eliminate criticism of the cooperative movement and a "do nothing" attitude among the populace.[4]

Loudspeakers announced the election and encouraged attendance. About midmorning, the local police ordered the shops in the market closed. According to one of the two Sanʿa officials who presided over the election, about 1,000 men attended. Others estimated as many as 2,000. All who attended were eligible to vote. The great majority were native ʿAmranis. Recent settlers, perhaps feeling their political weakness, did not attend. A number of ʿAmrani shopkeepers as well as settlers, hid in their shops until the police had cleared the marketplace, kept their businesses open, and did not participate.

The election procedure was simple. Names of candidates were called out from the crowd and a show of hands was tallied. The twenty-four highest vote-getters were seated on the advisory board. Although the votes are useful in establishing those men ʿAmranis consider important, the organization of the election may have affected its outcome. In the absence of a predetermined slate to be put before the electorate, the candidates presented may have been haphazardly selected and may not fully represent the men highly regarded by the voters. In other words, some men may have been accidentally or intentionally overlooked. A few wealthy and prominent men were not nominated.

The results are summarized in table 6. There were, of course, a number of unsuccessful candidates, some of whom were men of money and connections. One name, drawing two votes, also drew laughter from the crowd. The votes for the unsuccessful nominees ranged from 0 to 70.

The results indicate several general points. First, the young men, largely the educated youth, were able to seat a number of their group on the board. The youth had, prior to the election, taken a great interest in the cooperative and were the most obvious voting block. They avowed concern that the town would not reach its development potential unless some of the electees were more worldly than the town's traditional leaders. In this and other functions, the youth set themselves apart as a unique group, often referred to by other townsmen as the "children of June 13th," after the day in 1974 on which Ibrahim al-Hamdi seized political control of Yemen. Two of the young men were elected unanimously.

Second, the largest number of seats was gained by men of tribal ancestry. The *shaykh*'s descent group (*ḥabl* I) and another closely allied to it (*ḥabl* IV) were the most successful. Elected were the *shaykh*, the leader of his *ḥabl*, the leader of the allied *ḥabl*, and seven

162 / ʿAmrani Perceptions of Social Change

Table 6. Advisory Board Election Results

Electee	Ancestry	Habl Affiliation[1]	Age[2]	Occupation[3]	Residence	Votes[4]
A	gabīlī	I	40	shaykh	ʿAmran/Sanʿa	Unanimous
B	gabīlī	I	20	govt. empl.	ʿAmran/Sanʿa	Unanimous
C	gabīlī	I	55	landowner	ʿAmran	Unknown
D	gabīlī	II	30	former govt. empl.	ʿAmran	Unanimous
E	sayyid	—	45	physician	Sanʿa	Unanimous
F	gabīlī	III	45	well operator	ʿAmran	Unanimous
G	bayāʿ	with III	45	merchant	ʿAmran	Unanimous
H	bayāʿ	—	30	welder	ʿAmran	165
I	gabīlī	with I	25	military officer	(army posts)	Unanimous
J	bayāʿ	—	35	merchant	ʿAmran	175
K	gabīlī	IV	40	carpenter	ʿAmran	Unknown
L	gāḍi	—	50	ḥākam	ʿAmran	Unanimous
M	gabīlī	I	30	govt. empl.	Sanʿa	94
N	gabīlī	I	20	school teacher	ʿAmran	Unknown
O	gabīlī	I	50	landowner	ʿAmran	120
P	gabīlī	IV	25	govt. empl.	ʿAmran	Unanimous
Q	gabīlī	V	35	govt. empl.	Sanʿa	94
R	gabīlī	III	—	—	ʿAmran	Unknown
S	bayāʿ	—	30	merchant	ʿAmran	110
T	gabīlī	VI	—	—	ʿAmran	94
U	bayāʿ	—	—	merchant	ʿAmran	94
V	gabīlī	IV	45	elec. motor owner	ʿAmran	Unanimous
W	gabīlī	IV	35	govt. empl.	Sanʿa	94
X	bayāʿ	—	40	merchant	ʿAmran	Unanimous

Note: I did not know R, T, or V. I was casually acquainted with H and K. Although Q and W were in Sanʿa, I did see them occasionally. I knew all the rest.

¹ These are actual alignments and do not include those who may have had informal alliances. Roman numerals refer to separate *ḥabls*; I = *shaykh*'s descent group; III = "new" *shaykh*'s descent group; IV = allied with I.

²These are my estimates.

³This is the primary occupation.

⁴These results are unofficial. They were gathered from informants and the *qaḍi* who presided. I was not permitted to copy the totals.

other members of these two groups. The "new" *shaykh*'s *ḥabl* (III) did not fare well, a point emphasized by several informants after the election. Those two men who did succeed, won their seats, according to informants, purely on the force of their personalities rather than political affiliations. This same point was also made about most of the other winners since some of the unsuccessful nominees came from prominent groups.

Third, although tribesmen dominate the membership, a number of "merchants" were also elected. Some men told me that this would have been impossible in the past, but events in the last fifteen to twenty years seem to indicate that some men of the "merchant" substratum have been well regarded at least since the 1960s and seem to represent a sizeable constituency. Only one *sayyid* was elected. This may reflect the social and political aloofness of the *sāda* (who are viewed as silent supporters of the traditional leadership) more than a change in attitudes.

Fourth, at least nine of the electees have obvious, although sometimes limited, connections with central government ministries. At least a few of them may have been nominated as much for their possible influence in the capital as their personal appeal. This is particularly true of those who have permanent residence in the capital. However, electees "L" and "P" (see table 6) would have been assured seats even without Sanʿa connections.

A more personal analysis of some of the successful candidates reveals other important features:

Candidate A: *Shaykh* of ʿAmran. He spends most of his time in Sanʿa, but is sought out for his counsel in both of his homes. When in ʿAmran he is rarely seen; his behavior conveys the image of a man busy with many affairs. Although he is not aloof, his demeanor is reserved. His importance in the community is based on his family's extensive holdings and history of political leadership, but the *shaykh* is respected as an arbiter and a man able to get things accomplished. He chews *gāt* rarely.

Candidate B: Patrilateral cousin of the *shaykh* and part-time government employee. He has a secondary school education. While studying in Sanʿa he worked in a number of government ministries. He has made several trips both inside and outside Yemen studying cooperative programs. Some of his prestige derives from his family's wealth and power, but he is primarily respected by the younger men for his willingness to get involved in town affairs. He has taken an active role on several issues, including initiating the building of a soccer field, during which he was successful in getting some senior men to contribute the necessary land. He is very outgoing, but also gives the impression of having many important affairs requiring his attention. He rarely hangs out in the market with the other students. He chews *gāt* and freely associates with a wide variety of men.

Candidate D: A former government employee. Although he is somewhat older than most of the students, he is well regarded by the younger generation with whom he chews *gāt* in his house. Prior to the election he was often found hanging out around the market. After his selection his demeanor changed. His dress improved and he was seen rarely. He no longer spent as much time with his former associates, a change the latter sometimes criticized.

Candidate E: A physician. He is from a prominent *sayyid* family, his father having held a number of important posts under the imam. His present status within the community is based less on his ancestry and marriage ties to San'a than on his occupation and foreign education. Both his unique skill and government connections contribute to his prestige. Although he is mainly in San'a, when in 'Amran he prefers to meet people in his home where he chews *gāt*. He has few associates.

Candidate F: A land and well owner. Since his home and well are somewhat outside the town, he is seen rarely. However, he is consulted on a variety of issues. He is considered extremely hardworking, preferring work to *gāt* chewing. He is pious, honest, and community oriented. He contributed land and money to build a small elementary school near his home so younger children would not have to walk to school in 'Amran.

Candidate G: A wealthy cloth merchant, wholesaler, and landowner. He displays his position with his attire and expensive *gāt* purchases. He lives with his older brother in a large house. Although he has a shop on the outskirts of the old *sūq*, he is rarely in the market. He is well respected (in contrast to his brother) for his piety and sense of humor. Occasionally he chews *gāt* outside his home, but only as a guest at a special event.

Candidate J: A wealthy general-goods merchant. His father was a respected leader of the *walad al-sūq*. This may have contributed to his position, but his wealth and landholdings are extensive. He is viewed as extremely devout and somewhat of an expert in religious matters. He conveys an image of importance in his dress and by not socializing in the market even though his shop sits in the central square. He is generally inconspicuous but is reputed to be able to get things done, both because of his leadership within his patronymic descent group and his connections with other merchants. He chews *gāt* in his shop with a few friends.

Candidate L: Judge (*ḥākam*) of ʿAmran. Although his office is in the marketplace, he is virtually invisible. He is considered religious, fair, and honest. He is respected for maintaining the honor of his household; his wife does not leave it. Also he is well known for having married his daughter without a bride-price and to have given her the dowry. He does not chew *gāt* and visits other homes rarely.

Candidate S: A merchant with connections to *gāt* sellers. He is highly visible, having opened a general-goods shop in the vicinity of the *gāt* market. His shop's sign proclaims him as the "headman" of the market. Unlike many *gāt* sellers who are considered unscrupulous traders, he is respected as being honest and fair. He has been successful and had made several pilgrimages to Mecca.

Candidate X: Arms, ammunition, and money merchant. He is sometimes referred to as the head of all those without shops who squat in vacant areas of the market. Despite being in the market, and without a shop, he maintains a low profile. Unlike some others in his field, he dresses well. Perhaps because of his location he is often among the first to intervene in any disputes. He chews *gāt* with friends.

Informants claimed that in contrast to the outgoing advisory board members, some of whom had been appointed by the central government rather than locally elected, the new members were genuinely concerned with ʿAmran's growth and development. This widespread confidence shows that the electees were well-respected men. Their esteem was based on these qualities: (1) ability to get things done; (2) opinions and advice considered intelligent and responsible; (3) personal styles that were markedly unflamboyant (maintained a low-key, hardworking image); (4) for those engaged in commerce, reputations for honesty, often unlike others in the same occupations; (5) all appeared religious (those not known for their devoutness were still not among those who drank alcohol or did not pray).

With few exceptions, the electees were wealthy men although the sources of wealth vary. Only a few have large landholdings. As indicated earlier, land is considerably less significant now than in the past. Still, most of those with considerable property, including some of the "merchants," always have had land and were well off financially even before the revolution.

Several of the electees appear to have been selected because of their connections with power sectors in the capital. The majority of board members are better viewed as local leaders whose influence and popularity would be sufficient to sustain community support for cooperative programs. Whether explicitly or not, ʿAmranis appear to have recognized the need for both types of leaders—some with local influence, others with Sanʿa connections. This view is supported by the unanimous election of eleven men and by the broad support drawn by the other thirteen electees.

What can be inferred from the election results? To what extent do they suggest movement away from traditional bases of political authority? The fact that only one *sayyid* was selected suggests the departure is sharp, but then what can be made of the town's failure to select a single *muzayyin*? How significant is the fact that six of the twenty-four electees were "merchants?"

That six "merchants" were elected might suggest to some that ancestry is no longer a significant component of status. They would claim that if men of "merchant" descent are sufficiently wealthy and have enough influence in economic or political affairs, then their ancestry is no longer socially significant. However, were this true, these men should be able to marry their children outside the "merchant" stratum. This has not been the case. With very few exceptions, tribesmen, no matter how poor or unimportant, have continued to avoid marriage alliances with "merchant" families. Successful "merchants" may have a rightful place on the development association advisory board because of their influence and connections, and perhaps because of their personal virtues, but descent differences continue to be of intense social significance in other domains. It is more correct to see the election of six "merchants" (along with the other selections) as a concretization of muted aspects of a long-standing social reality. That is, despite the tribesman's stated abhorrence for the marketplace and the *walad al-sūq* families, and even though the stratum did not form political alliances, there were informal leaders who have had considerable influence. The fact, for example, that during the revolution, several tribesmen from prominent families formed a business partnership with a prominent "merchant" supports my claim that much interaction and compromise is concealed behind the tribesman's overt social ideology. Only if the tribesman's model is accepted as an accurate depiction of past ʿAmrani social relations will the election results appear as evidence of dramatic change. When its self-serving thrust is recognized and one begins to see through or beyond it, there is the realization that political influence was never the exclusive property of the tribesman or *sayyid* and that prestige was based on a combination of factors: descent, economic position, personality, and others. Given these realizations, little in the election results is cause for surprise.

CONCLUSION

Peters (1972) has discussed at length the limited utility of informants' views in discovering social hierarchy. His point is that although the simplicity of the rules informants provide is almost painfully appealing, it is a wholly false simplicity. The speciousness of informants' depictions derives in part from a real discrepancy between socialized values and attitudes on the one hand and actual perceptions of individuals on the other. The disparity stems as well from the human tendency to emphasize those rules or components of status that make oneself look best.

I discovered the profound insufficiency of ʿAmranis' stated social model whenever I used it in specific rather than theoretical discussions. Almost without exception, when I attempted to apply to particular individuals or actions the general rules I had been so carefully taught, my assessment was corrected or amended by informants who then went on to explain, usually in vague terms, that the rule did not apply in that specific instance. I have not been able to develop a formula for when, and to what extent, the rules do or do not apply in specific instances. I was not alone in this. Although informants adopted authoritarian demeanors when they modified status assessments, they were not demonstrating so much the errors made in specific cases as they were saying that with very few exceptions all status determinations are subject to manipulation. What this reveals is that in many situations the formal and informal bases of status overlap, but not uniformly. There is a strong situational element in the grammar of status assessment. The lack of concreteness evident now was always inherent in the social structure, but it is just more obvious. Increased opportunities for individual status manipulation have broadened the range of mobility beyond that allowed in the overt model, but status ingredients have remained vague and veiled. This is evident in the following examples:

ʿAbdalla, a man of extremely low status, settled in ʿAmran about the time of the revolution. He bought a house in a residential area and his children grew up as ʿAmranis, a point that helped to establish his position in the community. Drawing on repatriated funds, he has been successful both as a wholesaler and more recently as a distributor for Yemeni manufactured, commercial products.

He is well respected. His children are all educated and associate freely with other educated youth, particularly those from tribal families. More important, he has maintained a low profile. His counsel is sought on many matters, but he tends to keep to himself. He is seen in the marketplace rarely. He spends his time in his shop or at prayer. His piety is well known. Although a soft-spoken man, his background and knowledge convey an image of strength and virtue. He does not chew *gāt*.

He is extremely wealthy, but he is not at all pretentious. He dresses well but without flamboyance. This is one of his many honorable qualities. Furthermore, he exercises firm control over his wife and daughters who leave the house only occasionally.

Ahmad, a "merchant" in town, imported goods from Saudi Arabia. First he tried selling these in a modern Sanʿa-style shop but he had few customers. Thereafter he confined his activities to sales of items from his house, and was absent for long periods buying new inventory. During most of this time he was supported by the earnings of his sons.

When it was time for the annual pilgrimage, he announced that he was once again going to Mecca and added that he would then stop off in Cairo for medical treatment. Only the wealthy usually spend time abroad, and this side trip, in addition to his going to Saudi Arabia, was well noted.

Before his trip he was known for his generosity. Daily his second wife prepared food for some poor neighbors. He was, however, somewhat of a recluse. He avoided the marketplace and his errands were handled by his sons from his first wife. Upon his return he dramatically altered his patterns. Instead of chewing *gāt* alone or with some friends in the market, he began to chew in the house of a tribal family of former importance, then a gathering place for some influential men. Unlike some guests, he was scrupulous in bringing the necessary provisions for the water-pipe and was always the first to leave to pray, usually departing just prior to the first evening prayer call.

During this period he was building a large house and shop complex. He spent long hours overseeing the project but avoided reference to its obvious size or cost unless prompted by others.

Soon men began referring to him as *Hajj* Ahmad. This was a title he had held for many years but which was not used.

In these cases, an essential status ingredient was business success. Commercial achievements, however, are not sufficient in and of themselves. Some men have made great economic gains but are neither respected nor liked. Both these men, on the other hand, have altered their public images in ways almost guaranteed to heighten their prestige. While both are of "deficient" ancestry, they present themselves with such honorable discretion that even the most traditional tribesman could not in fairness fault them. Both have effectively reinforced and enhanced the status gains that come from affluence by emulating the ideal styles of the *sayyid* and the tribesman.

Their tactics, however, are far from identical. One chewed *gāt* of high quality, always purchased by his son; the other never chewed. One was polygynous, the other monogamous. One was known for his innovative and clever business practices, the other for honesty and piety. One rose above a steady stream of family fights, the other controlled his family to avoid any embarrassment. What these men have in common is their emulation of the ideal style. Both avoid the marketplace, loud public behavior, bragging, and overt preoccupation with economic matters.

Interestingly, men of tribal descent need not expend such effort putting across an image of honor, although some certainly do. If they are extremely ambitious, of course, they must work hard at impression management; but if they are satisfied with a private life, they can afford to let the ideal tribal image drop occasionally without much fear of status loss. They can, in fact, even laugh when among friends about such lapses.

> Hassan had often told me how his family had been among the first to enter the market after the revolution. He said it was not really shameful to be in commerce, that the difference between tribesmen and *walad al-sūq* centered on their attitudes toward money. The *walad al-sūq*, he said, had no honor; they charged high prices because of a love of money. The tribesman, he argued, simply took his share. A profit was all right if it was fair payment for one's work, but the *walad al-sūq* had no honor when it came to money.
>
> Sometime later we were strolling through the fields during a holiday. Most of the shops were closed and would remain so until the five-day celebration was completed. The open shops belonged to some of the *walad al-sūq*. Hassan told me how the *walad al-sūq* couldn't stay away from business, and added that he would open his shop the next day. I accused him jokingly of being like the *walad al-sūq*. We argued the point for a while, trading insults. A little while later he said to me in a conspiratorial whisper, that when he had first gone into the business he had a monopoly on some imported goods.
>
> "We paid only three riyals for one," he said, "but we sold them for seven. We were shameful, weren't we? We were just like the *walad al-sūq*."

What then is the key to the system? The hierarchy establishes patterns of interaction; but because it attempts to describe and dictate all aspects of life, it is not able to restrict how an individual behaves. Thus if a man is "trapped" by his ancestry (itself subject to some modification) or other formal status criteria, he can still, to a degree, modify his status by adopting the values and following the rules of those with preferred descent. The increased role of informal status criteria has eased or eliminated the barriers of the formal model.

As we have seen, there have been increasing modifications in the ground rules for ʿAmranis' formal relationships. These deviations both indicate differential compliance with the social norms and reflect actual status shifts. In the past these alterations might have been overlooked since the range of variation was relatively small. Now, the opportunities for dramatic, and therefore less easily denied, changes are greater. The formal model never was an accurate depiction of social reality, but it used to be a much better approximation than it is now. ʿAmranis' ambivalence has increased as the discordance between the ideal of the past and the reality of the present has grown. Even those who have thrived in the postrevolutionary climate remain unsure how to evaluate the changes or their new status. Others have found that recognizing social reality is uncomfortable, requiring acceptance that their position is less than it used to be or what they would like to think it had been.

ʿAmranis are clearly discomforted not only by the declining importance of the formal bases upon which their social determinations were made, but also by the implications these changes have for their relationships. There is an increasing sense that collective or stratum identity, action, and support typical in the past are being supplanted by a social system in which individuality and self-reliance are paramount. If in the past a few men stood out, they did so in accordance with accepted standards and without disregarding their ties to others. The new values are those related to personal achievement. Prestige, connections, occupation, community respect, and so forth are all seen as less related to ascribed characteristics than in the past. In many respects the cooperative election reveals this shift in status determination. It also shows that ʿAmranis are willing to accept changes as long as they tend to conform to the rough outlines of the past.

ʿAmranis' social structure is a modified version of that existing or thought to exist in the prerevolutionary era. The modifications evident now are outgrowths and expansions of small transformations that were established under the imamate. The change has been one of emphasis, not so much altering the parameters of formal status as allowing informal, achievable criteria a more important role. The shifts have altered relationships. These trends suggest that as more emphasis is placed on achieved status, a more open class-stratification system will replace the ascriptive social structure.

Notes

Chapter 1. *A Day in ʿAmran*

1. Tomas Gerholm (1977) has made an extensive study of social status in the town of Manakha in central Yemen. He provides a detailed description of *mafraj* seating as a status indicator.

Chapter 2. *ʿAmrani Views of the Past*

1. In using the term *hierarchy*, I follow Béteille (1974:60), who defines hierarchy as a rigid system of ranking based on well-defined boundaries between strata with little mobility. This is how ʿAmranis would characterize their social structure.

2. Although a plural form of *walad al-sūq* is occasionally used by ʿAmranis, they commonly employ the singular. This may be a verbal device to de-emphasize the collective nature of these denizens of the marketplace.

3. A *libna* is a variable measure of land. In the ʿAmran area, 100 *libna* is roughly equal to one acre (Federal Agency for Economic Development 1974).

4. Prior to the advent of paper currency after the revolution, the Maria Theresa thaler (also called a *faransī*) was the standard monetary unit. The thaler was imported, but the coins representing its subunits (*bugsha*) were minted in Yemen.

5. The principal references made by al-Hamdāni to ʿAmran deal with the Himyarite period (cf. al-Hamdāni 1938).

6. See note 3 above.

7. One *gadāh* is the standard unit of dry measure. Based on volume, the weight of each unit depends upon the grain being measured. A *gadāh* is composed of sixty-four units. The standard measuring procedure, the *mikiyāl* system, requires the use of a standardized measuring container, generally one-eighth *gadāh*. The measurer (*kayāl*) fills this with grain until a cone stands above the lip of the container. This is one unit. After it has been tallied, it is poured into a storage container. The measurer receives a small portion of the grain for his labor.

8. The World Bank (1979:8) states that the decline in agricultural production is a result of the drought of 1969–70.

Chapter 3. *Affiliation: Changing Bases of the Social Order*

1. *Hijra*, referring to Muhammad's migration to Madina, is the institutional domain of the *sāda* whose ancestors were among the *muhājirūn*, those who migrated

with Muhammad. The idea of a sacred zone where disputes could be mediated is discussed by Gerholm (1977) and Chelhod (1970, 1976).

2. Chelhod (1970) describes Yemeni tribal structure in terms of his interpretation of their Bedouin ancestry. Many of the categories he describes are known to ʿAmranis, but they do not use them. Those informants who chose to use historical sources for their explanations of tribal categories always cited al-Hamdāni.

3. This variable use of kinship terms is also found among the bilateral kindred of the United States.

4. A slightly different form of this oath is as follows:

> In the name of Allah. As my signature attests, I have severed my (previous) connections and joined *ḥabl* (name). I have become one of them, both in debt and arms. To me they pledge their property and I agree to support them likewise. Allah is my witness. Signed (name).

5. Barth (1959, cited in Bailey 1969:39–40), states that failure to fulfill one's obligations results in punishment. Beyond the clear example related in the text of the coward failing to kill his Janati enemy, however, I could find no instances of this practice in ʿAmran.

6. Bailey (1969:43) contends that in stratified groups a premise of equality can exist: "Insofar as both leaders and followers are servants of the same cause, some sense of equivalence between them is created."

7. In this case, all parties of the dispute attended the meeting: about 4,000 Bakil men on the side of the *walad al-sūq* and 3,000 men from ʿAmran, according to estimates. The latter figure makes sense only if men from tribal villages are counted. As in any dispute between tribes, the two groups met across a field in an elliptical formation and the spokesmen for each side, standing in the center, made speeches through the "poetic messenger" (*dawshān*). The leaders, after exchanging formalized greetings and settling the issue of expenses, asked for someone to come forward to present the case. As was part of normal procedure, when no one came forward the leaders continued, formally presenting the case; and a committee was elected to seek the actual resolution. All disputants shook hands indicating they would abide by the decision.

8. After this event, some say the *walad al-sūq* came to be called *bani al-thalath*, or tribe of one-third, a reference term found elsewhere in Yemen.

9. The term for neighbor is *jār*, the root of *jiwār*, the term used for those under tribal protection. If one could ask a neighbor for assistance, one was acting both as a neighbor and in a sense as a *jiwār*.

Chapter 4. OCCUPATION: ASCRIPTION AND ACHIEVEMENT

1. Low-status groups in the Arabian Peninsula have been described by Henninger (1951), Doughty (1979), and Dostal (1964). Bujra (1966–67, 1971) has provided a detailed description of a stratified village in Hadramaut, South Yemen, that shares many characteristics with highland Yemen villages.

2. The young, educated group (referred to as the "children of June 13th," after the date the progressive leader al-Hamdi seized power) are a new, vocal group. Education has largely been the domain of the *sayyid* and wealthy tribesmen families. The number of secondary school graduates for 1977 and 1978 was twenty-two, including one woman. This figure represents virtually all graduates. Of these, thirteen were from tribesman families, three from *sayyid* families, and the remaining six from either the *walad al-sūq* or families of uncertain ancestry.

3. Chelhod (1970:77) has suggested that the word *dawshān* derives from *dhu sha'an*, the possessor of affairs or knowledge.

4. Women often contributed to the success of their husband's labor, particularly those engaged in agriculture. The "bath attendant" women are unique only in the extent to which they work on their own.

5. Some information on items in the marketplace can be gathered from Niebuhr (1792[2]:93-94), Bury (1915:119-20), Helfritz (1958:118), and an accounting of imports from Faroughy (1947). Messick (1978:291) provides a list of some items sold in the Ibb market before the revolution.

6. The term *nāgiṣ* is known to ʿAmranis, who attempted to explain the *walad al-sūq* "deficiency" in terms of their having fewer teeth. Unlike Gerholm's (1977) reports for Manakha, the term is rarely used in ʿAmran.

7. Not all of Saudi Arabia's influence on Yemen may be viewed positively. The effects cited are those generally noted by ʿAmranis. Heavy emphasis must be placed on the Saudi contribution, which often overshadows the efforts of Yemen's government; however, I do not mean to suggest that Saudi Arabia is the sole source of economic stimulation or that it is the locus of new ideas. It is clear that many changes in ʿAmran are adaptations to events unique to the town, and reasons for modifications to deal with these changes need not be sought elsewhere.

8. The one *walad al-sūq* generator owner is, coincidentally, unique in having the only power plant that produces 110-volt electricity.

Chapter 5. *MARRIAGE: INDIVIDUAL CONNECTIONS AND STATUS ASSESSMENT*

1. The issue of seniority is made more complex among brothers who have different mothers. Half-brothers seem to have less solidarity than full brothers do. A further complication is that fathers sometimes show preference for a son other than the eldest.

2. In terms of kinship categories, such a group of related minimal agnatic units, a descent *ḥabl* (see chapter 3), is roughly equivalent to a lineage.

3. Kirchoff (1955.6-8) distinguishes two types of clan: one unilateral, exogamous, and egalitarian; the other typified by unequal relationships in which status is based on genealogic proximity to the group's common ancestor. This second type of clan is conical, "the whole tribe being one such cone, with the legendary ancestor at its top, but within it are a larger or smaller number of similar cones, the top of each coinciding with or being connected with the top of the whole cone."

Ripinsky (1968:227) carries the point further by defining unilineal endogamous groups as vertical clans. Again genealogic distance is important to status and the clan is hierarchically ordered, a process that is directly traceable to the superior position of the patriarch. "In other words, the distance of the relationship is directly proportional to the social rank to which such a bond of descent is entitled."

In ʿAmran, the "clans" of the tribe do not actually hive off from a common ancestor, as in Kirchoff's model, but there is an ideology corresponding to this structure. Rather, like Ripinsky's vertical clan, ʿAmran maximal or patronymic descent groups are small-scale hierarchies. It should be noted that while status is based on genealogic distance, this is an arbitrary point and can change (as when ascendency is altered) over time.

4. There is a lengthy literature on patrilateral parallel cousin marriage in the Middle East. A sampling of this topic, as well as further references, can be found in Khuri (1970), Barth (1954; 1973), and Murphy and Kasdan (1959; 1967).

5. I know of two hypogamous marriages among the *sāda*. Both were arrangements between friends. Each involved at least one non-ᶜAmrani descent group. The first occurred some years ago and as neither party still resides in ᶜAmran (and both are prominent in Sanᶜa), it has been "forgotten." The second occurred while I was in ᶜAmran and was the subject of some discussion, although soon it was no longer mentioned.

6. Bride-price is different from *mahr*, usually translated as "dowry." In ᶜAmran the *mahr* is a sum, today normally in the range of 2,000 to 3,000 YR that is exchanged with the bride-price as part of the many additional wedding gifts designated for the bride. Some fathers keep this sum; others give it to their daughters, usually in the form of gold.

7. Bujra (1971:104–5) found that in Hureidah, like ᶜAmran, upward mobility was slowed by the necessity of solidifying gains through marriage.

8. There were also some interstrata kinship networks that resulted from individuals being demoted (see chapter 3). I have no information on how these connections were effected.

Chapter 6. ᶜAMRANI PERCEPTIONS OF SOCIAL CHANGE: ACCEPTANCE AND DENIAL

1. It is not uncommon for some ᶜAmranis to travel to Cairo for medical treatments. Obtaining the necessary papers is not an easy matter and the costs of travel, lodging and medical expenses are high. Some men describe the illnesses as not physical but merely the "sickness of money." Many ᶜAmranis have made the pilgrimage to Mecca. Many have been several times. Even the very poor have scraped together the necessary funds, sometimes with the help of their pseudo-kin.

2. Messick (1978) provides a detailed description of wealth concepts in Ibb. He notes in particular that it is the use rather than mere possession of wealth that contributes to status gain or loss. Among other factors, he found that excessive spending on *gāt* was viewed negatively. ᶜAmranis do not make this equation. Men who are known to use their money in improper ways, as on alcohol, are not respected; but immoderate *gāt* consumption is viewed as incorrect only if one spends beyond his means.

3. The cooperative movement in ᶜAmran began after the coup d'etat in 1962. The *shaykh*, who was then the local administrator, established a municipal administration to coordinate activities in the marketplace and to set aside a special area for the "butchers." Vendors without shops, who squatted in open areas in the central square, were assessed a fee by the municipality and *gāt* sellers were taxed on sales. The *shaykh* contributed some land to the municipality. Revenues from fees and land sales were used to maintain the marketplace and to regulate the building of new houses.

Later, a cooperative association was formed, also under the *shaykh*'s direction. Its purpose was to further ᶜAmran's development into a major commercial center. Funding for projects came from levies on all residents. The assessments were based on the ability to pay.

In its early years, the cooperative was largely the recipient of foreign-aid projects. The first such program was the building of the elementary school by the Kuwaiti Fund. This was followed by grants financed by Saudi Arabia for another school and a clinic.

Locally conceived and initiated projects were less successful. These included abortive attempts to purchase tractors and to build a power plant to electrify the town.

The latter reached the construction stage, but the government diverted the generating equipment to another town. It was about this time that the political split occurred (see chapter 3).

The most successful program was the construction of a piped water system. Some of the funds for well drilling came from foreign grants (including Iraqi and United States funding). The balance of expenses came from local assessments. Several wells were developed and a pumping station was constructed.

In 1973 the central government established a national association of local development boards to facilitate projects and to coordinate development schemes. Approval of projects was to be issued in Sanʿa and a bank was set up to help in project financing. Funding for all projects was apportioned, with shares contributed by the government, from local taxes, and by direct assessments.

Under the government's plan, development boards were established in those areas without them. Boards already in existence were incorporated into the national organization. Each local board was to have two governing bodies. The first, a sort of general assembly, was to oversee the administrative board responsible for the day-to-day affairs of the local cooperative. Elections were held to select members of the general advisory board, after which those elected selected some of their members to be the administrative board. The first election was in 1975.

4. Several examples of the government-sponsored posters include:

(1) Fellow citizens: Be alert for fast talkers, liars, and hirelings and keep them out of your cooperative activities.

(2) Fellow Yemeni: The government has responded to your requests and given you three-fourths of the tax for developing your area. So supervise and audit where and why the money is spent.

(3) As the state has implemented a major campaign to assist you, you must select those you agree with. It is your responsibility to elect those like yourselves to the cooperative.

Glossary

The transliteration system used in the text and the glossary is described in "Note on Transliteration." Where two words form an entry, the first, unless otherwise noted, is the singular, the second the plural.

ᶜāgal Headman of an alliance or a descent group.

ᶜāmil Government administrator of a subdistrict. Before the revolution the office was usually held by a *sayyid*.

asra, asrāt Kinship category referring to groups ranging from the nuclear household to the extended family. Here the term is translated as minimal agnatic group.

ᶜayāl ᶜamm Literally, "father's brother's children," the term may be extended beyond actual cousins to include any relatives on the father's side.

badl Exchange marriage in which a man gives his sister to another in exchange for the latter's sister.

bani al-khamis Polite reference term for the *walad al-sūq*, rarely used in ᶜAmran.

bayāᶜ, bayāᶜīn The "merchant" substratum of the *walad al-sūq*.

bayt Kinship term referring to all those who bear the same patronym. In this sense the term is translated as "maximal agnatic group." The term may also be applied to groups as small as a household or used with an accompanying patronym to refer to either a particular descent group or an alliance founded on the named descent group.

bint ᶜamm Literally, "father's brother's daughter," the term also used loosely to refer to any woman, of the speaker's generation, in the father's maximal descent group.

dawshān "Poetic messenger," the most despised substratum in the *walad al-sūq* stratum.

fagih "Literate man." A title given to men who have acquired religious or other forms of expertise without formal training.

gabīla The tribe; the institutional representation of the *gabīlī* stratum.

gabīlī Tribesman or warrior; the social stratum composed of tribespeople.

gaḍī, guḍā' Expert in religious law.

gashām "Vegetable peddler"; one of the *walad al-sūq* substrata sometimes called *muzayyin*.

gāt Catha edulis; a shrub cultivated for its succulent leaves, the chewing of which produces a sense of euphoria.
gishr Coffee husks or the beverage brewed from them.
gudā' See *gaḍī* above.
guriyya Former Jewish quarter of ʿAmran.
ḥabl Kinship-political term of variable meanings, all of which are used abstractly: (1) a single descent line in a large descent group; (2) the core descent group of an alliance; (3) the alliance between descent groups.
ḥajjām "Bleeder" or cupper; a *walad al-sūq* substratum on a level near that of the *dawshān*.
ḥākam Judge schooled in Islamic law; the holder of this office is often a *gaḍī*.
ḥammāmī "Bath attendant"; one of the *walad al-sūq* substrata sometimes called *muzayyin*.
hijra Sacred enclave; the institutional representation of the *sayyid* stratum. A neutral zone in which religious teaching and mediation of disputes could be obtained.
imam Prior to the revolution, the political and religious head of state selected from among the *sāda*.
janbiyya Large curved dagger worn by Yemeni men.
jazzār "Butcher"; one of the *walad al-sūq* substrata sometimes labeled *muzayyin*.
jihāz Scabbard for the dagger or *janbiyya*.
jiwār Person who is protected by another.
kafāʾa Islamic rule requiring marriage partners to be of equivalent status.
kayāl, kayālīn "Measurer"; a low-status substratum falling between the *bayāʿ* and the *muzayyin*.
libna, liban (1) Land measure (100 *libna* equals 1 acre); (2) sun-baked mud and straw brick used in building.
madīna The original walled town.
mafraj Well-appointed room in a house designated for entertaining and *gāt* chewing.
maṣlaḥī, maṣlaḥīn Middlemen; a term applied to both tribesmen and *walad al-sūq* middlemen who served as intermediaries between producers and consumers.
muʾdhdhin Announcer of prayers.
mugahwī "Innkeeper"; one of the *walad al-sūq* substrata sometimes labeled *muzayyin*.
muhājir Man of religious knowledge who receives gifts for Quranic readings; term usually applied to a *sayyid*, but is not exclusive to that group.
muzayyin "Barber-circumciser"; part of the *walad al-sūq* substratum. Term also is applied in a generic sense to include butcher, innkeeper, bath attendant, vegetable peddler, and dagger polisher, in addition to barber-circumciser.
nāgis Term meaning "defiled" or "deficient," applied generally to the *walad al-sūq*.
nāḥiyya Administrative subdistrict, formerly called a *maktaba*.
nasab Brother-in-law.
rafīq Protector; usually a man of importance who guarantees another's safety.
sāda See *sayyid*.

sagāl Dagger "polisher-cleaner-appraiser"; one of the *walad al-sūq* substrata sometimes called *muzayyin*.

sayyid, sāda Descendants of ʿAli, Muhammad's nephew from whom the imams of Yemen were elected; the social stratum associated with religious ancestry and expertise.

Shafiʿi Sunni sect dominant in nonhighland areas of Yemen.

shāgī Hired laborer.

Shariʿa Islamic legal system.

sharīk Sharecropper.

shart Bride-price.

shaykh Tribal leader; in ʿAmran the term refers to those heads of alliances with significant followings.

sūq Market; the institutional representation of the *walad al-sūq* stratum since it is the locus of commerce.

walad al-sūq Social stratum whose ascriptive occupations were in the marketplace. A derogatory term.

waqf As used in the text, those religious endowments held by mosques.

Yemeni riyal (YR) During the period of this study, the riyal had an exchange rate of 4.5 to the U.S. dollar. The riyal was worth about $.22.

Zaydi Shiʿa sect dominant in the Yemeni highlands.

References

Abraham, Nabeel
    1977   Detroit's Yemeni Workers. *MERIP* (Middle East Research and Information Project) *Reports* 57:3–9, 13.

Arab Report and Record (ARR)
    1976   *Arab Report and Record.* London.

al-Ati, Hammudah Abd
    1977   *The Family Structure in Islam.* American Trust Publications.

al-Attar, Said
    1964   *Le Sous-Développement économique et social du Yemen.* Algiers, Tiers Monde.

Bailey, F. G.
    1969   *Stratagems and Spoils: A Social Anthropology of Politics.* New York, Schocken Books.

Baldry, J.
    1976   Al Yaman and the Turkish Occupation, 1849–1914. *Arabica* 23:156–96.

Barth, Fredrik
    1954   Father's Brother's Daughter Marriage in Kurdistan. *Southwestern Journal of Anthropology* 10:164–71.
    1959   *Political Leadership among Swat Pathans.* London, Athlone Press.
    1973   Descent and Marriage Reconsidered. In *The Character of Kinship*, ed. J. Goody, 3–19. Cambridge, Cambridge University Press.

Béteille, André
    1965   *Caste, Class and Power.* Berkeley, University of California Press.
    1974   *Studies in Agrarian Social Structure.* Delhi, Oxford University Press.

Bornstein, Annika
    1974   *Food and Society in the Yemen Arab Republic.* Rome, Food and Agriculture Organization.

Bujra, Abdalla S.
    1966–
    1967   Political Conflict and Stratification in Hadramaut, I and II. *Middle East Studies* 3:355–75; 4:2–28.
    1971   *The Politics of Stratification.* Oxford, Oxford University Press.

Bury, George Wyman
    1915   *Arabia Infelix, or The Turks in Yemen.* London, MacMillan.

Central Planning Office, San ʿa
    1978   *Final Report on the Airphoto Interpretation Project of the Swiss Technical Co-Operation Service, Berne.* Sanʿa.
Chelhod, Joseph
    1970   L' Organisation sociale au Yémen. *L' Ethnographie* 64:61–86.
    1973   La Parenté et le marriage au Yémen. *L' Ethnographie* 67:47–90.
    1976   Le Droit intertribal dans les hauts plateaux du Yémen. In Al-Bahit: Festschrift Joseph Henninger. *Studia Instituti Anthropos* 28:49–76.
Dorsky, Susan
    1981   *Women's Lives in a North Yemeni Highlands Town.* Ann Arbor, University Microfilms. In press, 1985, University of Utah Press, Salt Lake City.
Dostal, W.
    1964   Paria Gruppen in Vorderasien. *Zeitschrift für Ethnologie* 89:190–203.
    1974   Sozio-okonomische Aspekte der Stammesdemokratie in Nordost-Yemen. *Sociologus* 24(i):14–15.
Doughty, Charles M.
    1979   *Travels in Arabia Deserta.* Vol. 2. New York, Dover Publications. Originally published 1888 by Cambridge University Press.
Faroughy, A.
    1947   *Introducing Yemen.* New York, Orientalia.
Federal Agency for Economic Development
    1974   *Yemen Agricultural Handbook.* Stuttgart, West Germany.
Gerholm, Tomas
    1977   *Market, Mosque, and Mafraj: Social Inequality in a Yemeni Town.* Stockholm Studies in Social Anthropology no. 5. Stockholm University.
Glaser, Eduard
    1885   Die Kastengliederung im Jemen. *Ausland* 58:201–5.
Goitein, S. D.
    1941   "Synopsis." *Travels in Yemen: An Account of Joseph Halevy's Journey to Najran in the Year 1870 Written in Sanʿani Arabic by His Guide, Hayyim Habshush.* Jerusalem, Hebrew University Press.
    1973   About the Jews in Yemen. In *From the Land of Sheba: Tales of the Jews of Yemen*, coll. and ed. S. D. Goitein, 1–30. New York, Schocken Books.
Halliday, Fred
    1974   *Arabia without Sultans: A Political Survey of Instability in the Arab World.* New York, Vintage Books.
al-Hamdāni, Al-Ḥasan ibn Aḥmad
    1938   *The Antiquities of South Arabia, Being a Translation from the Arabic with Linguistic, Geographic, and Historic Notes on the Eighth Book of al-Hamdāni's Al-Iklīl*, trans. Nabih Amin Faris. Princeton, Princeton University Press.
Harris, Walter B.
    1893   *A Journey Through Yemen and Some General Remarks upon That Country.* London, Blackwood and Sons.
Helfritz, Hans
    1958   *The Yemen: A Secret Journey.* trans. N. Heron. London, George Allen and Unwin, Ltd.

Henninger, J.
　1951　　Tribus et classes de parias en Arabie et en Égypte. *Actes de 14e Congrès International de Sociologie, Rome, 30 aout-3 septembre 1950 (s.a.) 1951* 4:266-78.
Khuri, Fuad I.
　1970　　Parallel Cousin Marriage Reconsidered: A Middle Eastern Practice that Nullifies the Effects of Marriage on the Intensity of Family Relationships. *Man* (ns) 5:597-618.
Kirchoff, Paul
　1955　　The Principles of Clanship in Human Society. *Davidson Journal of Anthropology* 1:1-10.
LaFontaine, Jean
　1973　　Descent in New Guinea: an Africanist View. In *The Character of Kinship*, ed. J. Goody, 35-52. Cambridge, Cambridge University Press.
Levy, Reuben
　1957　　*The Social Structure of Islam*. Cambridge, Cambridge University Press.
Linant de Bellefonds, Y.
　1978　　"Kafā'a." *Encyclopedia of Islam* (2d ed.), 4:404.
Macro, Eric
　1968　　*Yemen and the Western World Since 1571*. New York, Frederick A. Praeger.
Messick, Brinkley
　1978　　*Transactions in Ibb: Economy and Society in a Yemen Highland Town*. Ann Arbor, University Microfilms.
Munson, Henry
　1981　　The Mountain People of Northwestern Morocco: Tribesmen or Peasants? *Middle Eastern Studies* 17:249-55.
Murphy, Robert, and Leonard Kasdan
　1959　　The Structure of Parallel Cousin Marriage. *American Anthropologist* 61:17-29.
　1967　　Agnation and Endogamy: Some Further Considerations. *Southwestern Journal of Anthropology* 23:1-13.
Niebuhr, M. Carsten
　1792　　*Travels Through Arabia and Other Countries in the East*, trans. R. Heron, Vol. 2. Edinburgh, R. Morrison and Son.
Peters, Emrys L.
　1972　　Shifts in Power in a Lebanese Village. In *Rural Politics and Social Change*, ed. R. Antoun and I. Harik, 165-97. Bloomington, Indiana University Press.
Peterson, J. E.
　1982　　*Yemen: The Search for a Modern State*. Baltimore, Johns Hopkins University Press.
Rathjens, Carl
　1951　　*Tâghût gegen Scherî'a: Gewohnheitsrecht und islamicus Recht bei dem Gabilen des jemenitischen Hochlandes*. Jahrbuck des Linden Museums, 172-87. Stuttgart, West Germany.
　1953　　*Sabaeica*. Mitteilungen aus dem Museum für Völkerkunde in Hamburg no. 24. Hamburg, West Germany.
Ripinsky, Michael
　1968　　Middle Eastern Kinship as an Expression of a Culture-Environmental System. *Muslim World* 58:225-41.

Salzman, Philip C.
    1974   Tribal Chiefs as Middlemen: The Politics of Encapsulation in the Middle East. *Anthropological Quarterly* 47:203–10.
Serjeant, R. B.
    1967   Société et gouvernement en Arabie du Sud. *Arabica* 14:284–97.
Stookey, Robert W.
    1978   *Yemen: The Politics of the Yemen Arab Republic.* Boulder, Westview Press.
Swanson, Jon C.
    1979   *Emigration and Economic Development: The Case of the Yemen Arab Republic.* Boulder, Westview Press.
Tyan, E.
    1960   "Bayʿa." *Encyclopedia of Islam* (2nd ed.) 1:1113–14.
al-Wāsiʿī, ʿAbd al-Wāsiʿ bin Yahya
    1947   *Tārīkh al-Yaman.* 2d ed. Cairo, Maṭabaʿa al-Salifiyya.
Wenner, Manfred W.
    1967   *Modern Yemen, 1918–1966.* Baltimore, The Johns Hopkins Press.
The World Bank
    1979   *Yemen Arab Republic: Development of a Traditional Economy.* Washington, The World Bank.
Yemen Arab Republic (Y.A.R.)
    1971   The Permanent Constitution of the Yemen Arab Republic. *Middle East Journal* 25:389–401.

Index

Achievement, occupation and, 91–121
Affines, status of, 123
ʿAgal, status of, 94, 96
Agnatic groups, 67–69
Agriculture, xiv, 22; decline of, 108–10, 120; labor costs in, 109–10; status and, 106–7; women in, 22, 52
Ahmad, imam, xvi, 40
Aid, foreign, 160, 176 n. 3
Akhdām, status of, 94
Alliance(s), 62; bases for, 71, 72; formation of, 70, 74; kinship and, 67–69; marriage and, 136–39; in the postrevolutionary era, 81; primary, 73–74; status and, xxii. See also Ḥabl
ʿĀmil, xviii; status of, 103
ʿAmran: expansion of, 55–57; in national structure, 62
ʿAmrani identity, 61–63
Ancestry: of election candidates, 161–63; status and, xxii
ʿArab, status of, 94
Army, careers in, 155
Asra, 67–69
Assistants to government officials, 117

Baʿath Party, 83, 85
Badl (exchange) marriages, 133, 140–41, 144–45
al-Badr, Muhammad, imam, xvi
Bani Hasham, 69
Bani al-Khamis (walad al-sūq), 42
Barber-circumcisers: and marriage, 130; special functions of, 100; status of, 43, 96, 99, 100, 101, 128

Bargaining, 6–8, 15–16
Bath, public, 10
Bath attendants: status of, 43, 94, 96, 99, 129; women of, 100
Bayāʿ/bayāʿin (merchants), 117; dual meaning of, 64; rank/status of, 43, 94, 96, 100, 101, 128–29, 152–54; as shopkeepers, 112–13
Bayt, meaning of, 70
Blacksmiths/blacksmithing, 112; status of, 103
Bleeders/cuppers, 117; status of, 43, 94, 96, 98, 99, 129
Blood money, 72
Brazing, shop use for, 112
Bride(s), selling of, 140–45
Bride-price, 55, 83–84, 136, 140–43; marriage and, 131–32
Brokers: occupation of, 117–18; status of, 96, 109
Brother(s), seniority of, 125
Building materials, shop use for, 112
Business, status and, 169–70
Business formation, 110–16
Businessman, status of, 101, 120
Butchers, 4–5, 8, 10; special functions of, 99; status of, 7, 43, 94, 96–99; success of, 117

Carpenters: shop use by, 112; status of, 103; tribesmen as, 105
Caste system, 156
Catha edulis. See Gāt
Children, 12, 16; farm work by, 52

"Children of the revolution (June 13th)," xxi, 174 chap. 4 n. 2, 161
Civil war, Yemeni, 39
Clan(s), 125, 175 chap. 5 n. 3; *bayt* as, 67
Class system, 156
Cloth, shop use for, 112
Coffee, 4
Coffee sellers, status of, 94
Commerce: hierarchy and, 158; tribal/nontribal distinction in, 62
Connections: marriage and, 123–49; tribal/nontribal, 63–66
Constitution, Yemeni, 92
Cooperative movement, 176 n. 3
Cousin marriages, 132–36
Craftsmen, status of, 94, 102–3
Cultural divisions, xiv–xv

Dagger, investment in, 110. See also *Janbiyya*
Dagger craftsmen, status of, 100. See also *Jihāz* maker, status of
Dawshān, 72; status of, 43, 94, 95–99, 117, 128
Day laborer, status of, 96, 103
Debts, obligations for, 70–73
Descent: Bakil, 49; variable expressions of, 68
Descent group(s), 66–67; internal ranking in, 77, 125–26; relations of, 124–27
Descent-group exogamy, 129
Diyya (blood money), 72
Dorsky, Susan, xvii, xviii, xix
Dowry, 176 n. 6. See also Bride-price

Economic change, 120–21
Egypt: in Yemen politics, xvi, 41
Egyptians: as teachers, 6; as wives, 147
Election, advisory board, 160–68
Electric generators, 15, 21, 111, 112, 114
Electric lighting, 20, 21
Endogamy, xxii, 128, 129, 133, 136, 137, 138
Equality: concept of, 55; internal ranking and, 125–26; intrastratum, 128; social, in marriage, 127–32; in Yemen, 92, 93
Etiquette, *gāt*, 17–20

Exchange marriage, 133, 140–41, 144–45
Executioners, status of, 94
Exogamy, 129

Faqih/fuqahā', status of, 97, 104
Field workers, pay for, 109
Foreign aid, 160, 176 n. 3
Foreign exchange, 15
Fruit, shop use for, 112
Freezers: in shops, 111, 114
Funerals, 37, 159

Gabila. See Tribe
Gabili (tribesman), 63; in election, 161–64, 167–68; marriage patterns of, 127–32, 136–39; as shopkeepers 112–13; status of, 42–44, 96, 97, 102–5
Gadī/gudā', status of, 94, 97, 103
Garage, shop use for, 112
Gashām, status of, 96, 99, 129
Gāt (Catha edulis), xiv, xxi; aphrodisiac tradition of, 17; growing of, 111–12; marketing of, 14–15, 103; spending on, 176 n. 2
Gāt chewing, xx, 16–20; by candidates, 164–66, 169–70; etiquette of, 17–20
General stores, 110
Gishr (coffee substitute), 3–4
Gold, investment in, 110
Government: careers in, 155; election management by, 160–61
Government administrator, xviii; status of, 103
Government employees: in election, 162, 164, 165
Government jobs, 117, 118
Grain, shop use for, 112
Grain dealers, status of, 96
Greengrocers, 8, 10; status of, 7, 43
Grocers, status of, 95

Ḥabl (kinship and alliance), 67–69; alliance and, 69–70; changing role of, 81–88; formation of, 74; leadership in, 75, 77; as lineage, 175 n. 2; marriage out of, 146–47; meanings of, xx–xxi, 69–74; "new," 152–53;

obligations of, 72; ranking within, 126; support function of, 73
Ḥabl leaders, status of, 102
Ḥajjam, 117; status of, 43, 94, 96, 98, 99, 129
Ḥākam, status of, 103
Ḥammāmī, status of, 43, 94, 96, 99, 129
Hanafi law, equality in, 127
Hashid tribes, 48–49, 52
Hierarchy(-ies), xv, 93, 94; in ʿAmran, 95–105; ascriptive, 156–57; commerce and, 158; formal system and, 158; imperfections in, 104–5; model of, and deviations, 95, 104–5, 168–71; sample, 94; sūq and, 105–8
Ḥijra sūq, 63, 65, 92
Himyarites, 40, 41, 43
History, ʿAmrani, 39–57
Hizam, shaykh, 50, 51
Holiday periods: obligatory visits in, 123–24; after Ramadhan, 22, 37
Holy market enclave, 63, 65, 92
Hotels, 11, 117; shop use for, 112
Household, relationships in, 124–25
Housing, 11–12, 45–46, 55
Hureidah, 152, 176 n. 7

Ibb, xiv, 176 n. 2
Identity, ʿAmrani, 61–63
Imam: attitude toward, 41; status of, 97
Inflation, 110–11
Innkeepers, 117; status of, 94, 96, 99, 101, 129
Insults, symbolic, 75
Intergenerational conflict, 84
Iraq, aid grants from, 160

Janbiyya (dagger), 6, 43–44
Jazzār. See Butchers
Jews, xvii–xviii, 53, 54, 56; attitudes toward, 42; occupations of, 45–46; living quarters for, 47, 48; social position of, 44–47
Jihāz (scabbard), 117
Jihāz makers, status of, 94, 96, 98
Judges, status of, 103

Kafāʾa, marriage principle of, 127
al-Kamal, Asad, 42, 43, 92, 93
Kayāl/kayālīn, status of, 96, 101, 102

Kerosene, shop use for, 112
Khadām, status of, 100
Khamir, marriage in, 133
Kin groups, relations of, 123–127
Kinship: alliance and, 66–69; model of, 68; pseudo, 124–27, 158–60. See also Ḥabl
Kinship terms, 123–25; variable usage in, 66, 67–69
Kuwaiti Fund, 176 n. 3

Labor costs: in agriculture, 109–10
Labor surplus, 115
Laborers, hired, status of, 96, 103
Land: status and, 118–20; values of, 46, 120
Land agent, status of, 103
Land ownership, xx
Landlord, status of, 119
Landowners: in election, 162–65; peasant, 96; status of, 96, 102
Leadership, ḥabl, 75, 77
Learned men, status of, 97, 104
Leather goods, shop use for, 112
Legal experts, status of, 97, 103, 104
Lighting, electric, 20–21
Lineage. See Descent group(s)
Literate men, status of, 97, 104
Lumber, shop use for, 112

Mahr (dowry), 176 n. 6. See also Bride-price
Maria Theresa thaler (currency), 46
Marketplace. See Sūq
Marriage, 123–49; alliance aspect of, 136–39; arrangement of, 147–49; of cousins, 132–36; endogamous, 133; exchange, 133, 140–41, 144–45; exogamous, 129; out of ḥabl, 146–47; hypergamous, 128, 136; hypogamous, 136; patterns of, 127–32, 136, 139; poverty and, 131–32; property control and, 133–35, 137–38; social mobility and, 147–49; social standing and, 129; status and, 123, 148–49
Maṣlāḥī/maṣlāḥīn, 117; status of, 96, 101, 103
Measurers: marriage of, 130, 131; status of, 96, 101, 102
Meat, 6–8. See also Butchers

Mechanics, shop use by, 112
Mediator, *shaykh* as, 79
Medicinal herbs, 117
Men: shopping activity, 9–10; social life, 13, 16–20
Merchandise: shop use for, 112; in *sūq*, 5–10
Merchants, 64; in election, 162, 164–66; influence of, 82–83; nonmigrants as, 117; rank/status of, 43, 94, 96, 100, 101, 128–29, 152–54; as shopkeepers, 112–13
Messengers, 72; status of, 43, 94, 95–99, 117, 128
Middlemen, 117; status of, 96, 101, 103
Migrants, returned, 110–16, 159
Migration: in ʿAmran economy, 108–10; occupations and, 106
Military service, 54
Minstrels, status of, 94
Mobility, social, marriage and, 147–49
Mosque, xix, 22; land owned by, 5, 99, 103; women forbidden in, 3
Mugahwī, 117; status of, 94, 96, 99, 101, 129
Muhājir, status of, 97
Municipal administration, 176 n. 3
Muzayyin; variable meanings of, 179. See also Barber-circumcisers

Nāgis, status of, 102. See also *Walad al-sūq*
al-Nasser, Gamal ʿAbd, 41
Nasserism, xvi
National identity, 61–63
Neighbors, 87; relationship between, 158–60
Non-ʿAmrani shopkeepers, 112–13
Nonmigrants, occupations of, 116–18
Nontribal peoples: connections with tribals, 63–66; distinguishing features, 62–63, 69

Oath of alliance, 70, 72
Occupation(s), xxii, 91–121; ancestral, 100; of candidates, 162–68; of Jews, 45–46; migration and, 106; nonstigmatized, 116–18; status and, 43, 91–93; stigmatized, 95–102, 114; titles of, as surnames, 99; of tribesmen, 105–7

Office, shop use for, 112
Ottomans, xi, xv–xvi, 50–52

Patrilateral cousin marriage, 132–36
Patrilateral endogamy, 137
Patrilineal descent, 126
Patrilineality, status and, 124
Patrilocal residence, 124
Peasants; 103; status of, 94, 96, 97
Pharmacy, 106; shop use for, 112
Pilgrims, return celebration for, 159
Pilgrimages: to Mecca, 176 n. 1; return from, 37
Poetic messengers, 72; status of, 43, 94, 95, 128
Polishers, status of, 96, 97, 99, 100
Posters, election, 160
Potters, status of, 94
Poverty, marriage and, 131–32
Power, status and access to, xxii
Prayer(s), 3–4; alms for, 13; daily, 3, 14, 16, 20, 21, 30
Prestige, status and, xxii
Property control, marriage and, 133–35, 137–38
Property inheritance and management, 125
Protected relationship, 65–66
Protection, tribal, 63–64, 87, 174 n. 9
Pseudo-kinship, 124–27, 158–60
Public criers, 72; status of, 43, 94, 95–99, 117, 128

Quran reading: alms for, 13; in *gāt* chews, 19

Radio repair, shop use for, 112
Rain-making, 99
Ramadhan, xix, 22, 37
Rank, in descent groups, 125–26. See also Status
Religion: in *gāt* conversation, 19
Religious ceremonies, xix
Religious divisions, in Yemen, xiv–xv
Religious endowments, 5, 99, 103
Religious experts, status of, 94, 97, 103
Rents: for business sites, 119–21
Residence, 62, 124; shop use for, 112
Restaurant, shop use for, 112
Revolution of *1968-1970*, xi, xvi, xxiii, 39, 41, 56; benefits of, 154–55; life before, 52–55; tribal role after, 81–88

Rifles, investment in, 110
Riyal, (currency), xxi, 6–7, 120
Roads, development of, xvi

Sacred enclaves/markets, 63, 65, 92
Sāda/sayyid (social stratum), in election, 162, 164, 165; electric generator operation by, 111, 114; in history, xiv, xv, xvi; marriage patterns of, 136–39; as shopkeepers, 112–13; status of, xiv, 43, 94, 95, 97, 103, 104; upward mobility of, 153–54
Saddle making, status of, 103
Sagāl, status of, 96, 97, 99, 100
Salesmen, status of, 94
Salt, shop use for, 112
Sana', status of, 94, 96, 97
Saudi Arabia, xii; aid grants from, 176 n. 3; in 'Amran economy, 107–8, 108–10; economic influences on Yemen, 175 n. 7; return from, 37; in Yemeni revolution, xvi
School administrators, 118
Segregation, sexual, xviii–xix
Seniority within family, 125
Servants, status of, 100
Shafi'i, xii, xiv, xv, xvi
Shāgī/shugā', status of, 96, 103
Sharecroppers, 53, 109; status of, 96, 102
Shari'a, xiv
Sharik/shuraka', status of, 96, 102
Shaykh(s), xv; in election, 162; 164; as Jew protectors, 45, 63; marriage in household of, 135; as mediator, 79, 82–83; "new," 85–86, 152–53, 161, 164; "old," 85, 86; role and functions of, 77–80, 82–83; selection of, 77–78; status of, 94, 96, 97, 102, 103, 104
Shi'a/Shi'ites, xiv; marriage rule of, 127
Shop(s): innovations in, 114–15; ownership of, 118, 119; outside sūq, 10–11
Shop use, distribution of, 110, 112–13
Shopkeepers, 112–13
Slave descendants, status of, 94
Social categories, 95–99
Social differences: origin of, 42–44; status and, xxii
Social divisions, xiv–xv

Social mobility, 151–71; marriage and, 147–49
Social position, 91–121
Social relationships, formal model of, 168–71
Social standing, marriage and, 129
South Yemen, xii
Status: achieved, 104; affines and, 123; agriculture and, 106–7; alliances and, xxii; ancestry and, xxii; assessment of, 152–57; changes in, 147–49; differentiations in, 92–120; land and, 118–20; marriage and, 123; 127–32, 148–49; occupation and, 43, 91–93; origin of, 42–44; power and, xxii; variables in, 157
Steel, shop use for, 112
Stereo tapes, shop use for, 112
Stonemasonry, status of, 102
Storeroom, shop use for, 112
Suburbia, 12
Sunni, xiv; marriage rule of, 127
Sūq (marketplace), 4–10, 14–15; expansion of, 56; hierarchy and, 105–8; Hijra (holy), 63, 65, 92; inviolate status of, 65
Surnames, occupational, 99

Tailors: shop use by, 112; status of, 103
Tanning/tanners, status of, 94, 103
Tax collectors, status of, 103
Taxation, xx, 102
Taxi(s), 11, 21, 114–16
Tea shop, 112
Teachers, 118; Egyptian, 6; status of, 97
Television, 21
Television repair, shop use for, 112
Topsoil, sale of, 110
Town criers, status of, 43
Tribal peoples: connections with non-tribals, 63–66; distinguishing features, 62–63, 69
Tribal villages, 74–75
Tribe: in postrevolutionary era, 81–88; in social order, 61; status of, 94
Tribesmen, 63; in election, 161–64, 167–68; marriage patterns of, 127–32, 136–39; occupations of, 105–7 112–13; status of, xv, 42–44, 95, 96, 97, 102–5
Tujjār, status of, 101, 120

Turks, xi, xv–xvi; relationships with, 50–52

United States, aid grants from, 176 n. 3
Vegetable peddlers, status of, 96, 99, 129
Verbal duels, symbolism of, 75

Wages, 53
Wakes, 37, 159
Walad al-sūq (social stratum): in election, 165–67; *ḥabl* absent in, 69; influence of, 82–88; marriage among, 128; nonmigrants in, 116–17; rank within, 128; as shopkeepers, 112–13; status of, xv, 42–44, 91–95, 96, 97, 101–2, 104, 105, 152–53
Warehouses: operation of, 117; shop use for, 112
Warrior-peasants. See *Gabīlī*
Watch repair, shop use for, 112
Water supply, 14, 53–54, 57, 160
Water workers, status of, 94
Wealth, status and, xxii, 121, 155–56
Weavers, status of, 94, 96, 97

Weddings, 37, 55, 159. *See also* Marriage
Welding, shop use for, 112
Well(s), 53, 54
Well diggers, status of, 103
Wholesale, shop use for, 112
Women: in agriculture, 22, 52; domestic duties of, 16, 17–18, 52; etiquette toward, 9, 17; field work by, 52; in *madīna* (walled city), 12; marriage eligibility of, 136; mosque prohibition for, 3; occupations of, 100; in Ramadhan, 22, 37; segregation of, xviii–xix; social life of, 13–14, 20
Women's Gate, 48

Yahya, imam (modern), xvi, 40
Yahya ibn Hussayn (ninth century), xiv, 43
Yemen: constitution of, 92; economic changes in, 108–9; history of, xv–xvii
Youth, 83–85, 93, 161

Zaydi/Zaydism, xiv, xv, xvi
Zaydi law, equality in, 127